IMAGES
of America

SAN GORGONIO PASS

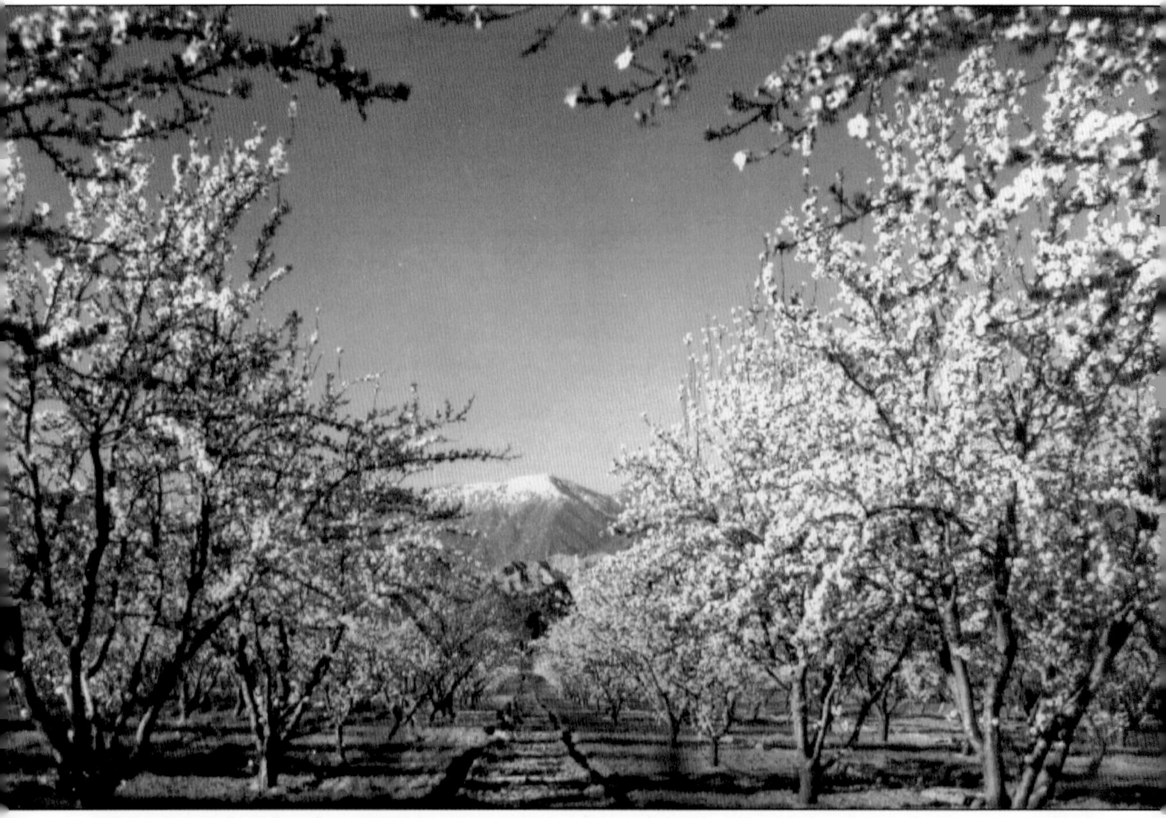

This almond orchard in full bloom was located in the San Gorgonio Pass, where many acres of almonds were once planted. In earlier times, almonds were a major crop in the area, perhaps reaching their peak in the 1920s but continuing well into the 1940s. At one time, there were over 1,000 acres planted in the pass. (Courtesy of Norman McGary.)

On the Cover: Between 1883 and 1884, the Banning Land and Water Company built two reservoirs beside San Gorgonio Avenue and Water Canyon. The upper reservoir at the mouth of the canyon is pictured here with a remote cabin on its bank. (Courtesy of Joan Coombs.)

IMAGES
of America

SAN GORGONIO PASS

Kenneth M. Holtzclaw and the
San Gorgonio Pass Historical Society

ARCADIA
PUBLISHING

ISBN 978-0-7385-3097-0

Published by Arcadia Publishing
Charleston, South Carolina

Printed in the United States of America

Library of Congress Catalog Card Number: 2005934849

For all general information contact Arcadia Publishing at:
Telephone 843-853-2070
Fax 843-853-0044
E-mail sales@arcadiapublishing.com
For customer service and orders:
Toll-Free 1-888-313-2665

Visit us on the Internet at www.arcadiapublishing.com

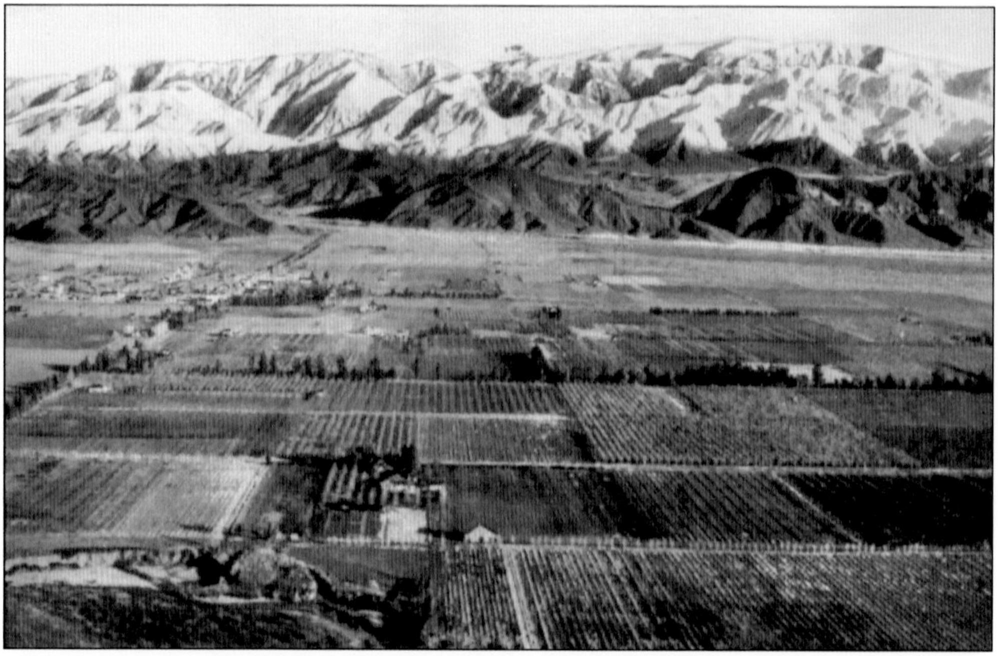

This image depicts the extensiveness of fruit growing in the San Gorgonio Pass in earlier years. Many such views were available throughout the pass, east of the small town of Banning. The checkerboard pattern of white and red blossoms made a beautiful blanket covering for the floor of the pass. (Courtesy of Norman McGary.)

Contents

ACKNOWLEDGMENTS

When a writer puts together a book like this, strangers become friends, and friends evolve into a large pool of resourceful information that helpfully adds to the quality of the book. I would like to mention that this book's compilation was enhanced in this manner and represents the effort of numerous people, all of whom I am grateful to have associated with. Many of the pictures entered within these pages were graciously presented to me and the research supplied was most helpful.

I would like to begin by thanking Marilyn Vonderheide, program manager of the Laura Mae Stewart Foundation, and the Laura Mae Stewart Foundation itself for their contributions within the pages of this book, which made up one chapter. Thanks to Steve Lech, Riverside County historian and author, for access to his large photograph collection and his contributed research. Nara Haskell spent much time touring the historical Haskell Ranch with me in San Timoteo Canyon and providing information about its buildings. She and her husband owned and operated the ranch for many years. It is soon to be razed by bulldozers, paving a path for development. Photographs were also provided by Nara through the San Gorgonio Pass Historical Society. Joan Coombs, longtime resident of Banning and affiliate of the Gilman Historical Ranch and Wagon Museum, provided vintage photographs and, most importantly, the one for the book's cover.

Marianne Bailiff provided pictures from her collection, including the rare photographs of pioneer Nellie Bailiff, who was a telegrapher for the Southern Pacific Railroad in Cabazon. Thanks is given to pro tem mayor Jeff Fox of Beaumont for pictures and research. Bud Mathewson, Banning businessman and longtime resident, contributed both photographs and research information. Bill Bell, of the Banning Public Library, provided advice and research during the preparation of this book. I would like to thank my wife, Margaret, as well for her editorial expertise and support during the preparation of the book. In addition, Charles G. Ferrell, editor and associate publisher of the *Record Gazette* in Banning, was helpful during its preparation. Claudia Keeling, chairman of the Beautification and Mural Committee of the Banning Chamber of Commerce is to be thanked for her contribution in relation to the mural section in the book.

Not to be omitted, several other helpful persons were: artist Norman McGary of Banning; author Maria Webster Weisbrod of the Banning Bench; Donald and Susan Echlin of the McCoy House in Beaumont; Ricka Showalter, manager of Bob's Big Boy restaurant in Calimesa; Ros Otero, recreation coordinator at the Beaumont-Cherry Valley Recreation and Park District; Gary J. Curto, director of development at the San Gorgonio Memorial Hospital in Banning; Beverly Lewis, auxiliary president of hospital volunteers at San Gorgonio Memorial Hospital; artist Joe Corda of the Corda Art Gallery in Banning; Christie Mitchell, curator of the Gilman Historical Ranch and Wagon Museum; Virginia Ross, president of the San Gorgonio Pass Historical Society; Jerry Cody, Riverside County district advisory commissioner; and Jack Dallas, son of Chris Dallas, owner of the historical San Gorgonio Inn.

INTRODUCTION

The San Gorgonio Pass is cradled between Mount San Gorgonio in the San Bernardino Mountains to the north and Mount San Jacinto in the San Jacinto Mountains to the south. Both mountain peaks are over 10,000 feet in height, the tallest being almost 12,000 feet. The pass is essentially a swath of land reaching from mountain range to mountain range in the west, passing east through San Timoteo Canyon, and extending farther east toward the desert as far as Whitewater, or even more distant. The seasonal, snowcapped mountain peaks portray a picturesque beauty, towering high above the pass's floor. The San Gorgonio Pass is the deepest pass in the continental 48 states and exceeds the Grand Canyon by 2,000 feet. However, it has its drawbacks too. Occasional strong winds sweeping down from the high desert and drifting sands wear the wooden electrical poles and billboard signs away so much that they have to be reinforced and protected at the base by railroad ties. It has been said that railroad workers coming through Whitewater had to tether themselves to the railroad cars when the winds were extremely strong.

The San Gorgonio Pass was doubtless a favorite passage for aboriginal Indians. It was the most convenient route from the coast to the desert, with plenty of game in the mountains, fish in the streams, and water along the way. There have been many stories of grizzly bears in the pass and how prevalent they were in the past. Allegedly, during the 1800s, visiting San Gabriel Franciscan Friars and wagon excursionists to the Salton Sea to obtain salt for the mission feared them as they came through the pass. It has been related that the Cahuilla Indians would carry torches at night when they had to travel between villages.

According to anthropologists, early Native Americans lived here beside the bubbling water springs for over 1,000 years. They survived by using numerous plants for food, thatched housing, and medicine. They built their villages and traversed an intermingled network of earthen footpaths, enabling them to move from one thatched village to the other. They reached out to the beautiful mountains of San Gorgonio, San Jacinto, and elsewhere to hunt game and search for food. Artifacts of large granite rocks with mortars for grinding acorns and other seeds have been found in the sloping mountain ranges of the San Gorgonio Pass, a firm indication that the Native American's presence was here.

But the calm serenity of Native Americans living peaceably by themselves in the San Gorgonio Pass was not to last. First arrived the exploring Mexicans, then the Spaniards, and finally the Europeans. Spanish expedition reached the area around 1774 and by 1824, the fathers of the San Gabriel Mission established an *asistencia* at the highest point in the San Gorgonio Pass, north of Beaumont. By that time, the area was known as Rancho San Gorgonio and was named after St. Gorgonio, a Latin martyr. It was the farthest eastern rancho that the San Gabriel Mission had established and it extended through the San Gorgonio Pass as far as Whitewater. Early in its existence, fathers at the San Gabriel Mission drove wagon trains through the pass to the Salton Trough in the desert to harvest salt from the salt flats. San Gabriel baptismal records note that some of the Native Americans from Whitewater Canyon were baptized as early as 1809.

Paulino Weaver, born in Tennessee about 1800, came to California in 1830 and perhaps was influential in bringing about some of the lifestyle changes for the Native Americans in the pass. He lived in what was alleged to be the abandoned adobe *assistencia* chapel of the San Gabriel Mission. He became well acquainted with the Native Americans in this area. He was a prospector and when he discovered gold at La Paz on the Colorado River in January 1862, it brought many a miner to frenzy—they had to go to the river and pan for gold.

This created a demand for a convenient route from California to the river. The solution was supplied by William Bradshaw, who discovered an old path that was once used extensively by Native Americans. Making this path the gateway to the Colorado River, it became a stagecoach line with stops in San Timoteo Canyon, Smith's Station, Gilman Ranch, and Whitewater. The path became known as the Bradshaw Trail.

When the Buchanan administration began on March 4, 1857, after Franklin Pierce ceased to be president of the United States, congress passed an act authorizing an overland mail line in Southern California. The route from San Francisco to Yuma roused intense rivalry between Los Angeles, San Bernardino, and San Diego. The route ultimately chosen was through the San Gorgonio Pass and the contract was given to the Butterfield Company in September 1857. In January 1858, the California legislature adopted a resolution introduced by a Los Angeles assemblyman to establish a weekly mail run from San Bernardino to Fort Yuma, via the San Gorgonio Pass.

Stage lines that routed through the pass brought about an influx of foreign adventurers and growth began to exponentially occur. Opportunists, fur trappers, miners, timber cutters, and fruit growers began to move to the pass. Some Native American footpaths were replaced by roads, built with mule-drawn road graders, for buggies. The stagecoach era added much to promote activity in the San Gorgonio Pass but when the Iron Horse came upon the scene in the late 1880s, it was an end of an era for the stage lines. They soon fell into oblivion because the railroad was faster, more reliable, and definitely preferred.

After the automobile came onto the scene near the turn of the 20th century and technology was improving, it became prudent to pave some of the roads in the area. The first major paved highway was Highway 99, which went through most of the towns that dotted the landscape throughout the pass. But as the population increased in the state and country, cars became more prevalent and tourists traveled more extensively. Roads like two-lane Highway 99 became inadequate.

Sometime around the mid-1950s, our country was building interstate highways throughout many parts of various states and California was no exception. Interstate 10 was brought through the San Gorgonio Pass but it bypassed the old route of Highway 99. Because I-10 was being built to the south, it took away traffic through the downtown areas of some of the towns and slowed growth. However, growth is on an incline today and population in the pass is growing fast, but the rural atmosphere may be in jeopardy.

Numerous trains traverse the San Gorgonio Pass daily, carrying hundreds of freight carriers filled with cargo to points east. Often it requires a number of engines to accomplish the task. The Amtrak comes by occasionally, its routes are usually scheduled at night. One hundred and forty thousand cars and trucks pass over I-10 daily.

One

San Timoteo Canyon

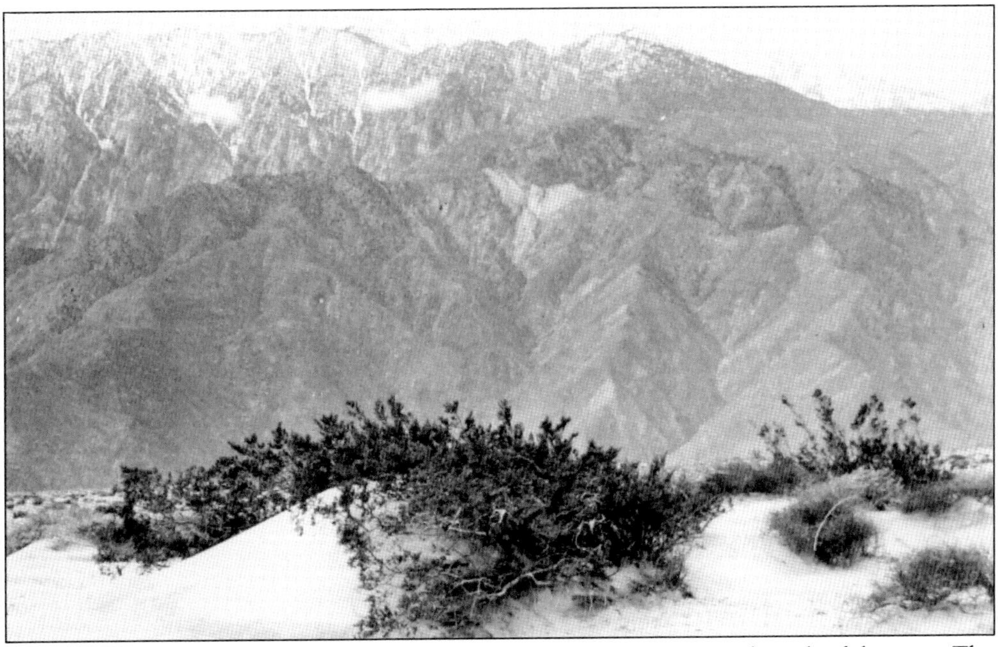

During the winter months, Mount San Gorgonio is heavily snowcapped much of the time. The mammoth San Gorgonio Mountain dwarfs everything that lies below it. The view provides an alluring spectacle to those living in the pass and those passing through. (Courtesy of Norman McGary.)

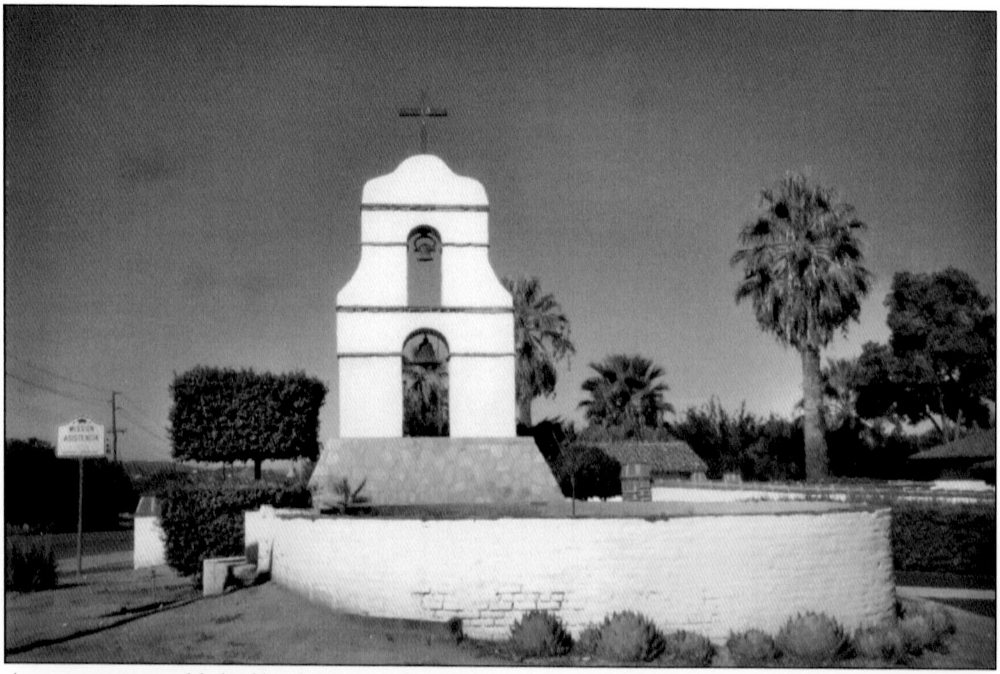

An *asistencia*, established by the San Gabriel Mission, was an adobe structure built near the bottom of San Timoteo Canyon. Supposedly it was used as a mission annex but was later abandoned and used to house farm animals. Exposed to the elements, it melted back into the earth. The mission was rescued in 1929 and restored, as pictured here. In 1937, it opened to the public. (Courtesy of the author.)

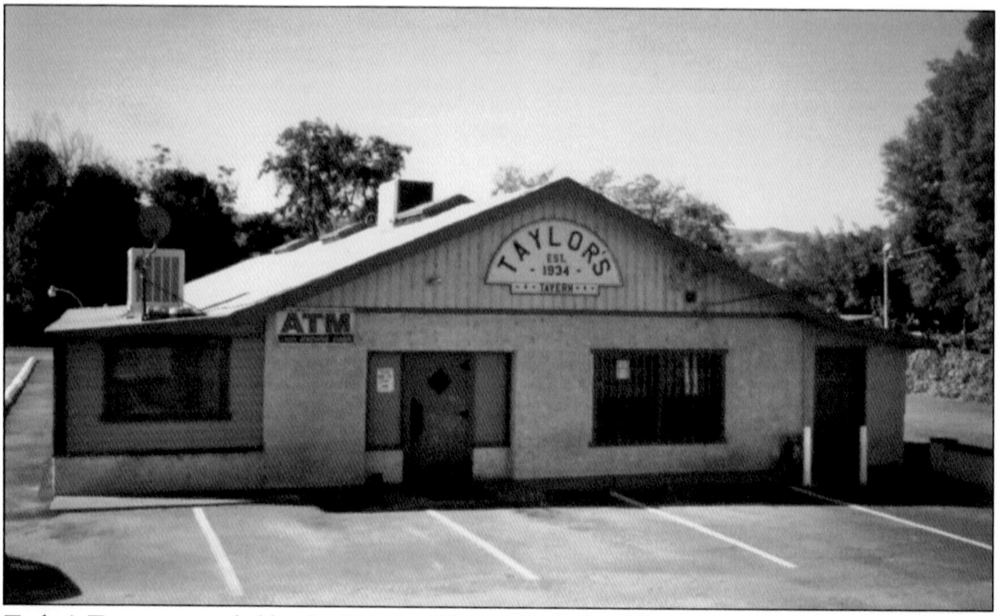

Taylor's Tavern, preceded by the Dine and Dance Corral and San Timoteo's three-pump service station, is located at the bottom of the San Timoteo Canyon. The structure was originally built in 1933 with bricks made at the old Verdugo Ranch. Today it is a popular stop at the foot of the canyon and a local historic site. (Courtesy of the author.)

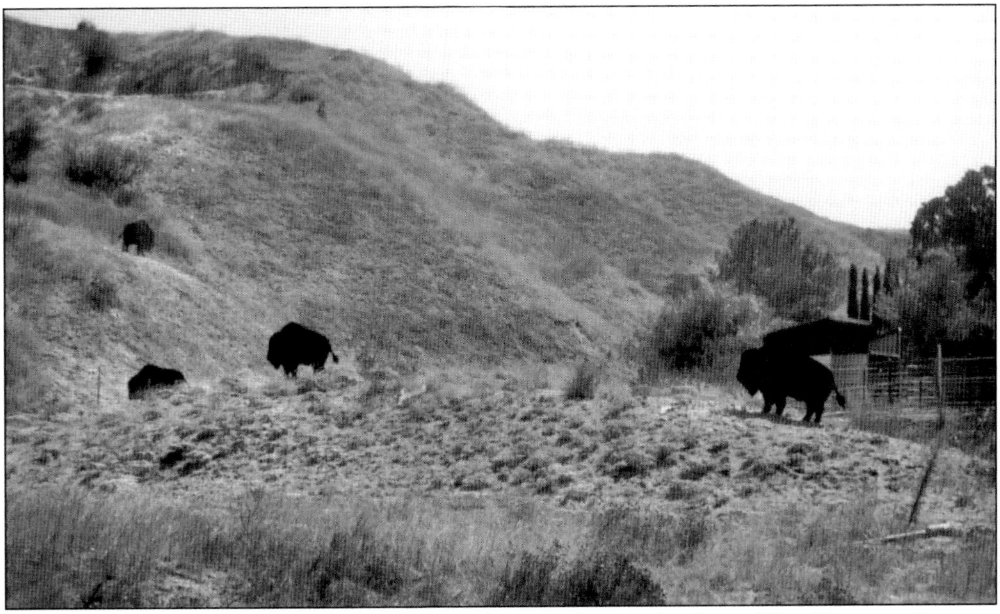

Buffalo Meadows Ranch is a large horse-boarding ranch near the foot of San Timoteo Canyon. Pictured here is a rather unique array of sculptured buffalo climbing the hillside near the ranch. The sight turns many heads. Horse ranches have become popular in the canyon, other ranches are beginning to plant citrus, and the housing boom has definitely reached the canyon. Several old ranches are being obliterated. (Courtesy of the author.)

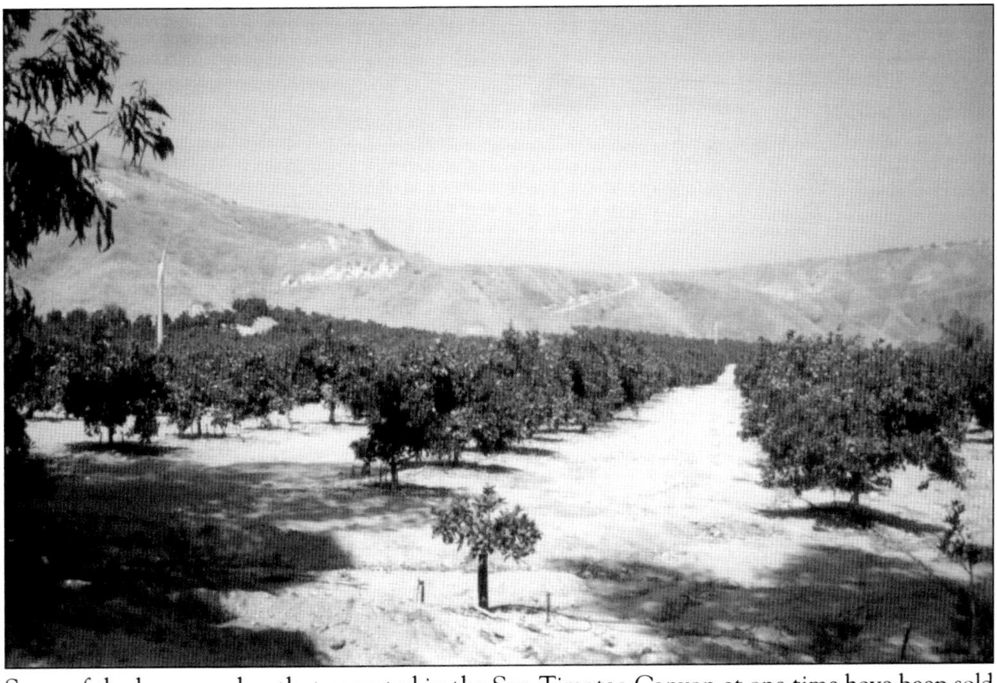

Some of the large ranches that operated in the San Timoteo Canyon at one time have been sold to land developers, but some have been divided into smaller units and sold off for other uses, such as chicken ranches, horse ranches, and citrus production. Shown here is an orchard of young Valencia orange trees. (Courtesy of the author.)

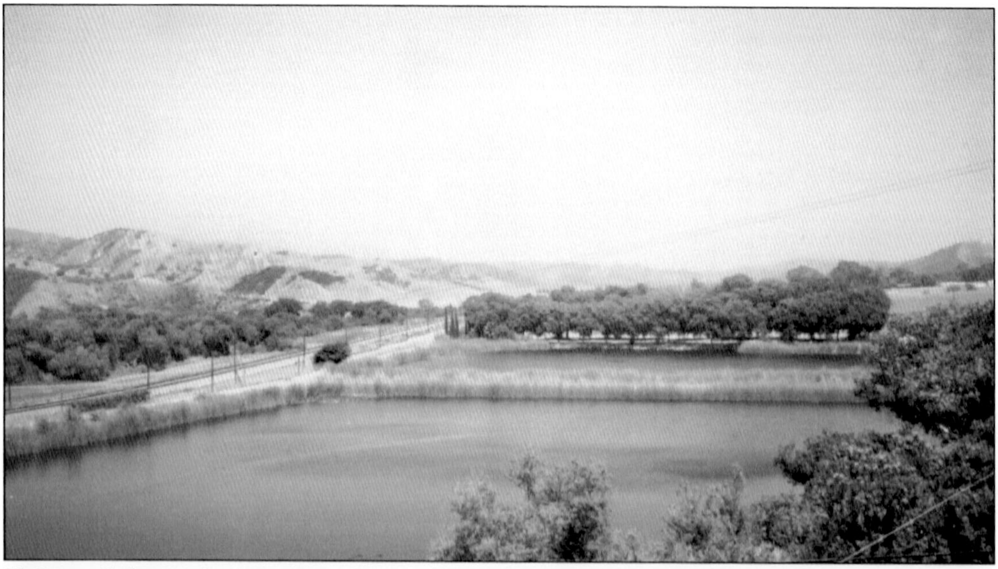

El Casco Lakes in San Timoteo Canyon, once fed by artesian springs, are now replenished by well water during the dry season. Completed in 1879, the lake's water is maintained by a 19-foot high, 116-foot crested earthen dam along the canyon road, known as dam No. 822. The lakes once served as a reservoir for the historic Frink ranch, but they and much of the surrounding land is now owned by the Riverside Land Conservancy. (Courtesy of the author.)

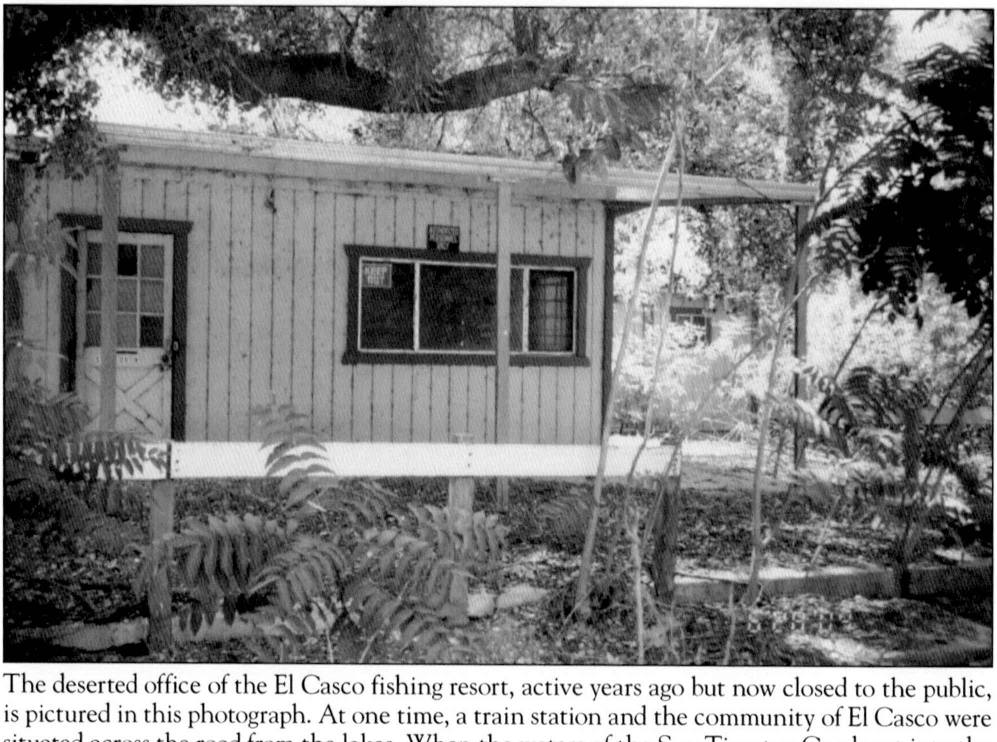

The deserted office of the El Casco fishing resort, active years ago but now closed to the public, is pictured in this photograph. At one time, a train station and the community of El Casco were situated across the road from the lakes. When the waters of the San Timoteo Creek cut into the south bank and threatened to undermine the train station, it was moved to another location and the community dwindled away. (Courtesy of the author.)

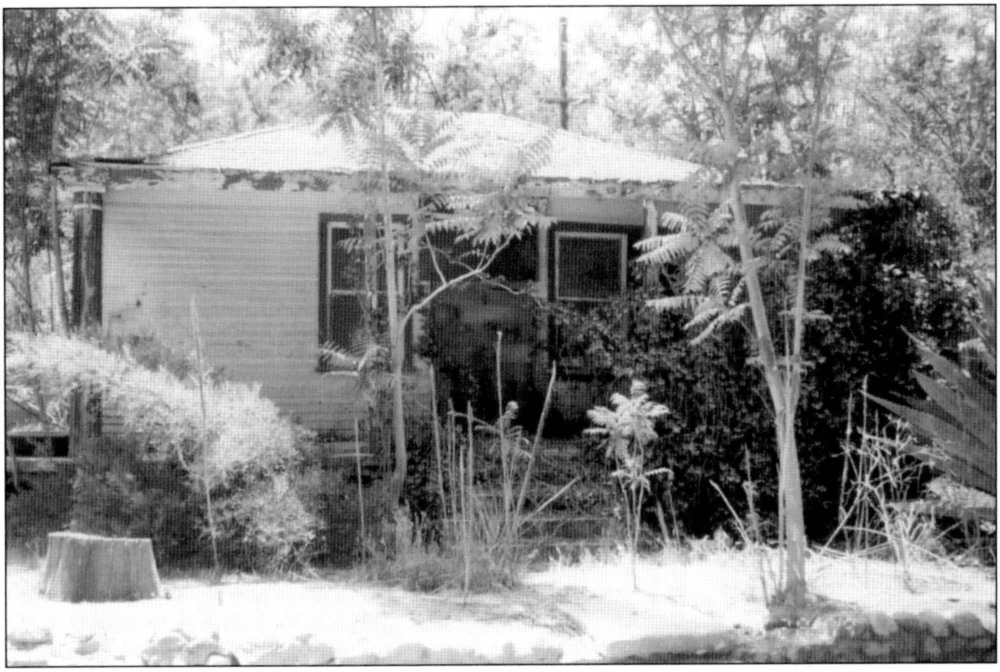

During the heyday of the El Casco Lakes resort, people purchased lots above the ridge of the lake to build vacation cabins. Others came to camp and fish. Pictured here is a typical cabin of that era, now deserted. Since the lake has been closed to the public, fishing has been suspended and numerous cabins left abandoned—although some are still occupied. (Courtesy of the author.)

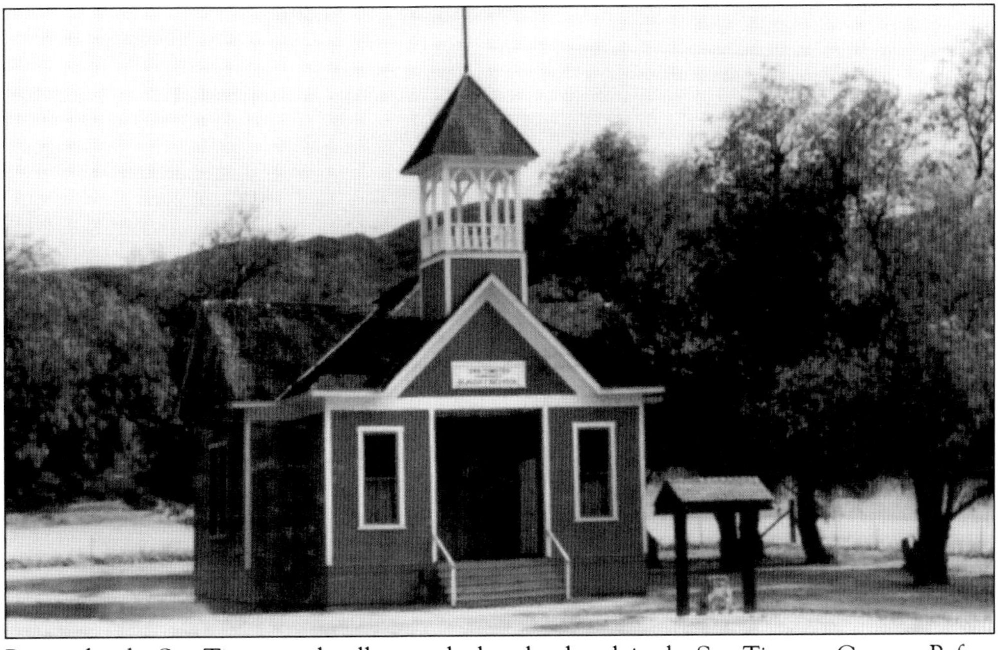

Pictured is the San Timoteo schoolhouse, the best landmark in the San Timoteo Canyon. Before construction of I-10, this canyon was a direct artery through the San Gorgonio Pass. The history of the pass would be diminished if the San Timoteo Canyon were to be ignored, for it existed even before the schoolhouse. (Courtesy of the author.)

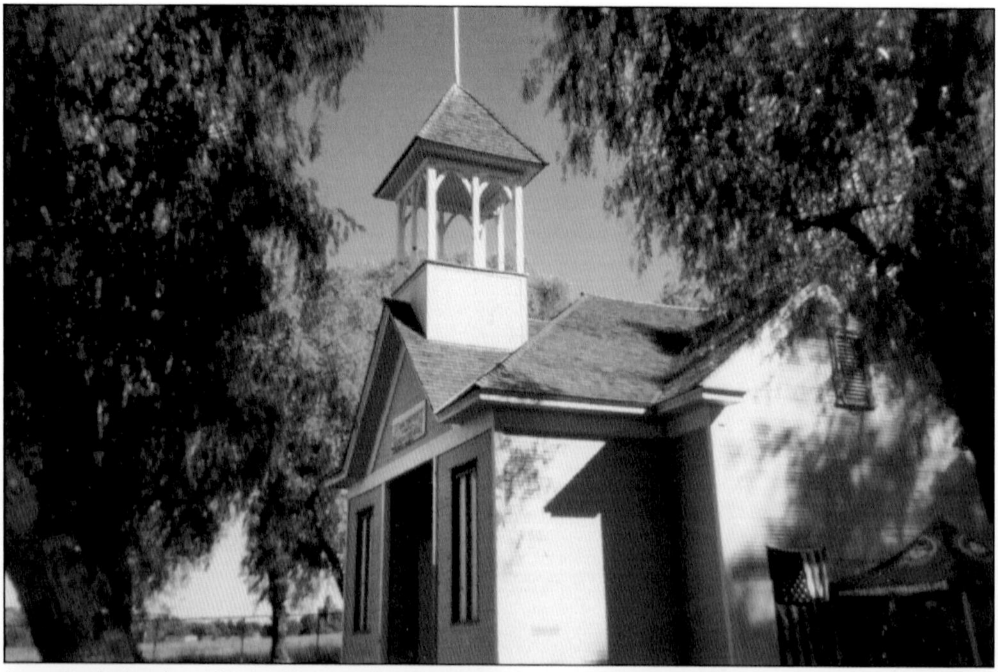

Jerry Cody fought to keep the one-room, San Timoteo Canyon schoolhouse standing. Thanks to his and other's efforts, it was bought and renovated by the Riverside County Regional Park and Open-Space District. The school is pictured here during a celebration in Ray Flores' honor on his 90th birthday, a graduate of the school in 1926. The photograph was taken before renovation was complete. (Courtesy of the author.)

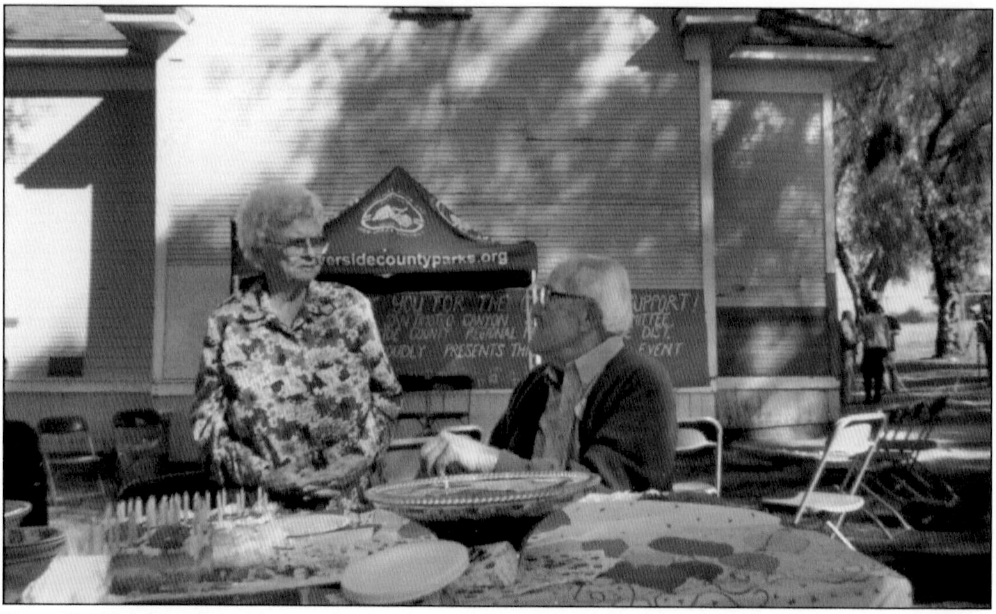

Betty DeWitt faces Ray Flores, who is relating a story about his boyhood days at the school. Betty and Ray were classmates and this celebration gave them a chance to reminisce about old times. Ray remembers climbing the trees in the school yard during recess and waving to the train engineer, who often slowed to wave back to the children at play. (Courtesy of Jerry Cody.)

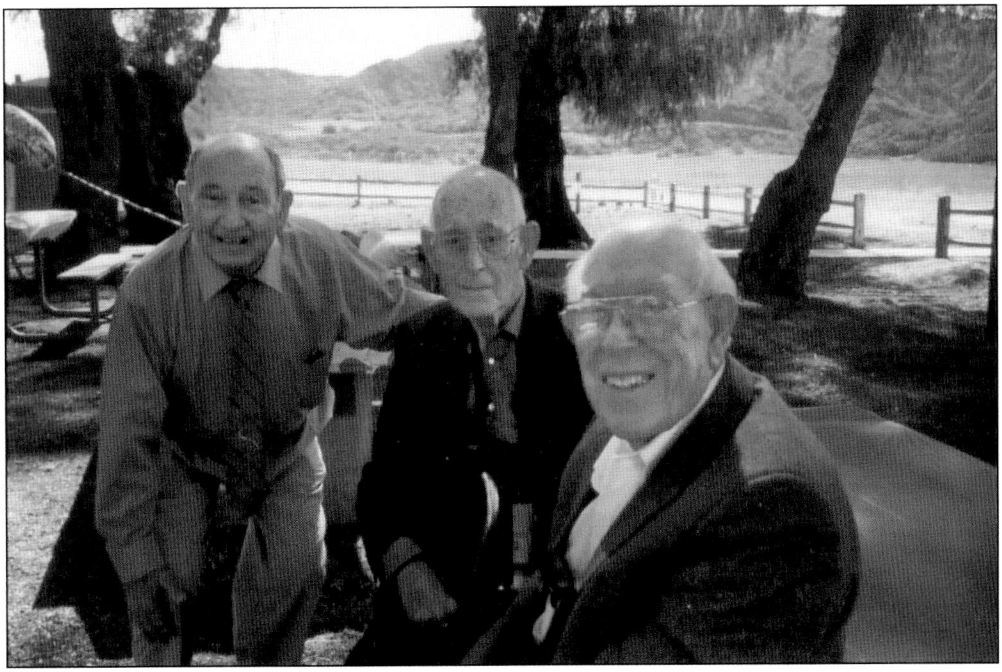

Jerry Cody, left, lives near the San Timoteo Canyon School and has worked hard to promote its restoration. Beside him are the Van de Vender brothers, whose grandfather built the one-room school. This celebration commemorated restoration progress and the installation of the school as a county park. (Courtesy of Jerry Cody.)

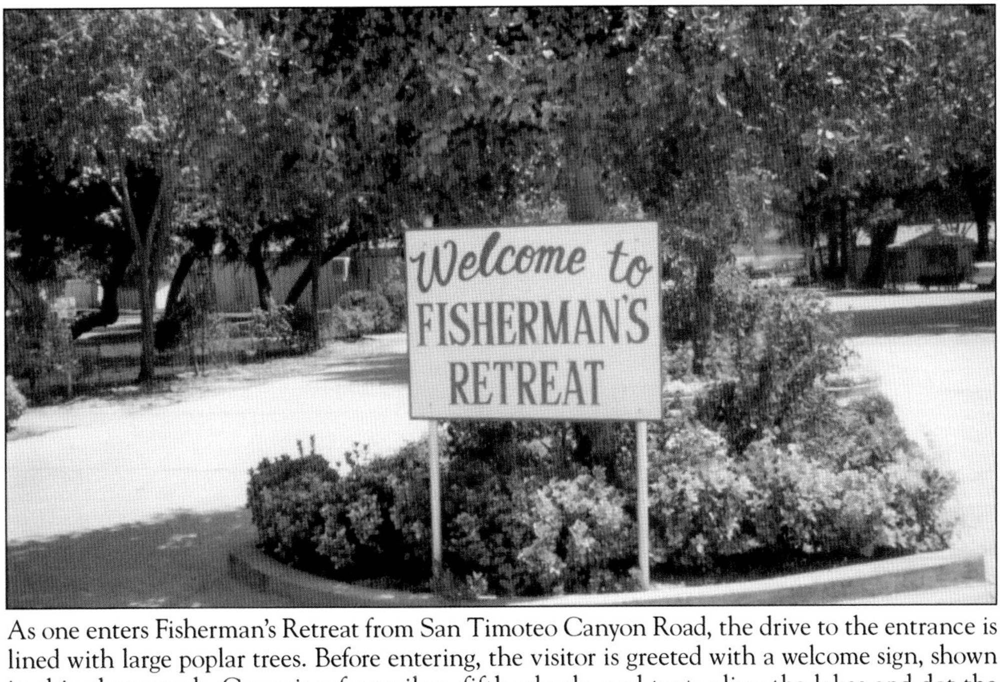

As one enters Fisherman's Retreat from San Timoteo Canyon Road, the drive to the entrance is lined with large poplar trees. Before entering, the visitor is greeted with a welcome sign, shown in this photograph. Campsites for trailers, fifth wheels, and tents align the lakes and dot the terrain throughout the park. Often fishermen sit around the levies of the lake fishing for bass, trout, perch, and catfish. (Courtesy of the author.)

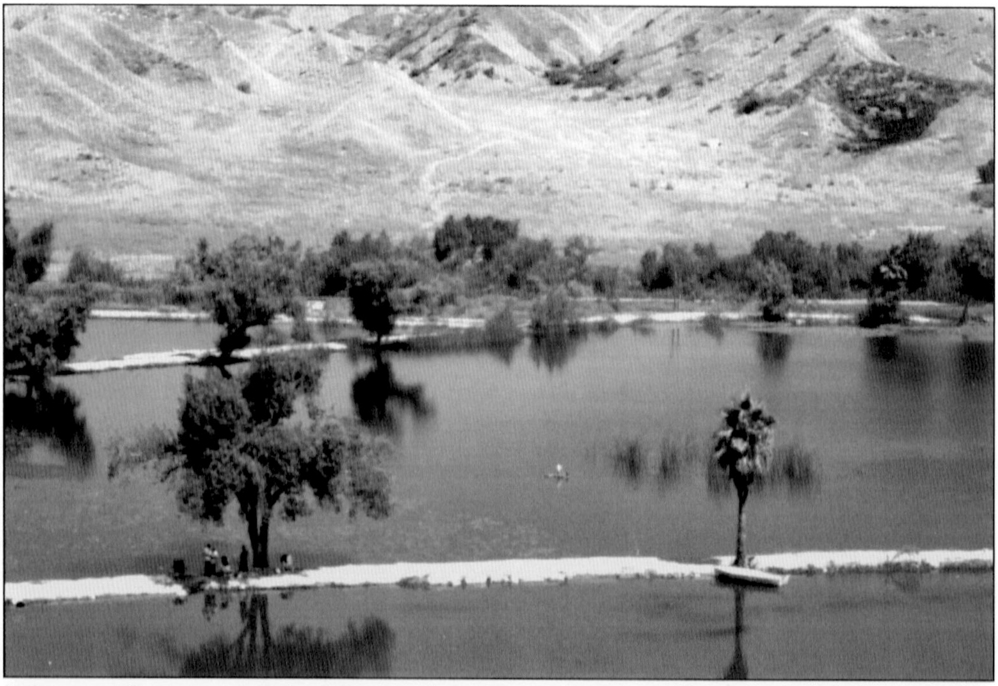

Fisherman's Retreat, a popular fishing and camping resort, is seen from the high ridge above the lakes. Resort homes and cabins have been built on the ridge, providing a wonderful view below. Fisherman's Retreat has become an affiliate of Coast to Coast Resorts and many people stop here to camp for a few days. (Courtesy of the author.)

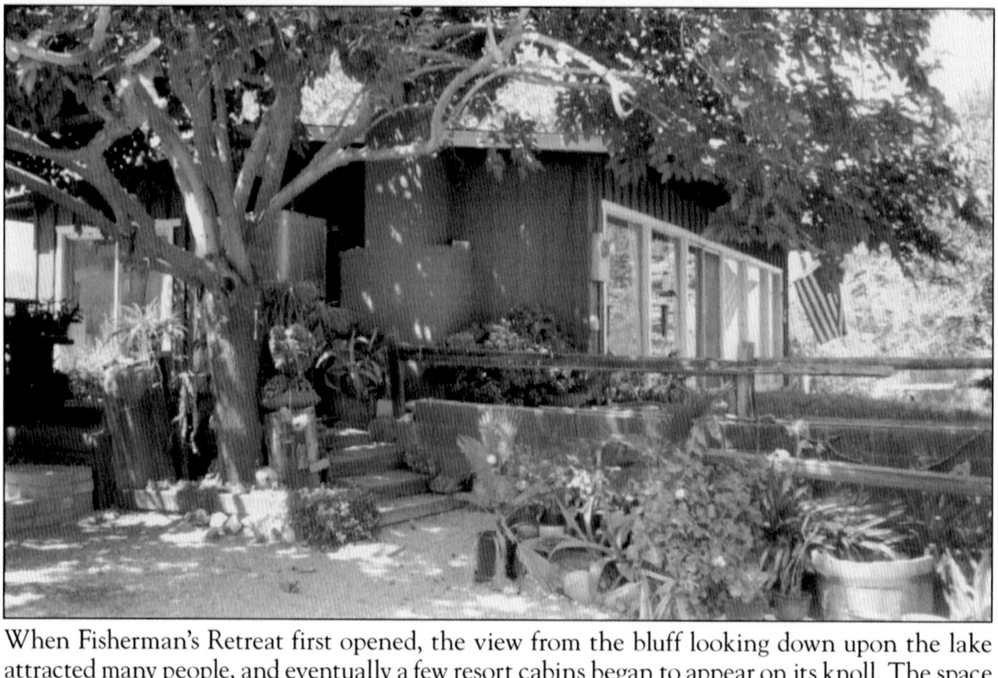

When Fisherman's Retreat first opened, the view from the bluff looking down upon the lake attracted many people, and eventually a few resort cabins began to appear on its knoll. The space was limited but in time it filled with cottages—some for weekend visits and several for permanent residents like the one pictured here. (Courtesy of the author.)

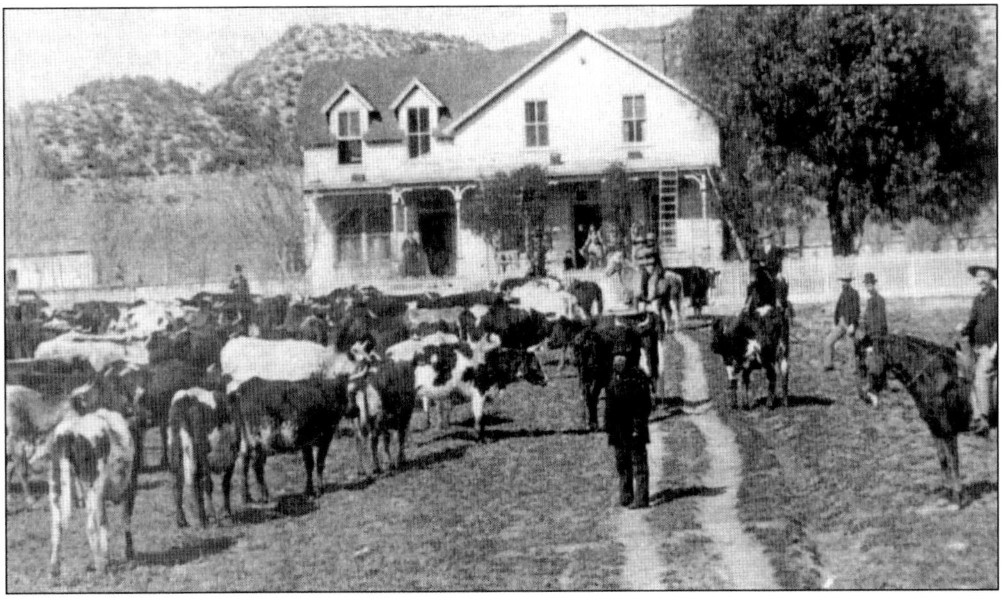

The original William Singleton ranch house sat on Woodhouse Road in San Timoteo Canyon. Singleton came to San Timoteo Canyon in 1875 with his wife, Ann, and their children Ann and William, eventually developing a 4,000-acre ranch. Singleton's wife, Ann, was the sister of George Cooley, who owned the vast acreage of the Cooley Ranch to the west. (Courtesy of Nara Haskell.)

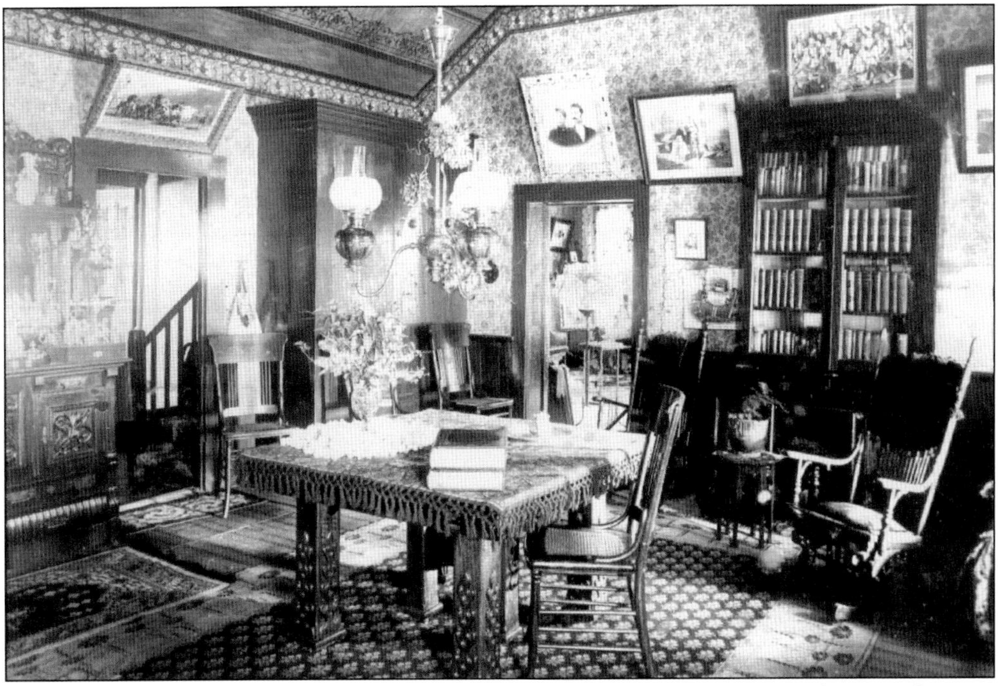

This is the dining and sitting room of the Cooley Ranch house in 1898. Ann Singleton used to visit her brother's family at the Cooley Ranch often. Their house, unlike the Singleton Ranch house, was elaborate and served as a showcase for the many people who visited there. The conductors of the Southern Pacific (SP) Railroad were often guests at the Cooley Ranch whenever they had a layover in Colton. (Courtesy of Nara Haskell.)

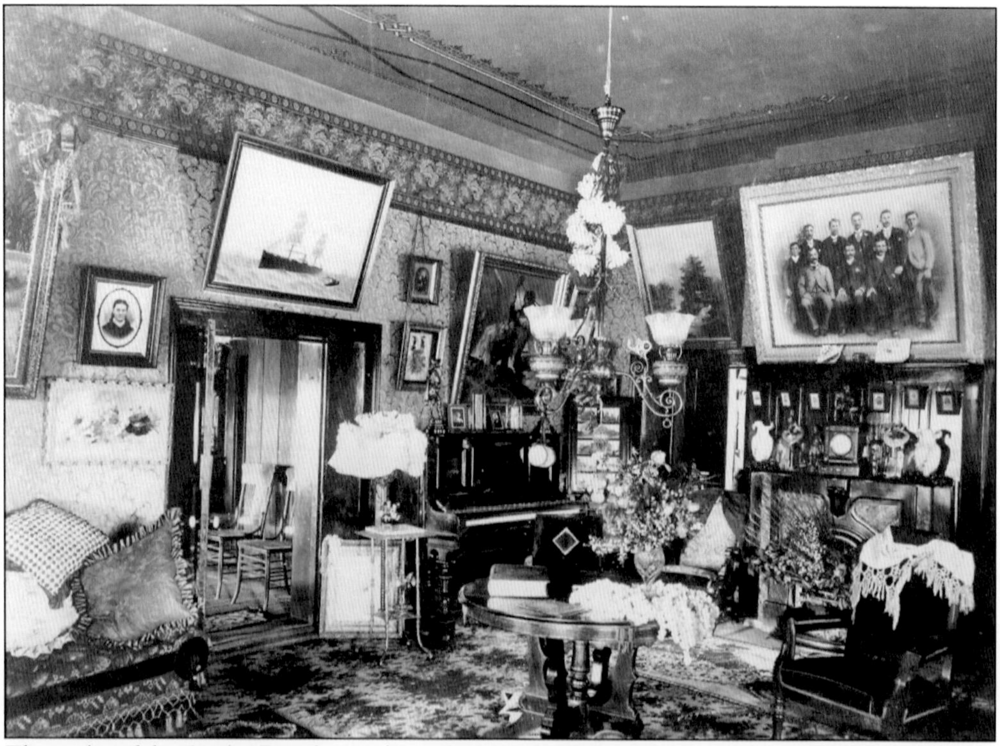

The parlor of the Cooley Ranch was the gathering site for family members and business associates of the Cooley family. The family residence had the reputation of being an important place to visit and numerous people sought entrance to see the elaborate decor; it often brought them back for other occasions. It is interesting to note the extremely high ceiling, as compared to many of today's homes. (Courtesy of Nara Haskell.)

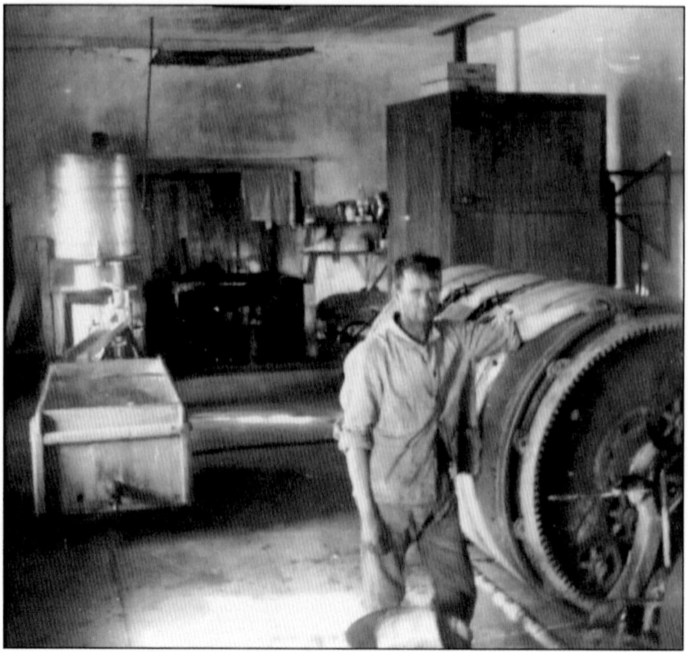

Behind the Singleton Ranch house was a large barn that housed a big butter churn, shown here. Used to churn milk from their large dairy, the butter was trucked daily to a creamery in Redlands. The barn also served as an entertainment center for dances and meetings, with people coming from as far as Redlands and Beaumont. It became known as Buttermilk Hall. (Courtesy of Nara Haskell.)

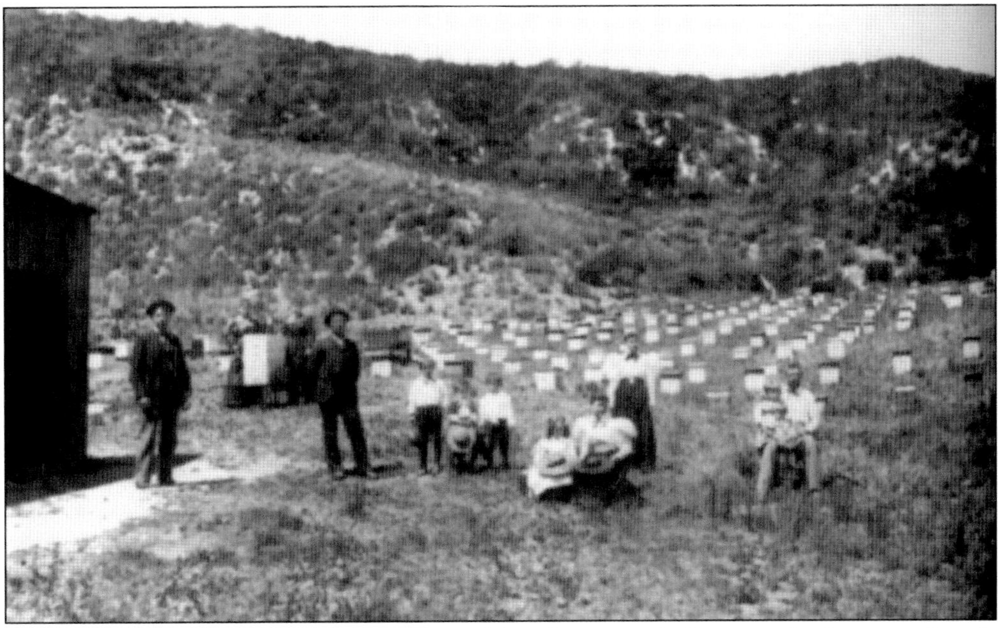

The Singleton family proudly poses in front of their large stand of bees on the Singleton Ranch in the San Timoteo Canyon. An important part of farm life was beekeeping. The handling of bees to obtain honey and wax was quite lucrative and consequently the family owned a large number of hives. (Courtesy of Nara Haskell.)

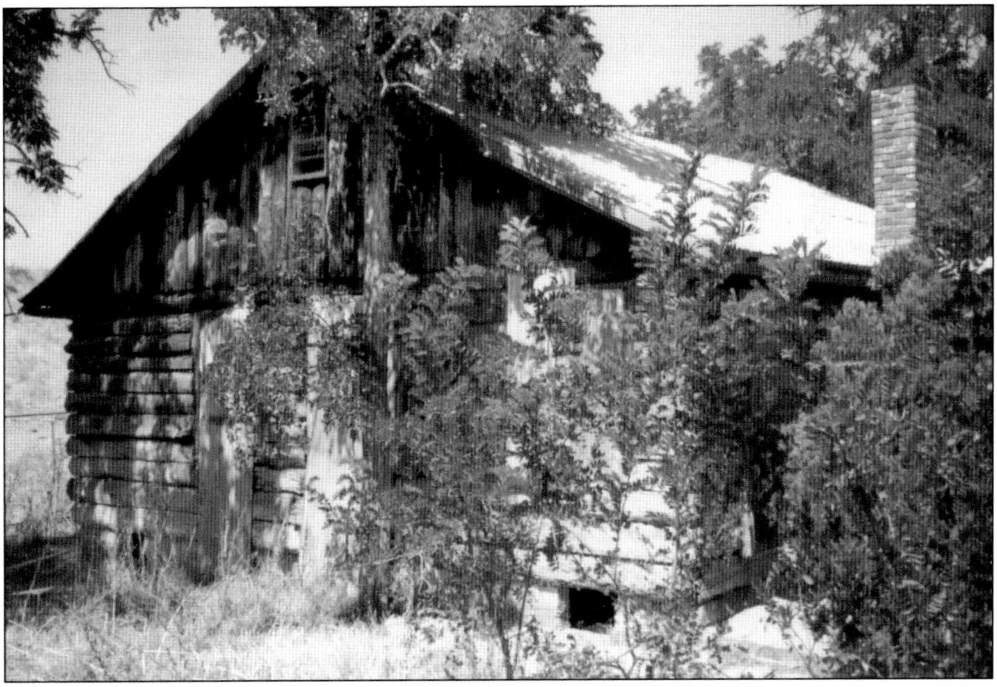

Pictured here is one of the few remaining structures on the old Singleton Ranch—a termite-ridden log cabin. A number of ranch hands and relatives lived on the large ranch and this house, like several others, has been abandoned. The original Singleton Ranch residence has been gone for some time, allegedly burned to the ground by fire. (Courtesy of the author.)

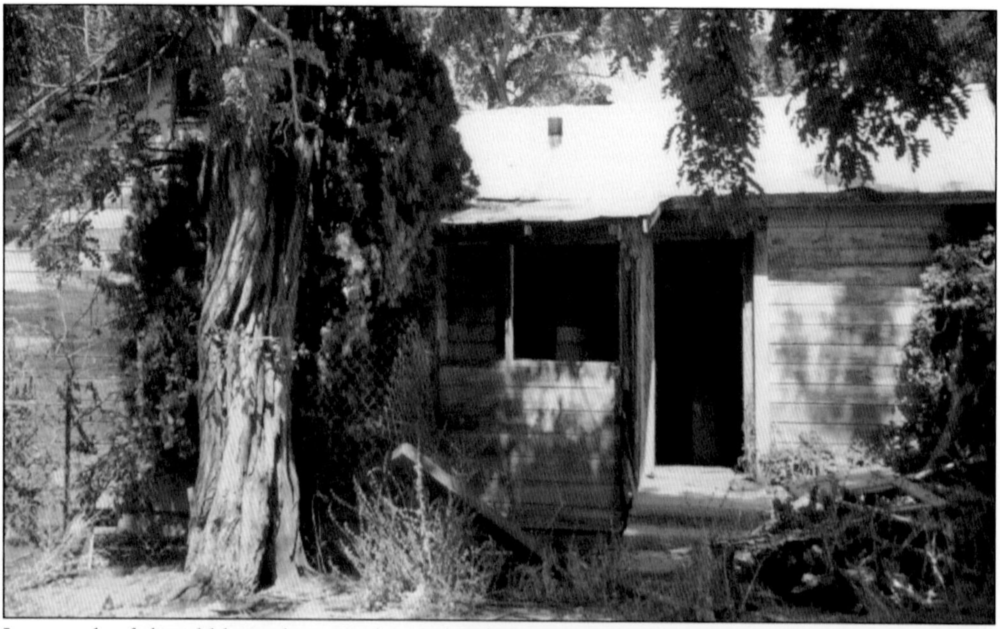

Just north of the old log cabin stands another house, seen in this photograph. Like a few other remaining structures on the site, it too is in a state of ruin and will soon be demolished. Images like this will be the last glimpses of the historic Singleton Ranch site, for drilling is now being performed on the ranch site for preliminary soil testing prior to housing development. (Courtesy of the author.)

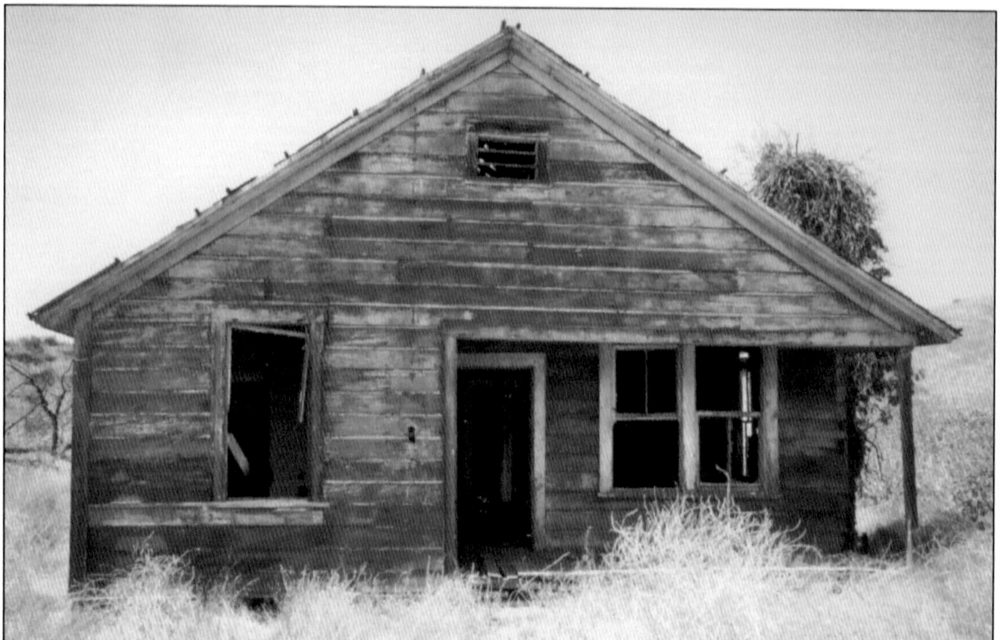

Because it is in the path of a large housing development, this dilapidated house on the Singleton Ranch is another structure that will soon be demolished. New construction will begin, and like numerous other sites in the area, rooftops will be added to the San Timoteo Canyon. (Courtesy of the author.)

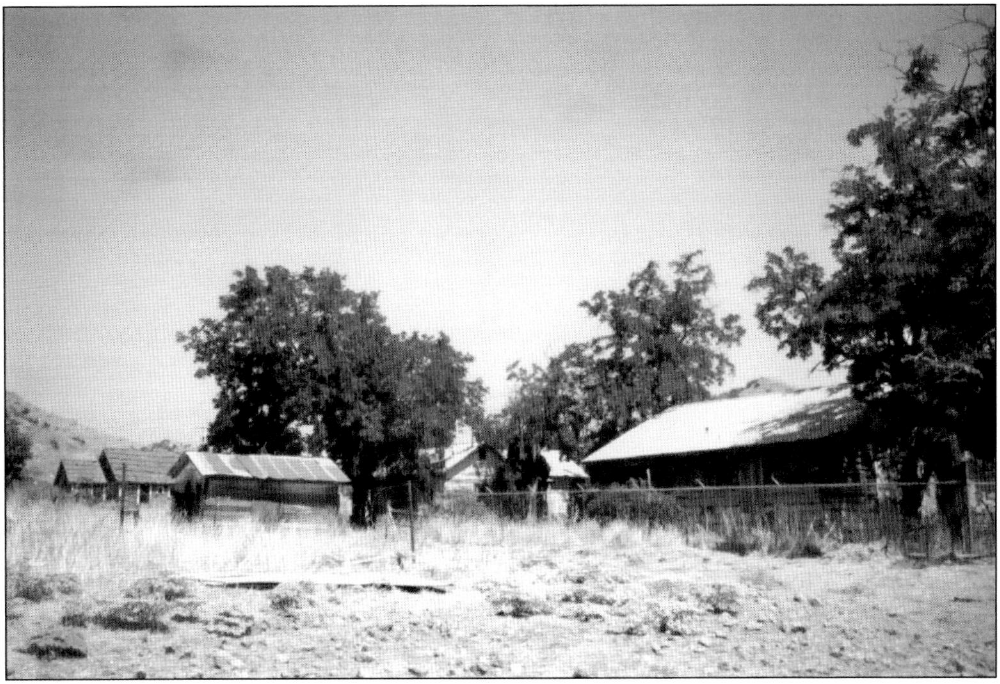

A row of worker's cabins was located behind a larger house on the Singleton Ranch. It took numerous farm workers to maintain a large farm like the Singleton Ranch and some lived on the ranch year-round. There are still a few structures on this property that have not yet succumbed to complete breakdown or fire. (Courtesy of the author.)

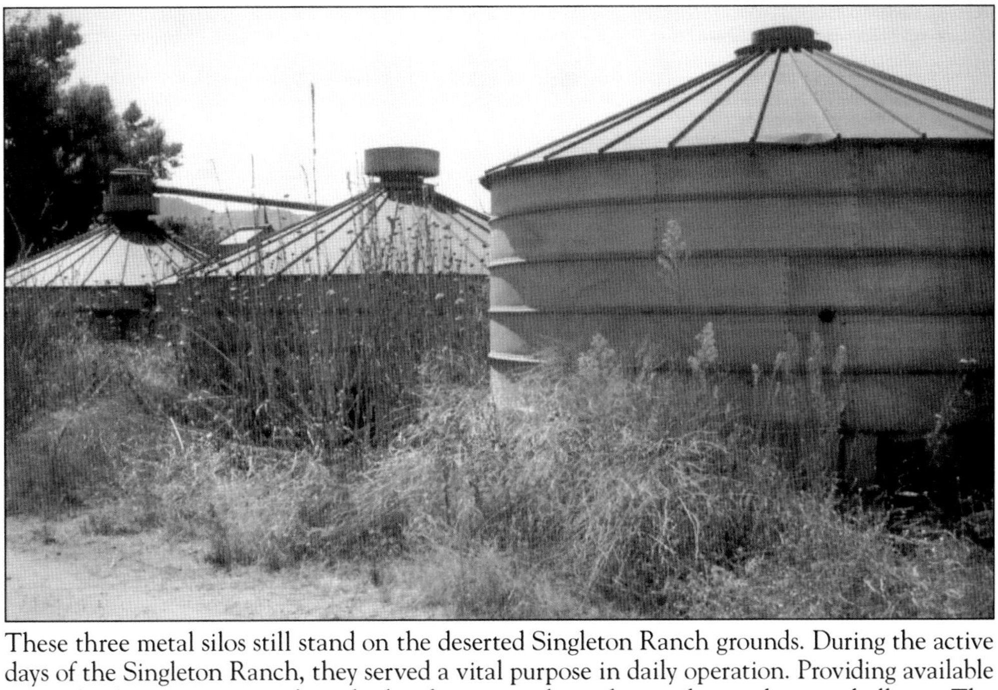

These three metal silos still stand on the deserted Singleton Ranch grounds. During the active days of the Singleton Ranch, they served a vital purpose in daily operation. Providing available forage for the numerous cattle and other farm animals on the ranch was always a challenge. The silos helped in this respect. (Courtesy of the author.)

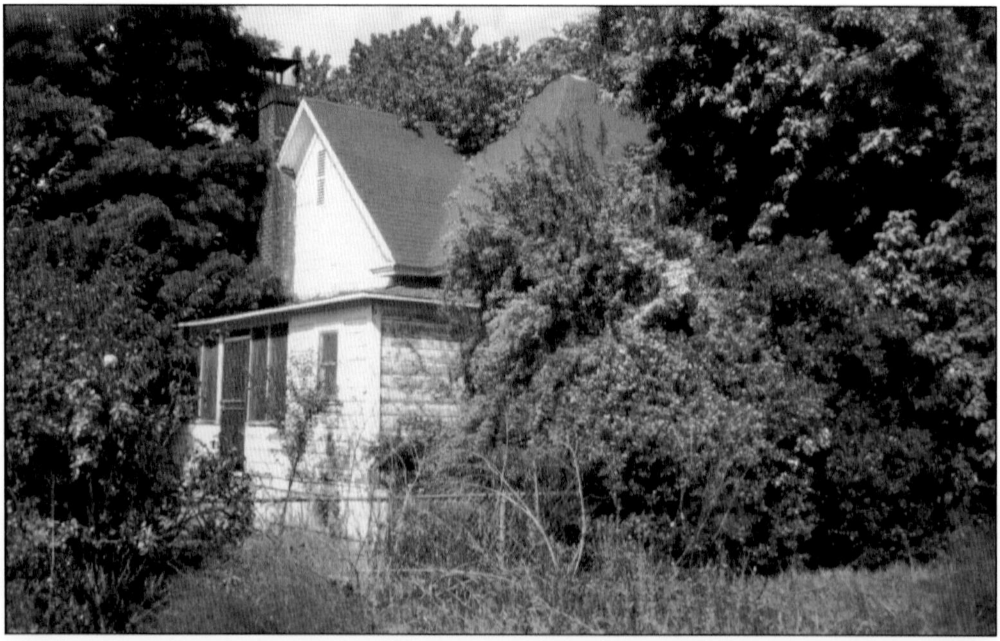

This house, now on the historic Haskell Ranch in San Timoteo Canyon, was the home of Will and Gerty Singleton. It was originally built on the Singleton Ranch and moved from Woodhouse Canyon Road to this location when the ranch was sold. Moved diagonally across a field on logs pulled by horses, it took six weeks to accomplish the task—all during the workers' spare time. (Courtesy of Nara Haskell.)

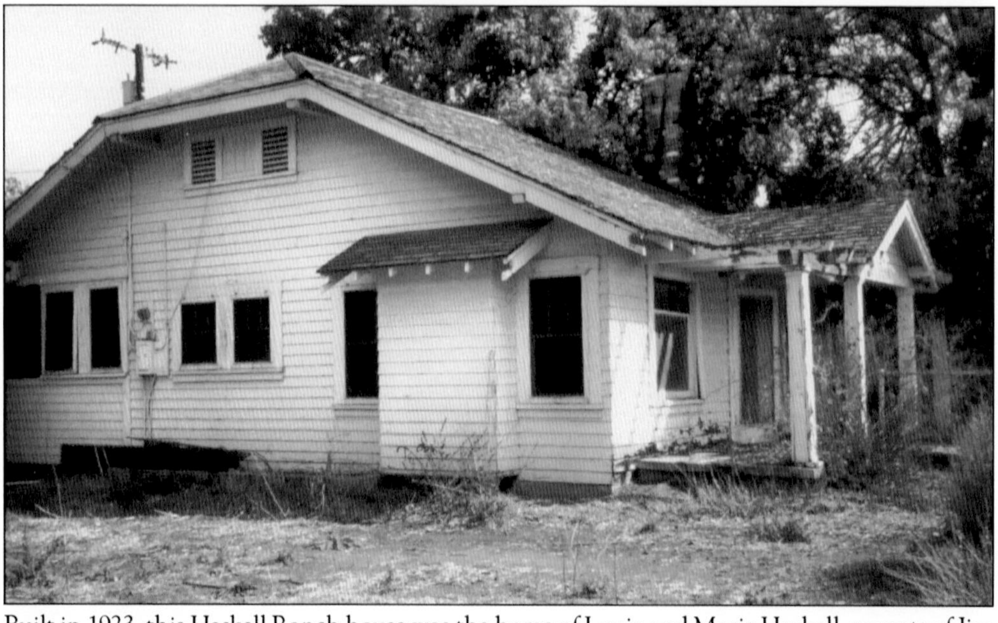

Built in 1923, this Haskell Ranch house was the home of Louie and Marie Haskell, parents of Jim Haskell, who married Nara Haskell. It faced San Timoteo Canyon Road and was, at one time, next to the original 1800s ranch house, once lived in by James and Ann Singleton-Haskell. Jim and Nara Haskell later lived in Jim's parent's house until about 1950, while operating the ranch. (Courtesy of Nara Haskell.)

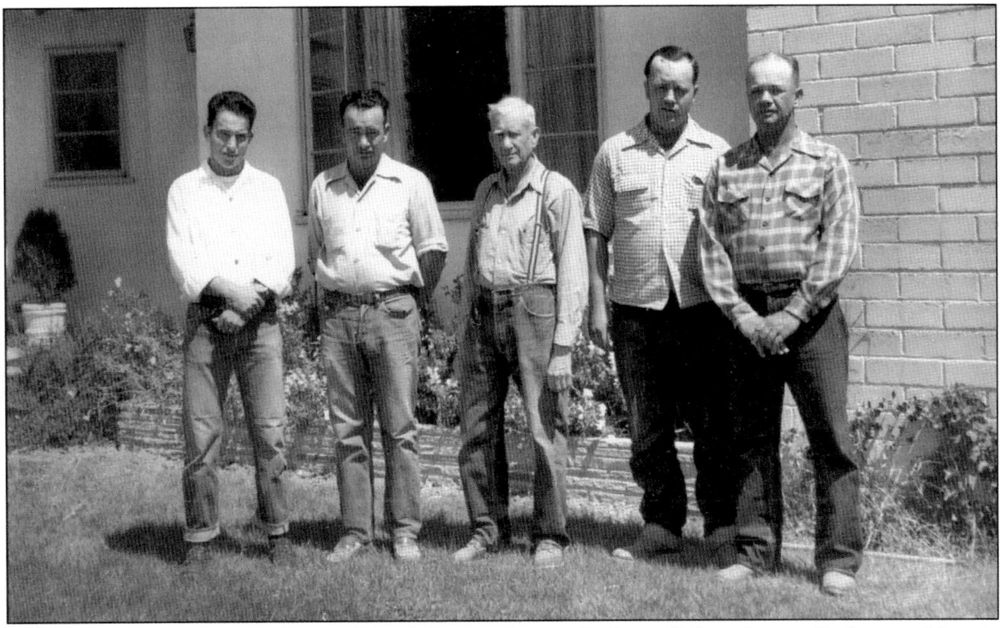

The Haskell clan, pictured here, from left to right, are Robert, Kelsey, James S., Jim, and Lewis Haskell. Lewis is Jim's dad and James S. is Lewis's dad. The picture was taken at a nearby farmhouse in San Timoteo Canyon. James S. Haskell, Jim's grandfather, and Will Singleton bought the Singleton/Haskell Ranch in 1913, and Jim and Nara Haskell owned it until 1950. (Courtesy of Nara Haskell.)

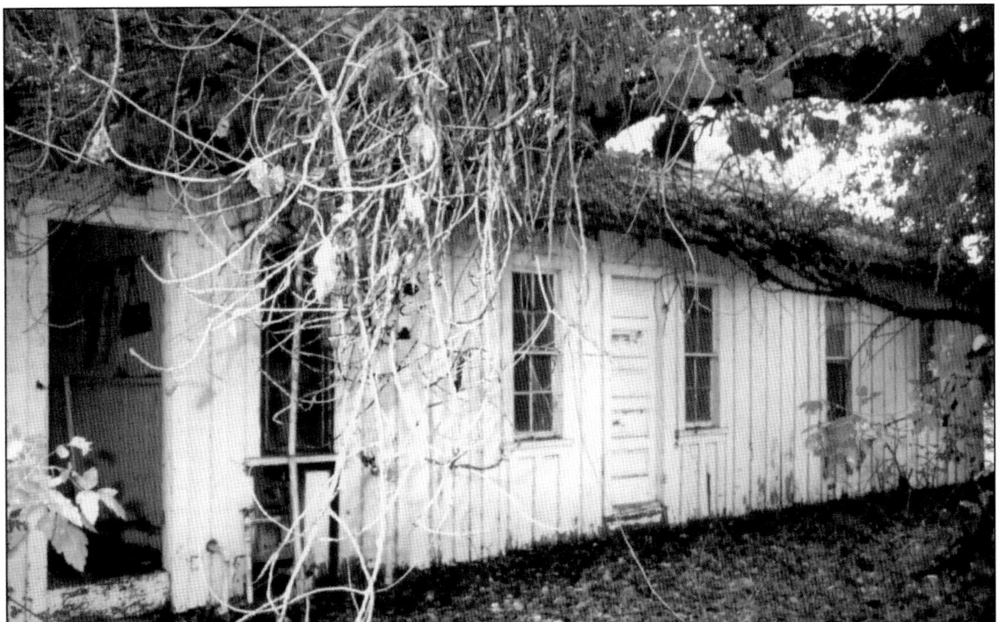

Located in the San Timoteo Canyon, this vine-covered bunkhouse once served the workers of the large Haskell Ranch. It was occupied year-round by workers who milked cows, did the tractor work, planted, harvested, and performed other jobs required to run the ranch. The bunkhouse was an important entity of the ranch. (Courtesy of Nara Haskell.)

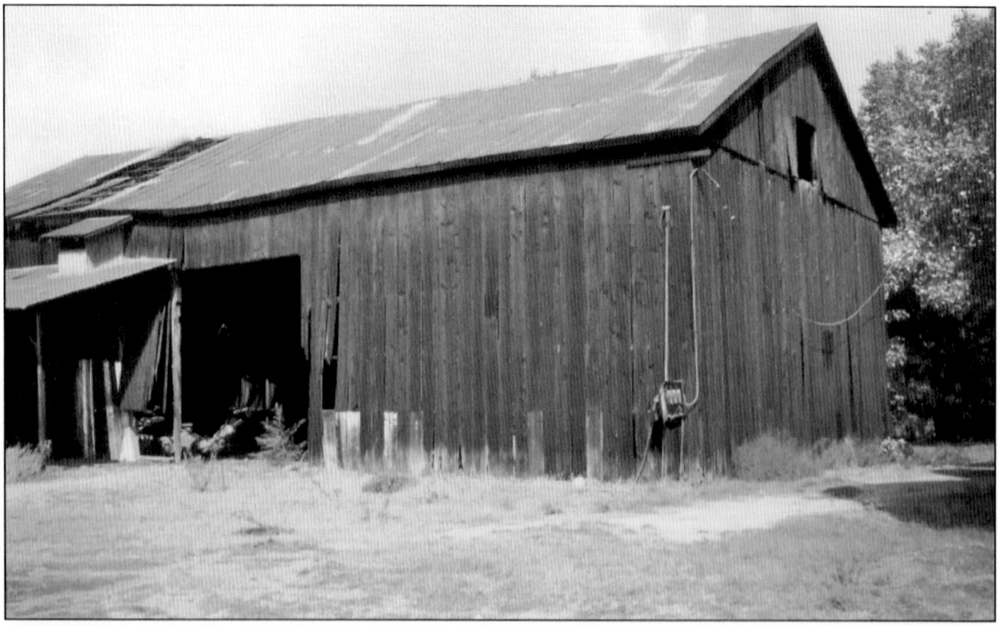

This barn, located on the Haskell Ranch, was an important part of ranch life. Most barns were the central locus of the ranch and were deemed so because they served many uses—not only to store hay and feed, but also to house farm equipment that was needed on a large ranch such as this one. (Courtesy of Nara Haskell.)

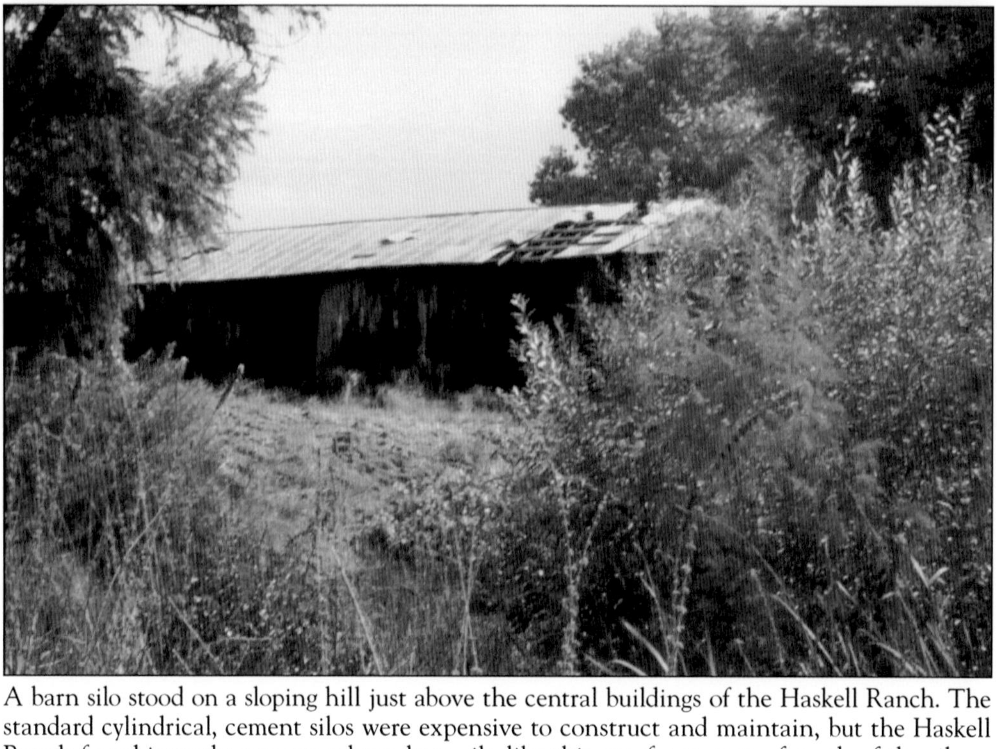

A barn silo stood on a sloping hill just above the central buildings of the Haskell Ranch. The standard cylindrical, cement silos were expensive to construct and maintain, but the Haskell Ranch found it prudent to use a large barn silo like this one for storage of much of the silage. Loading and unloading was easier on this type of silo. (Courtesy of Nara Haskell.)

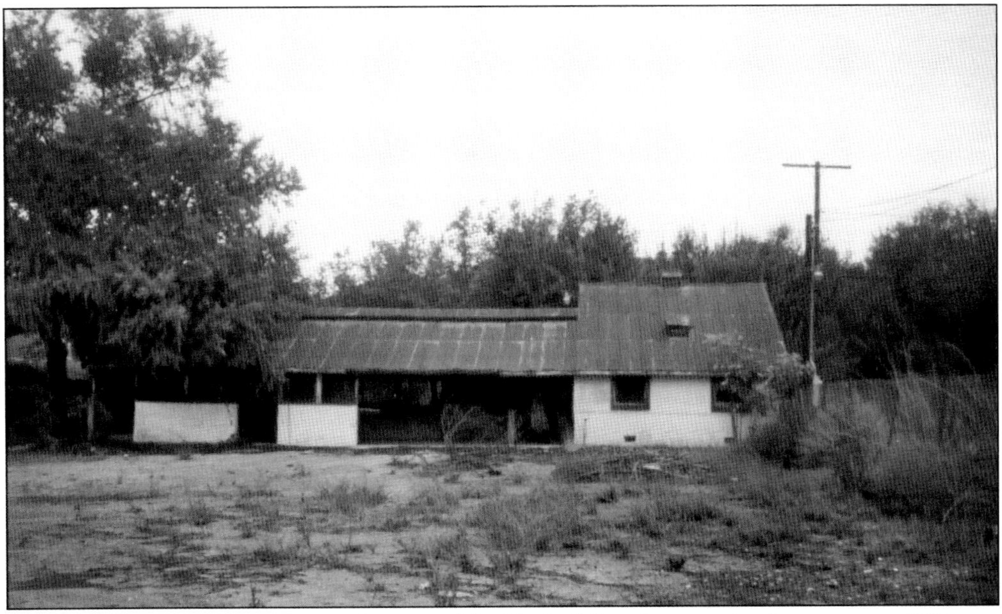

The milk barn was an important element of the Haskell Ranch operation because over 300 cows were milked daily. Maintaining a dairy was a never-ending task, as cows had to be milked morning and night, seven days a week. Properly maintaining the herd always kept the farm workers busy. (Courtesy of Nara Haskell.)

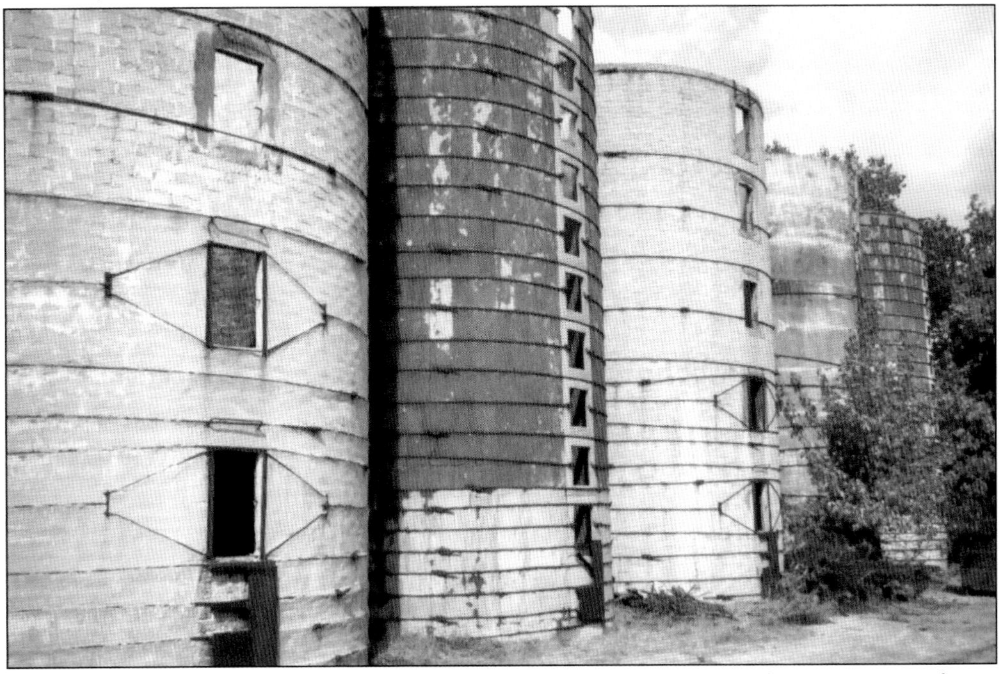

The Haskell Ranch had numerous silos, like the ones pictured here. They were a significant component of the ranch because the storage of silage was of utmost importance. Many hours of work were centered on the silos for loading and unloading silage material for cattle. During one particular loading operation, a man was killed when he fell from the top of one of the silos. (Courtesy of Nara Haskell.)

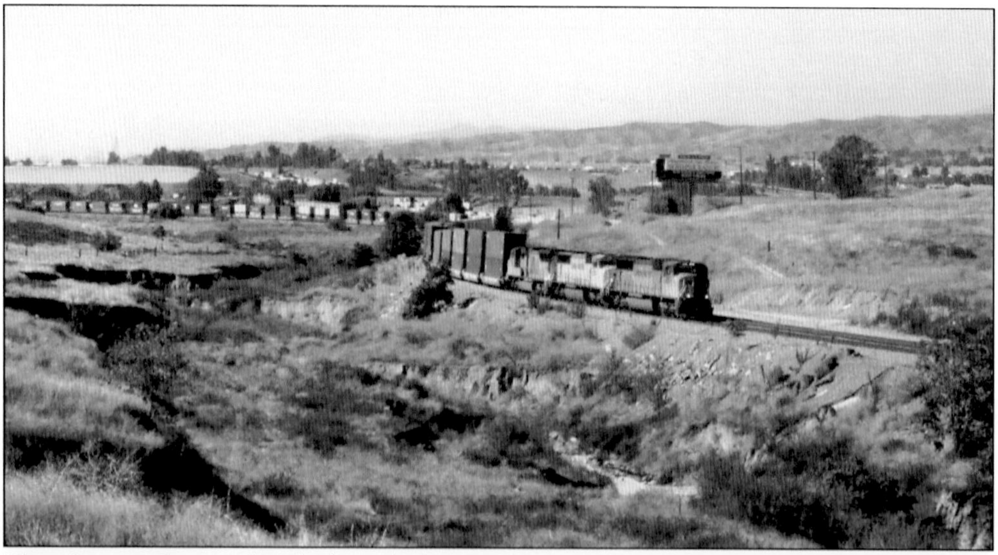

This photograph was taken looking down San Timoteo Canyon near the junction of I-10 and Highway 60. Trains, moving long trails of cargo carriers, stacked two high on each flatbed, are often seen traveling through San Timoteo Canyon. (Courtesy of the author.)

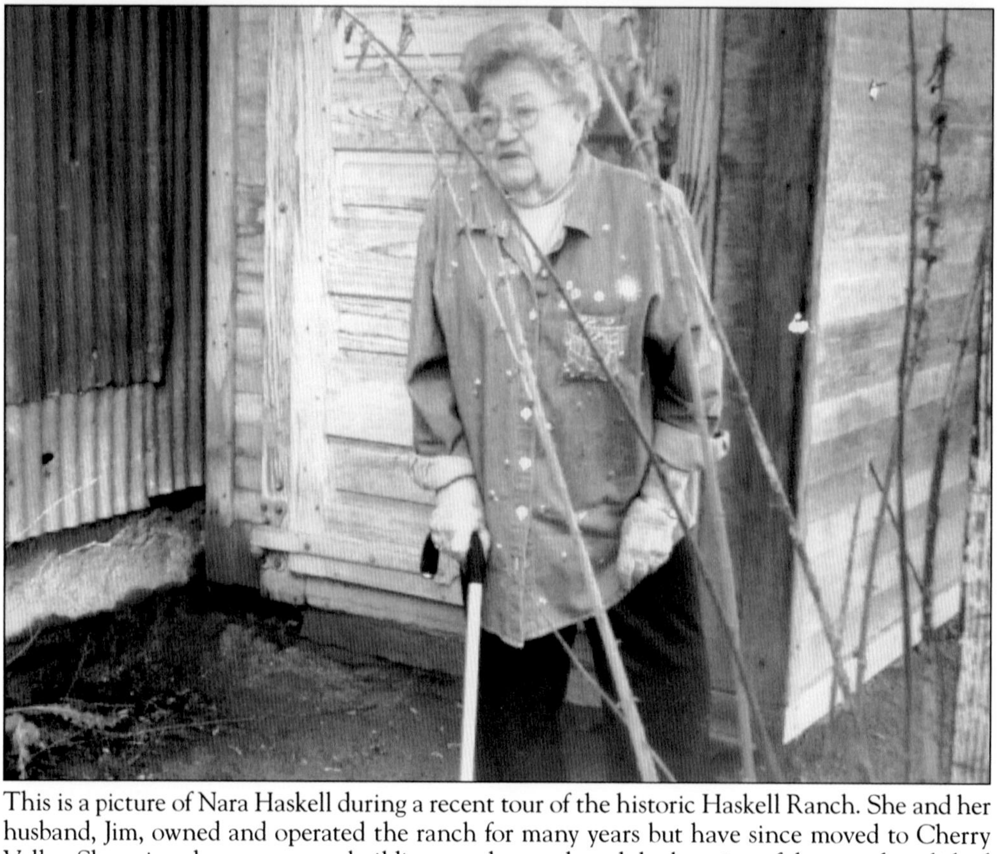

This is a picture of Nara Haskell during a recent tour of the historic Haskell Ranch. She and her husband, Jim, owned and operated the ranch for many years but have since moved to Cherry Valley. She pointed out numerous buildings on the ranch and the location of the now demolished Weaver adobe, once a stage stop. (Courtesy of Nara Haskell.)

Two

CALIMESA

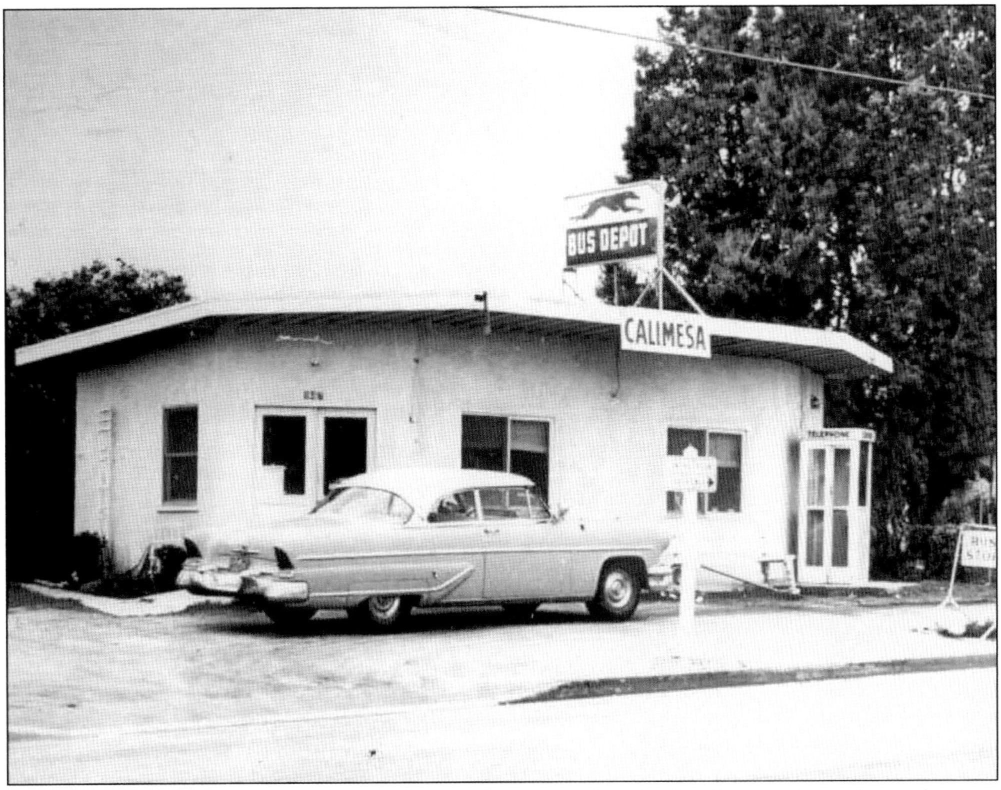

When small communities such as Calimesa began to dot the landscape throughout the San Gorgonio Pass, the demand for small Greyhound bus depots became evident. Shown here is the depot established in Calimesa in the mid-1950s. Though only a small one, it served Calimesa well during this period. Note the large V-8 Mercury car parked in front, now a vintage automobile. (Courtesy of the Yucaipa Valley Historical Society.)

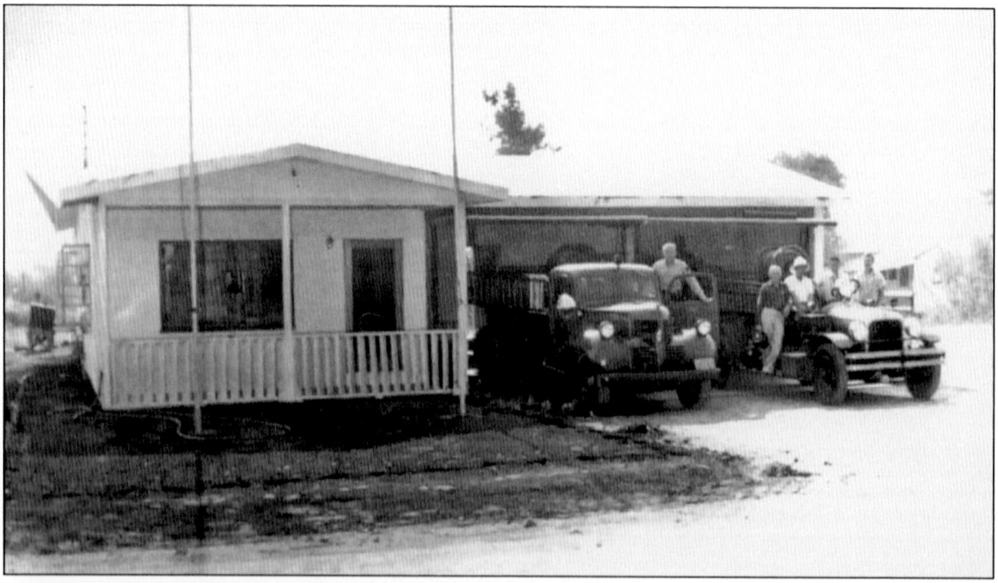

For the citizens of Calimesa, June 15, 1957, was a great day—it marked the dedication of their fire department. Joe Scarite, alert and ready to challenge any fire, stands by the old Segrames engine. During this time, it served the community well. (Courtesy of the Yucaipa Valley Historical Society.)

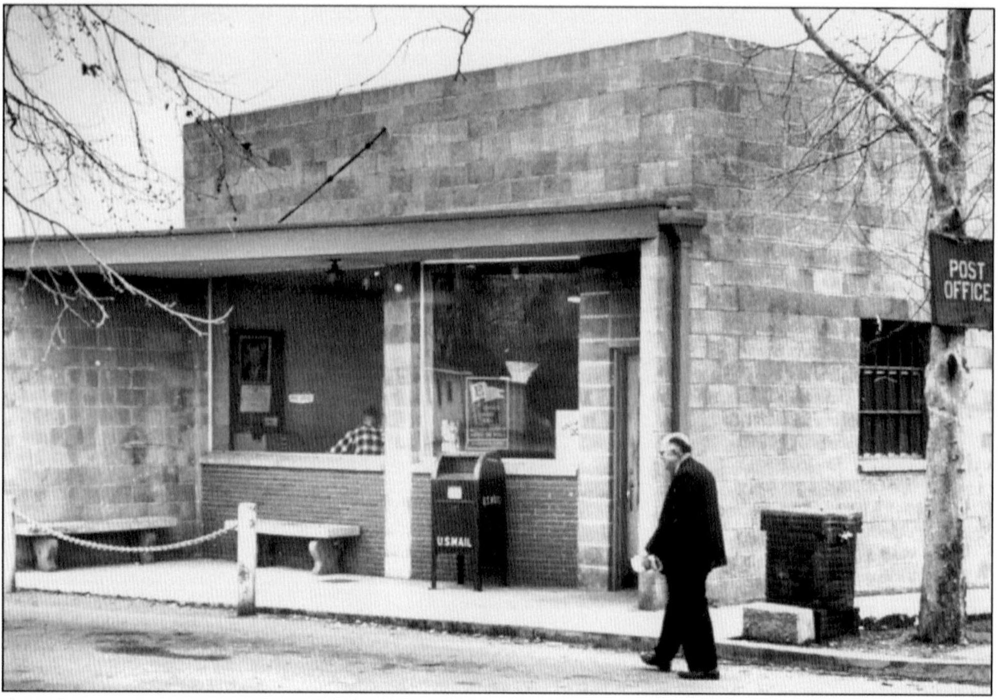

Another important entity established in Calimesa was the post office on Calimesa Boulevard. Communities in the pass took pride in their post offices and whenever one was established in their particular town, it was a time of joy for the townsfolk. Homer Carr, sales manager of the *News Mirror*, is shown in this 1960 photograph while walking near the Calimesa Post Office. (Courtesy of the Yucaipa Valley Historical Society.)

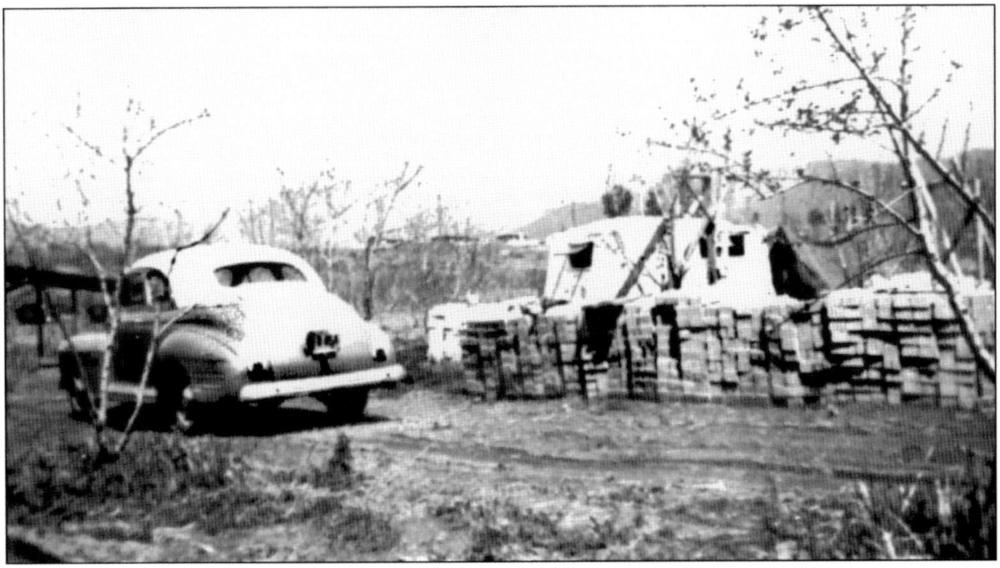

This was a common sight throughout the pass during its early growth. Some people migrated to the area with the means to build large homes, but others came with little money to do so. Pictured in Calimesa is a family with only a car, a trailer to live in, and a stack of bricks to begin building their house. (Courtesy of the Yucaipa Valley Historical Society.)

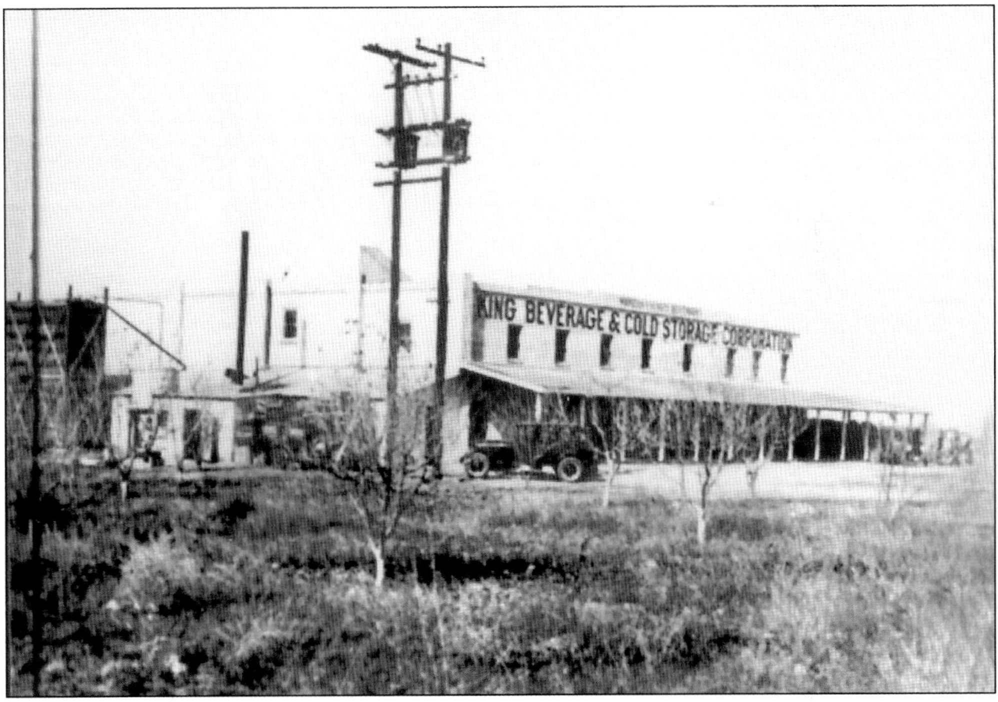

In the 1920s, Calimesa, like other communities in the San Gorgonio Pass, was beginning to expand. People were coming to settle and enjoy the pleasant weather and country living. For 10 years, from 1920 to 1930, the King Beverage plant on Calimesa Boulevard was a boom to the community's economy. It supplied a number of needed jobs for the small town. (Courtesy of the Yucaipa Valley Historical Society.)

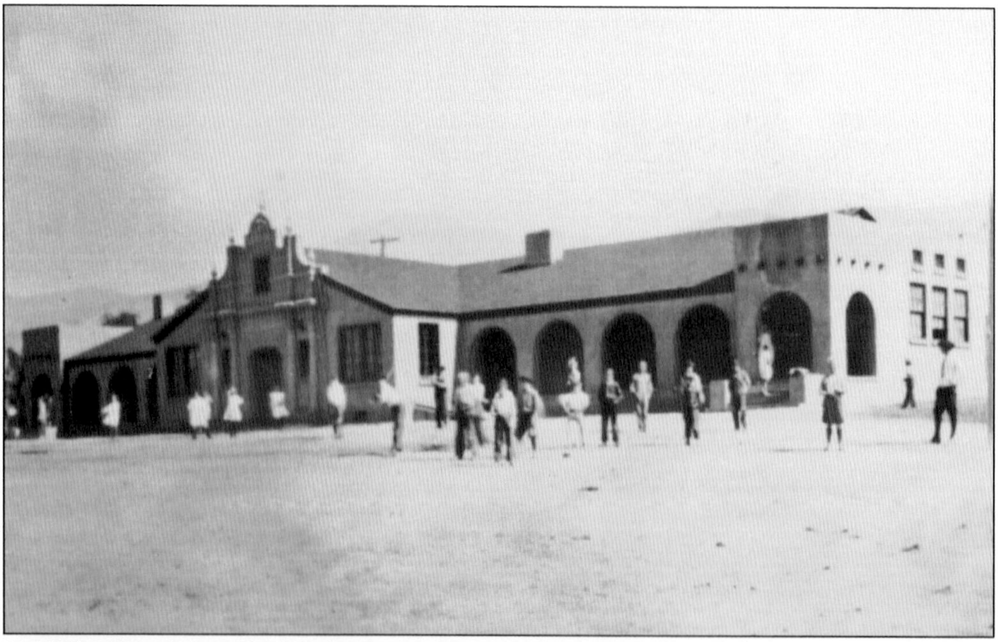

In 1925–1926, students from Calimesa traveled to the Yucaipa School before one opened in their own town. Note the unique architecture of the school, with a likeness to the structures of early missions. (Courtesy of the Yucaipa Valley Historical Society.)

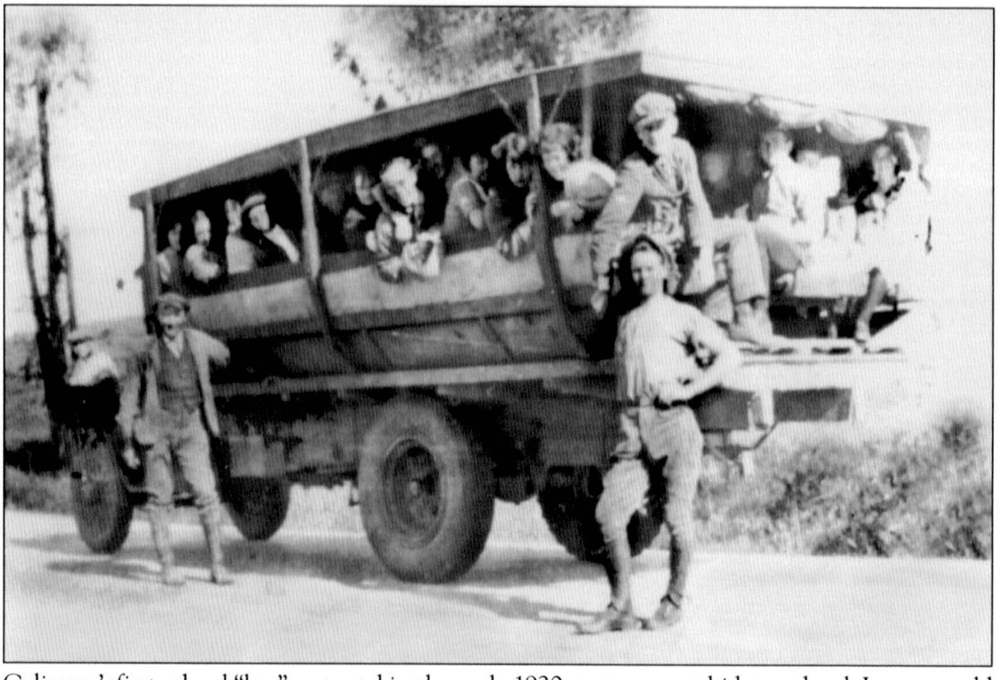

Calimesa's first school "bus" was used in the early 1920s to transport kids to school. It was an old farm truck that had been revamped with bench seats so that as many as possible could be carried to their destination. Even though it was not comfortable like the buses that are used today, these children appear to be enjoying the ride. (Courtesy of the Yucaipa Valley Historical Society.)

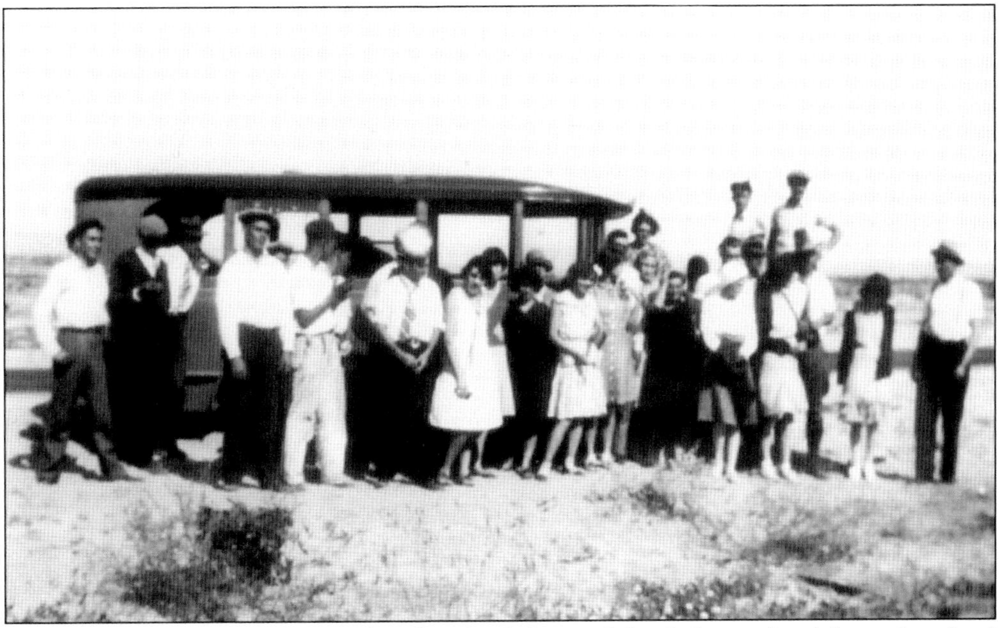

Shown here is the first real school bus that the Calimesa School obtained and deemed a school bus for its students. The man at the far right is believed to be Old Dad Hanson, the driver of the bus. It must have been a very cold ride to school in the winter months, with the windows that appear to be open. (Courtesy of the Yucaipa Valley Historical Society.)

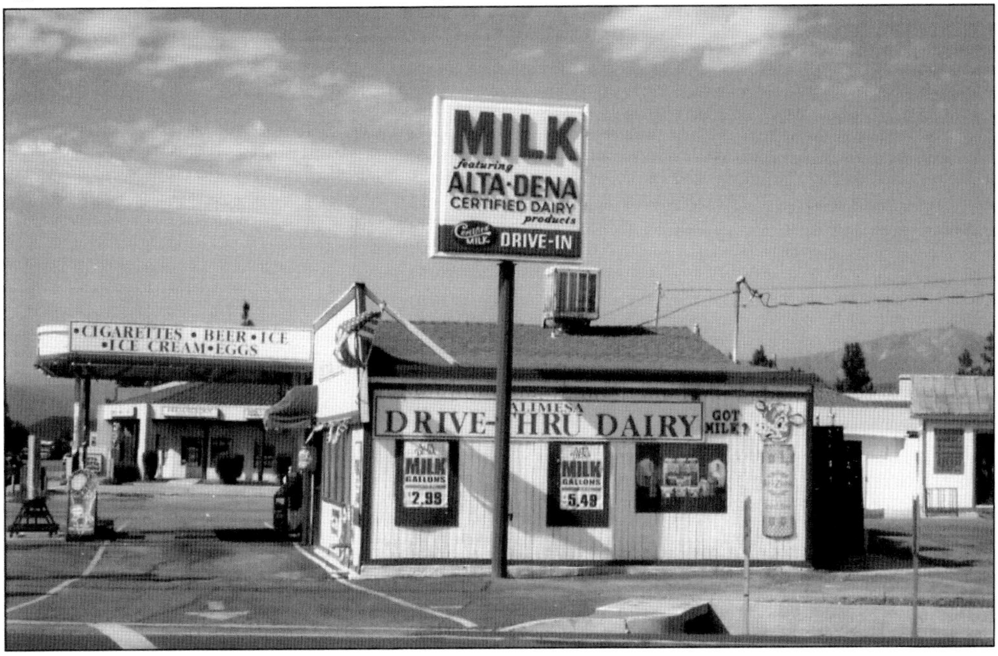

This Alta-Dena Dairy in Calimesa, located at 1045 Calimesa Boulevard, is one of three dairies in the pass area that once operated as a drive-through. The buildings of two other dairies can still be seen in Redlands and Beaumont. The one in Beaumont was originally a two-pump Standard Oil Station and was converted to the drive-through dairy in late 1964. The property is owned by Rich Rush of Calimesa and is leased to a tenant. (Courtesy of the author.)

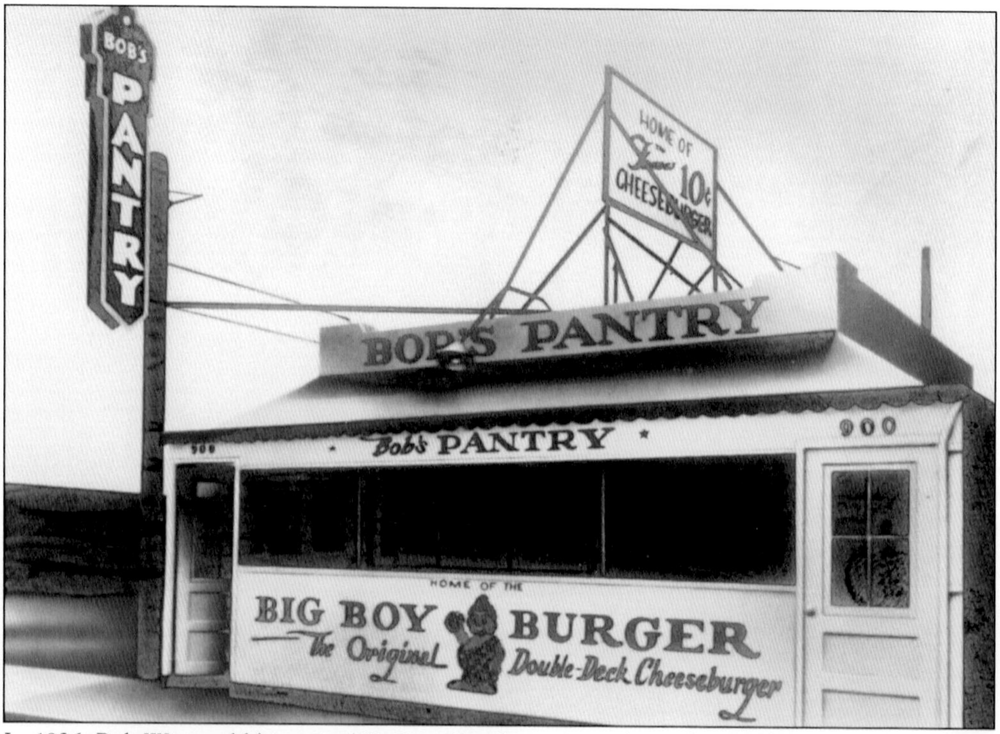

In 1936, Bob Wian sold his prized DeSoto Roadster to purchase this small hamburger stand in Glendale, California—Bob's Pantry, the precursor of Bob's Big Boy restaurant chain. In 1937, the first double-decker hamburger was born. Bob named it Big Boy in honor of a chubby, six-year-old boy with droopy overalls, who used to sweep up in exchange for a free burger. (Courtesy of Ricka Showalter.)

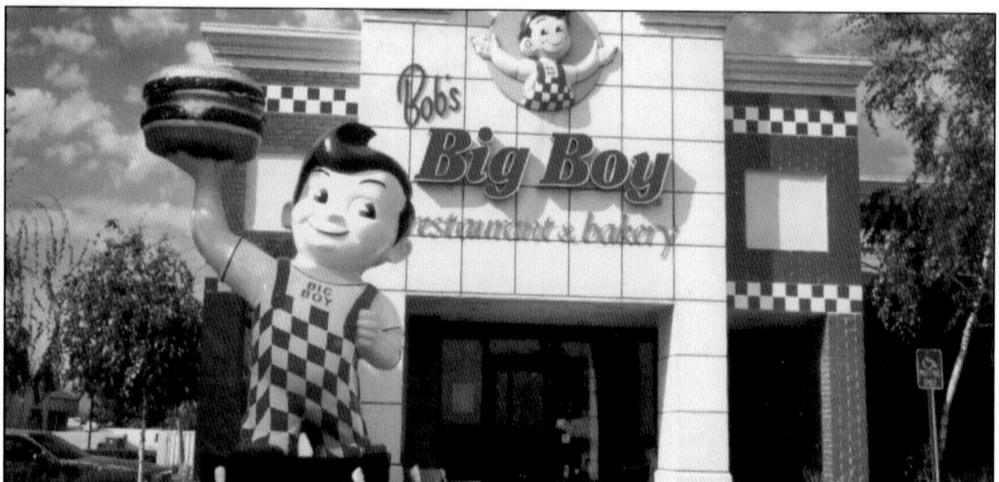

Big Boy has been an American institution since 1936. Pictured here in Calimesa is the first Big Boy restaurant, located on an interstate highway corridor. Its large caricature Big Boy, with an outstretched arm holding high a double hamburger, was held in captivity for almost two years because of Calimesa's sign laws governing the sign space businesses could use. Public outcry freed him, though, from the restaurant's trash. Only five Big Boy Restaurants remain in California. (Courtesy of the author.)

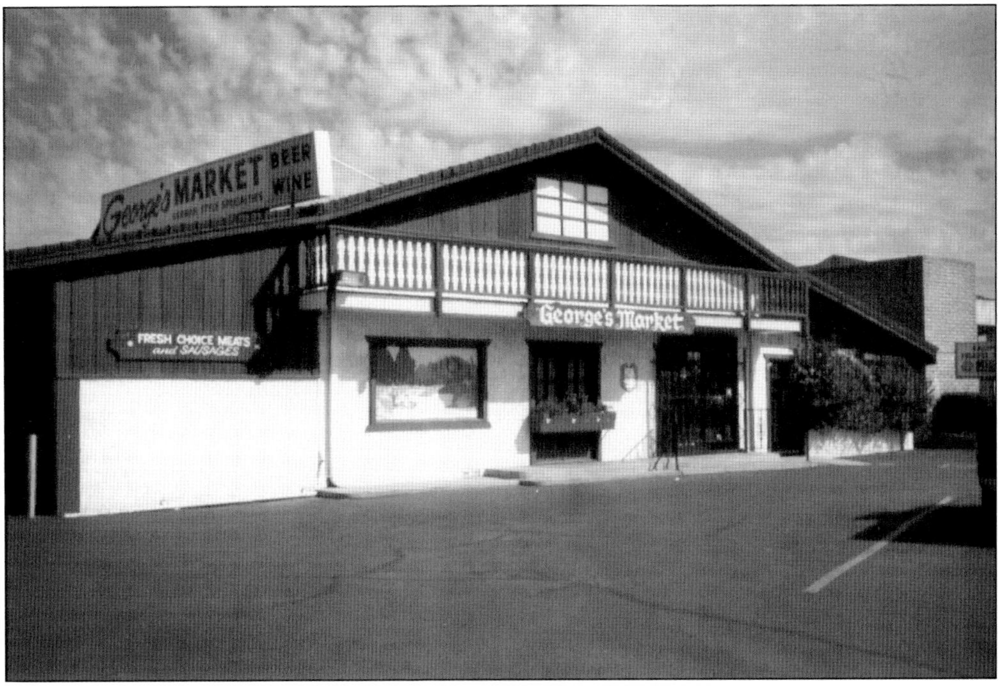

Pictured here is George's Market as it appears in Calimesa today. Around 1928, it was only a small fruit-packing shed, with a hitching post for horses. Frank and Minnie Swartz came here from Chicago with their 11-year-old daughter Rita and in 1950, bought the shed and opened a grocery store. In 1971, they sold it to George Troelenberg, who converted it to a German deli. (Courtesy of Rita Taylor.)

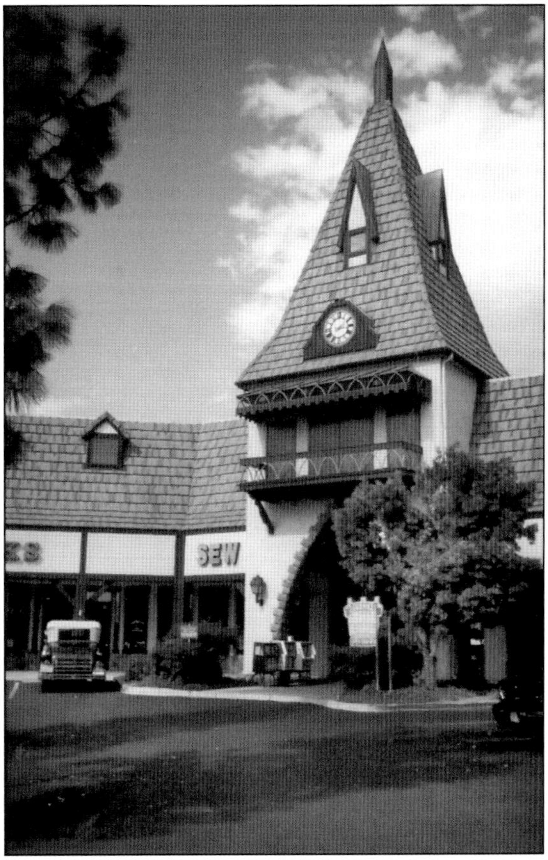

The Calimesa Royal Family Restaurant was one of the entities in Calimesa's small shopping center that was built over a decade ago. It is owned and operated by Eddie and Shannon Meeks and other family members. Its previous owners all strived to make it a favorite eatery for local people. (Courtesy of the author.)

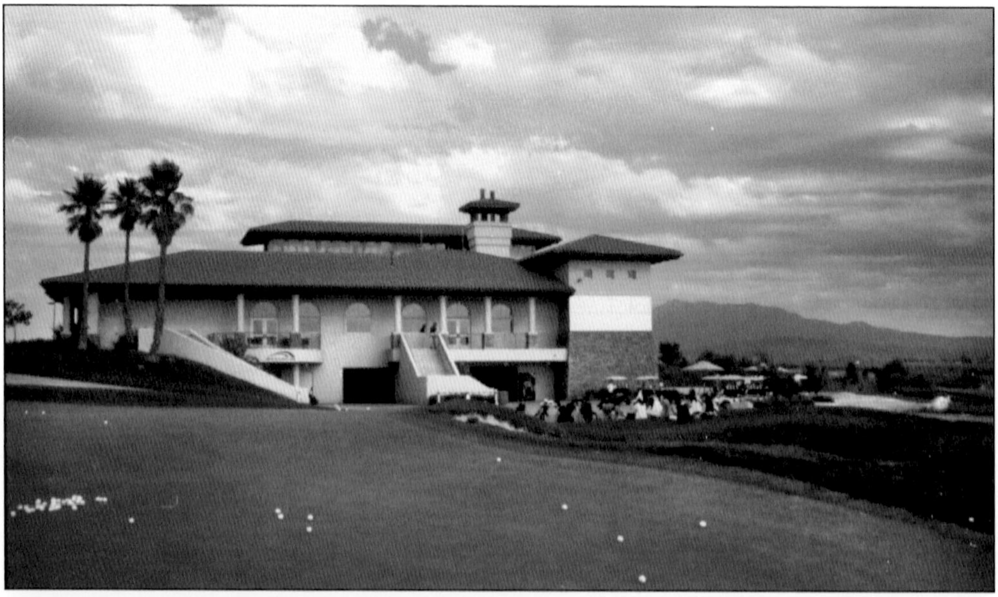

Calimesa recently become home to one of the Professional Golfers Association's (PGA) respected tournament courses. The clubhouse of the beautifully developed 18-hole course in Calimesa is pictured here. It conducts major events such as the PGA Championship, one of four major championships in golf. The course covers hills and slopes between Calimesa and San Timoteo Canyon, adding a swath of greenery between the two. (Courtesy of the author.)

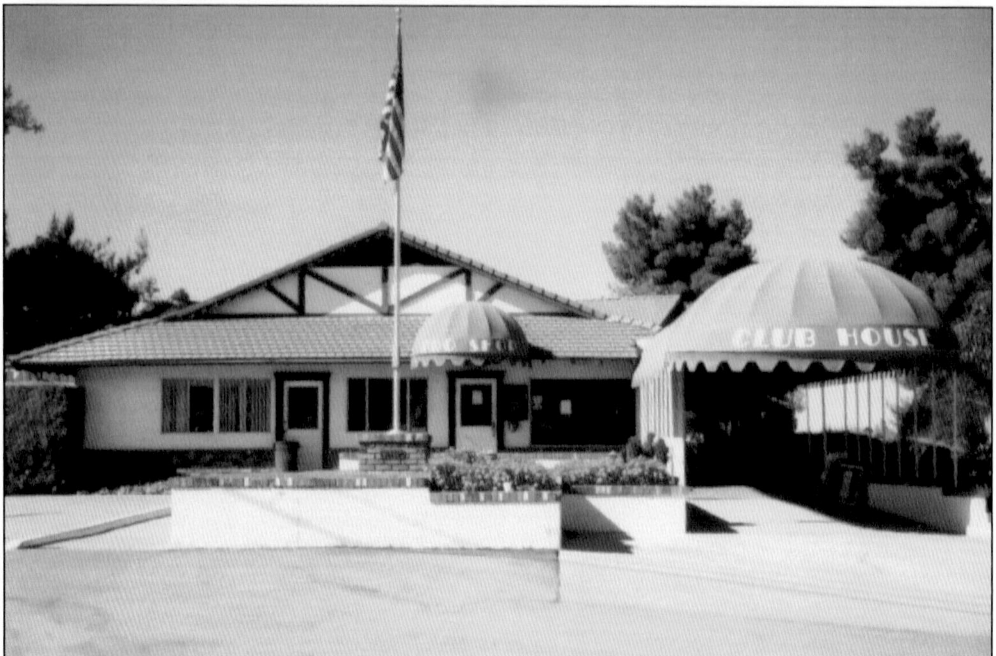

Here is the clubhouse of the 18-hole Calimesa Country Club. The club was started in the 1950s when large quantities of soil were scooped out of the area for use on I-10, creating a naturally sculptured terrain suitable for a golf course. George Gardner created it initially, followed later by the Calimesa Country Club. It is owned by the Braswells. (Courtesy of the author.)

Three

BEAUMONT

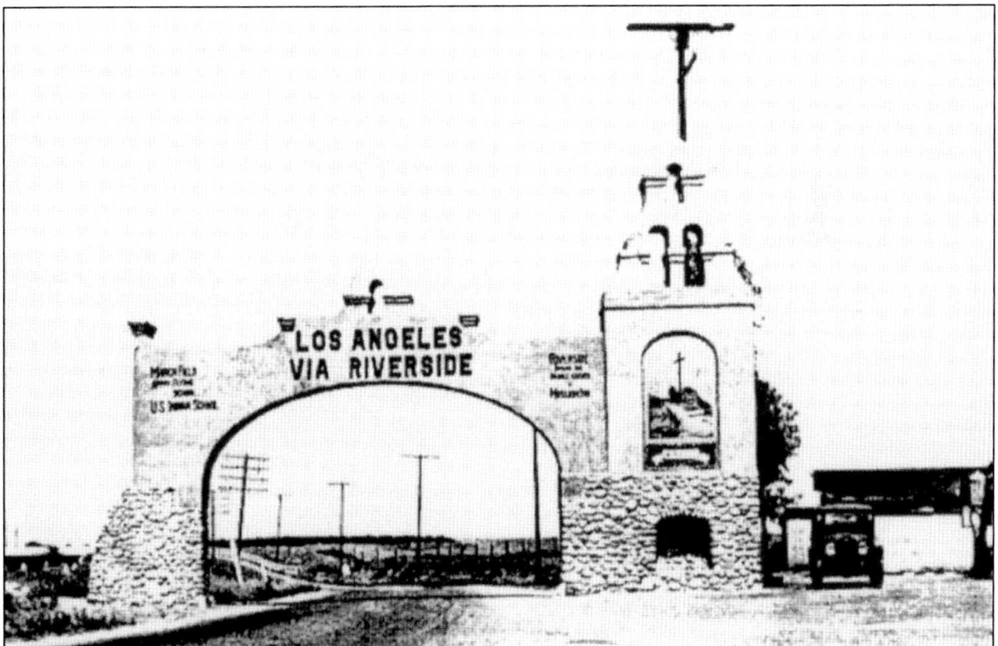

This arch once adorned the entrance to Beaumont. As one left Beaumont, it was evident that to reach Los Angeles, travel was eminent only through Riverside. I-10 had not been constructed yet, so travel via Redlands was not an option. The archway was demolished to make way for the construction of I-10. (Courtesy of Bill Bell.)

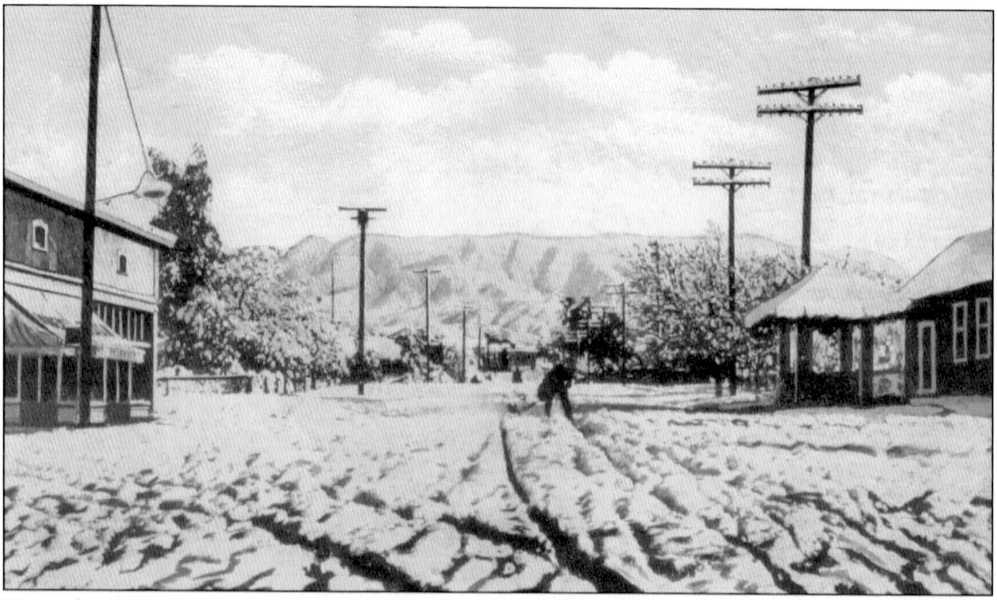

Never let it be said that it hasn't snowed heavily in Beaumont. On December 31, 1915, this photograph, taken in the heart of the small community of the San Gorgonio Pass, shows a significant snowfall. There have been snowfalls in Beaumont since but none have reached the level this photograph depicts. (Courtesy of Steve Lech.)

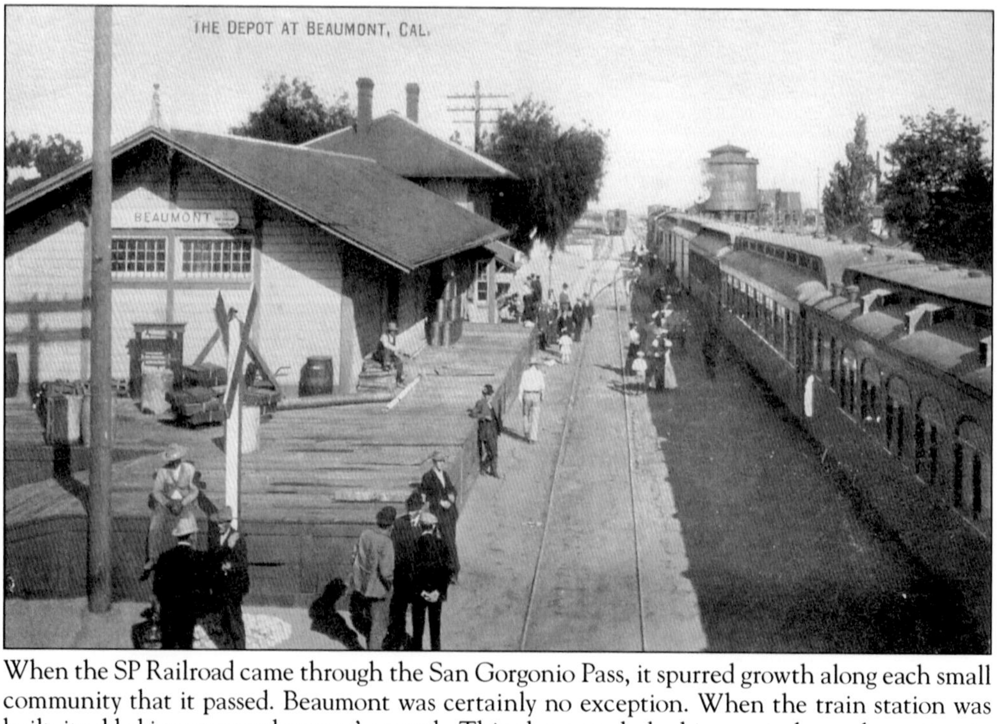

When the SP Railroad came through the San Gorgonio Pass, it spurred growth along each small community that it passed. Beaumont was certainly no exception. When the train station was built, it added impetus to the town's growth. This photograph, looking east, shows the station in its prime years. (Courtesy of Steve Lech.)

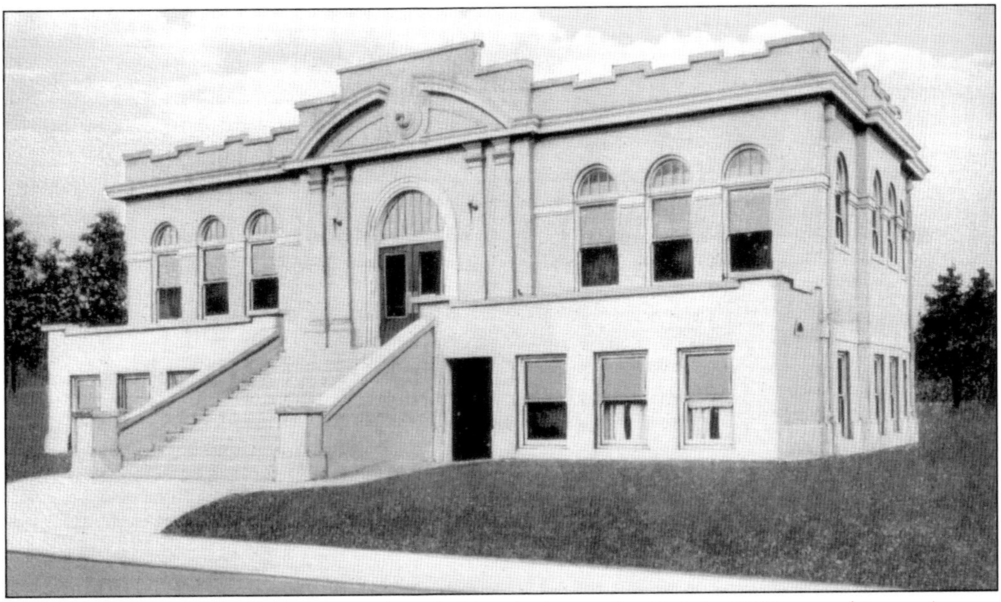

The *Gateway Gazette of Beaumont*, founded by Arthur J. Burdick in 1908, stated in its August 17, 1911, issue that the Beaumont Township was made a library district, established by a special election so that a library could be built. Immediately thereafter, steps were taken to get a library underway. The library building pictured here was completed in 1914 and funded by Carnegie. On June 16, 1914, it opened with much fanfare. (Courtesy of Steve Lech.)

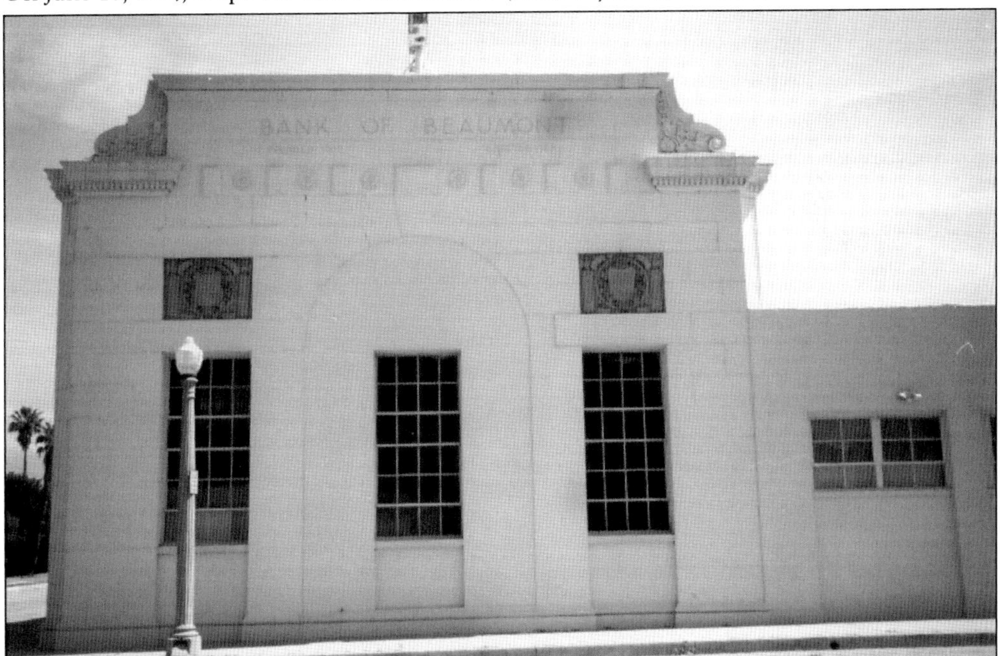

The Bank of Beaumont building, once bought by Bank of America, is now the home of Precision Printing. The Bank of Beaumont opened its doors in 1909 at the corner of Fifth and California Streets. It is silhouetted against the western part of town when looking north as one drives past Beaumont on I-10. (Courtesy of the author.)

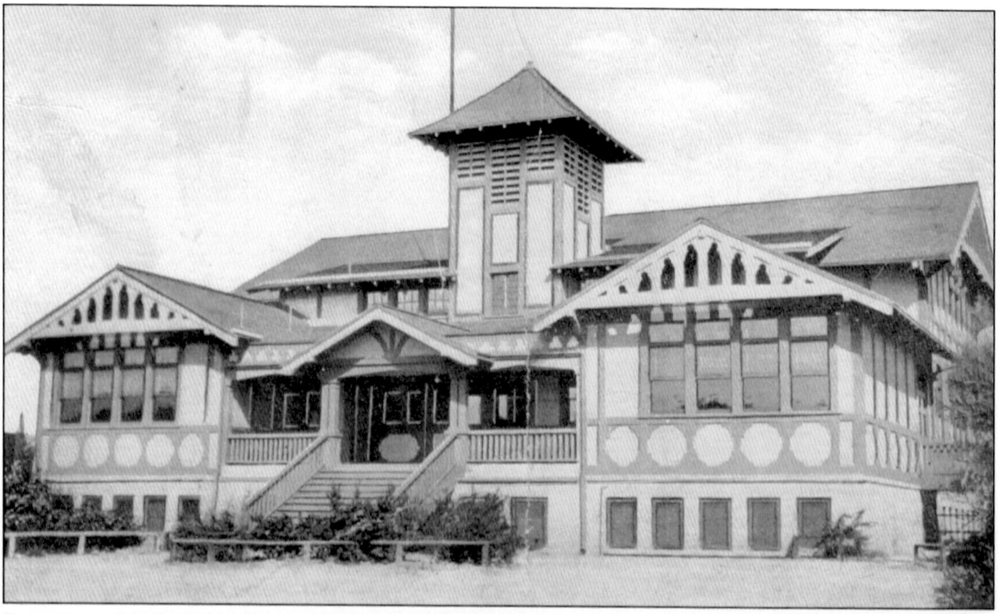

Beaumont High School was organized in September 1909, with 17 students enrolled the first year. C. S. Dodds and Miss Gall were the teachers. The school's meager start began in a 12-foot by 20-foot shack, located on Egan Street. It moved to an abandoned store on Fifth Street, then to tents, and later to the newly constructed school shown here. (Courtesy of Steve Lech.)

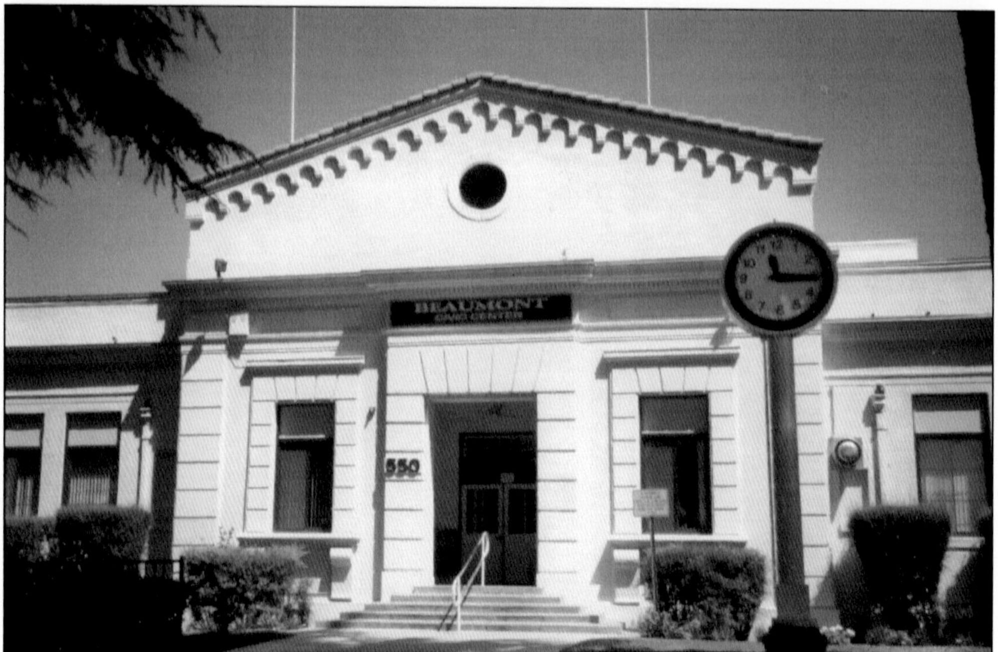

Beaumont's City Hall, seen on the north side of Sixth Street, was originally built in 1935 and used as a high school, later replaced by an elementary school. In the mid-1980s, the elementary school moved to a new location and city hall, located then at 500 Grace Street, moved to the school site. It remains there today. (Courtesy of the author.)

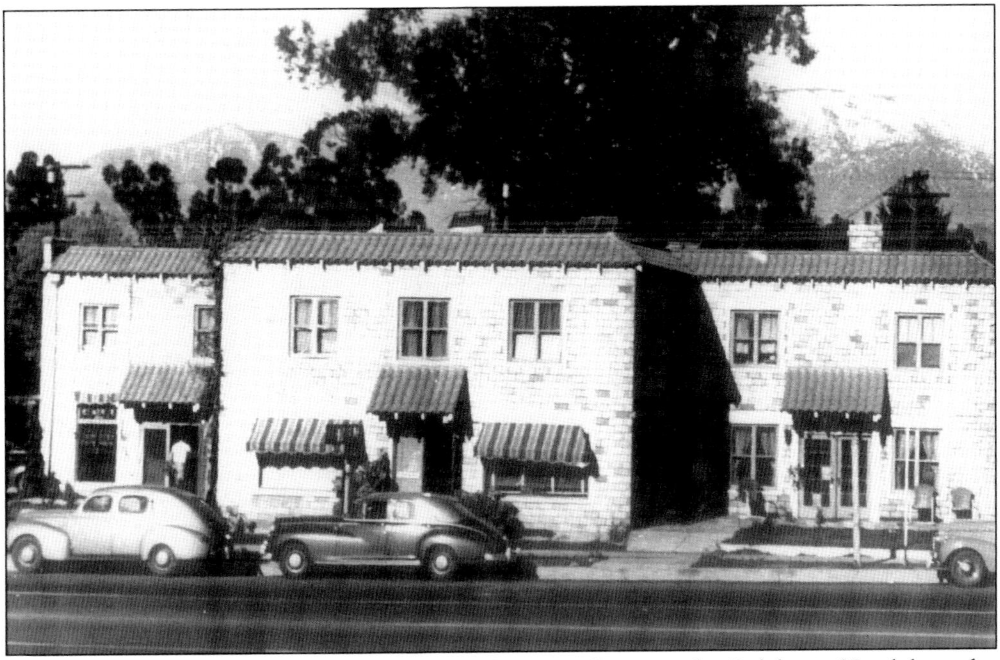

One of the main stops for travelers in the San Gorgonio Pass was the California Hotel, later the Beaumont Inn and Cafe, on the corner of California and Sixth Streets. In later years, the Beaumont Inn and Cafe closed and the building has since been converted to the House of Decision, a home for battered women and children. (Courtesy of the author.)

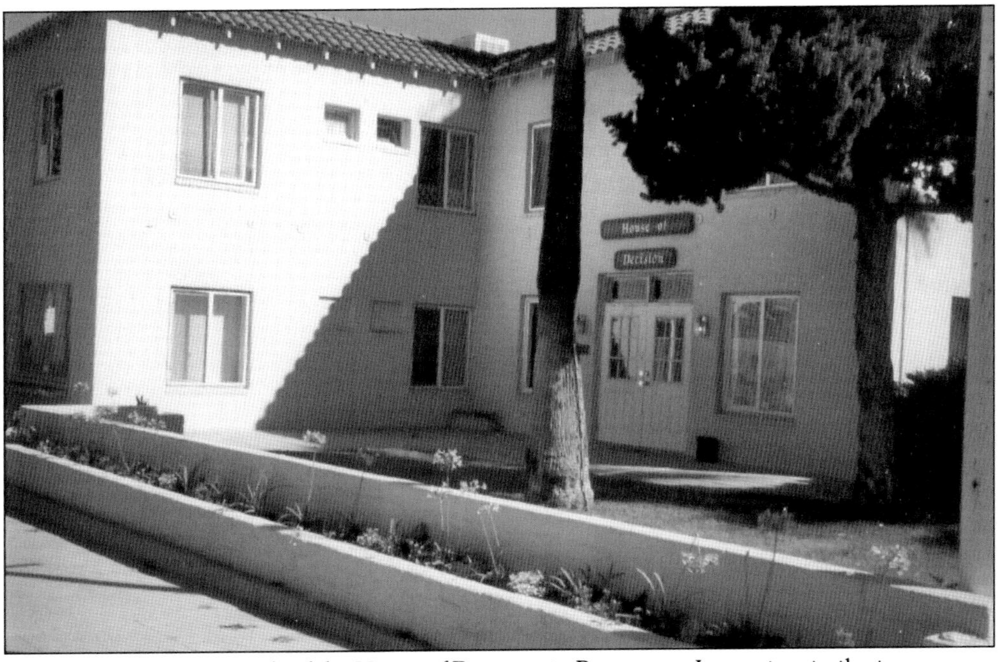

This is a recent photograph of the House of Decision in Beaumont. It remains similar in structure to the old California Hotel, with a few minor renovations. Missing are the old landmarks—the California Hotel and Beaumont Inn and Cafe signs—once adorning the front corner of the building. (Courtesy of the author.)

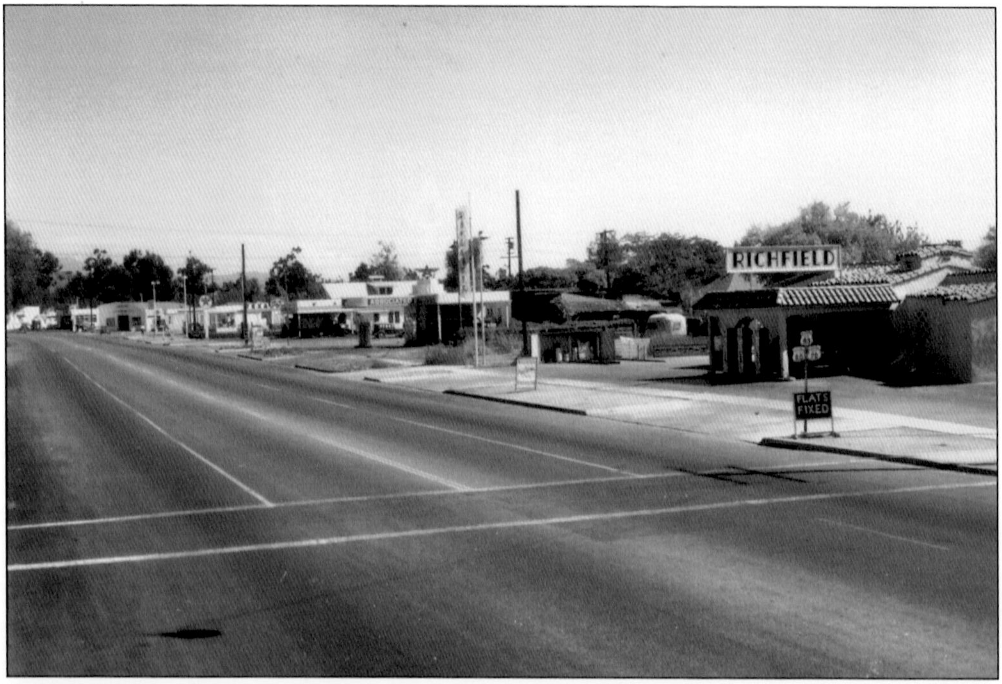

During the late 1930s or early 1940s, this view of Sixth Street was once evident when entering Beaumont from the west on Highways 60, 70, and 99. Note the row of gas stations at the highway's right. They include Richfield, Associated, and Texaco. The 76 station at the end of this row, on the southwest corner of Sixth and California Streets, had not yet been established. (Courtesy of Steve Lech.)

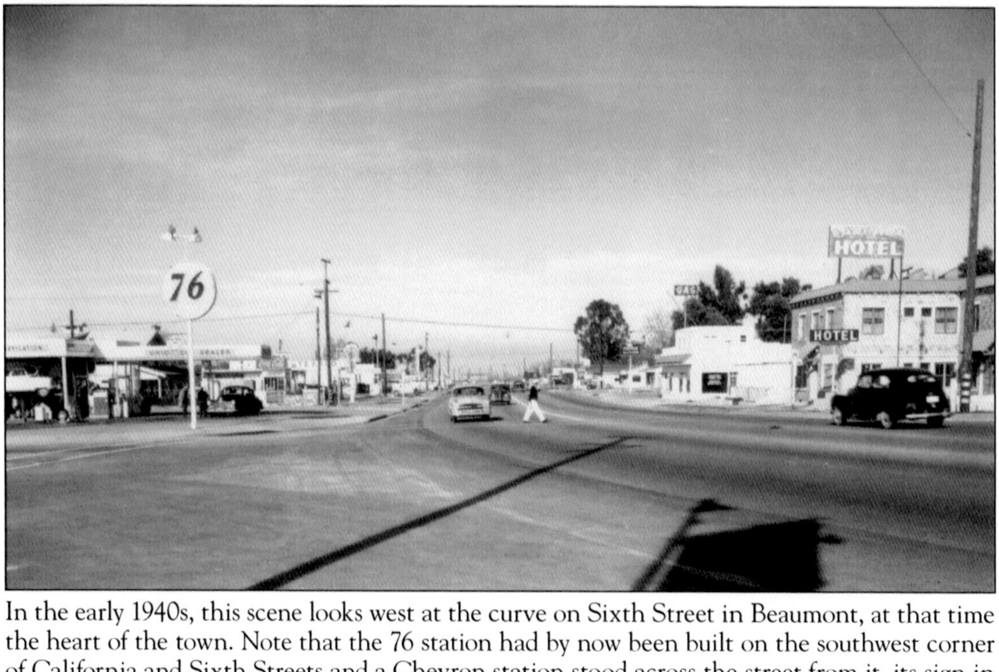

In the early 1940s, this scene looks west at the curve on Sixth Street in Beaumont, at that time the heart of the town. Note that the 76 station had by now been built on the southwest corner of California and Sixth Streets and a Chevron station stood across the street from it, its sign in front barley visible. (Courtesy of Steve Lech.)

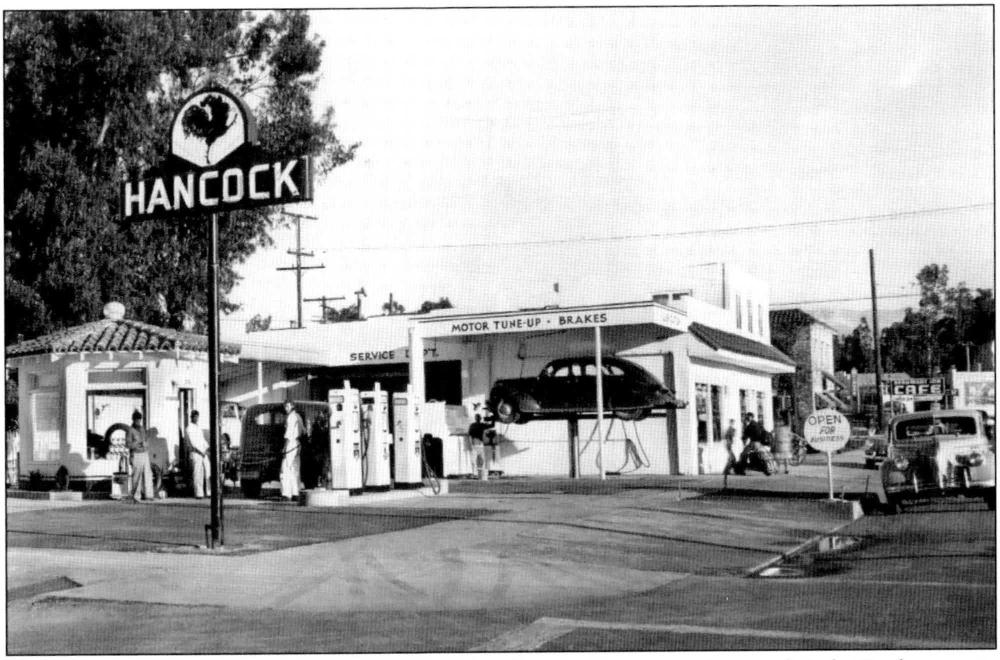

By 1946, the California Hotel, right, had changed to the Beaumont Inn and Cafe. To the west is the Hancock station, which bought the old Chevron station and updated it with a hydraulic car lift and auto parts store. The property was leased and operated by Clarence Lewis, who is pictured servicing a car on the lift. (Photograph by Steadman; courtesy of Beverly Lewis.)

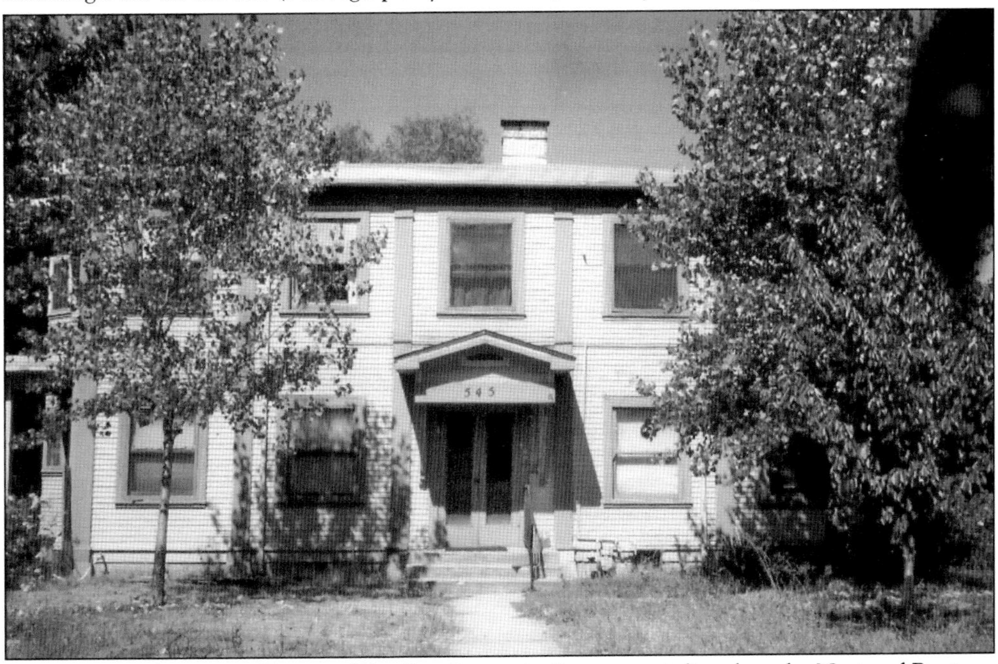

Built in 1924, the original home of Dr. Guy Bogart in Beaumont is listed on the National Register of Historic Homes. Bogart was mayor of Beaumont in the early 1920s and started the Cherry Festival. William and Deborah Lash bought and are restoring the Bogart house, a depiction of Colonial Revival architecture. (Courtesy of the author.)

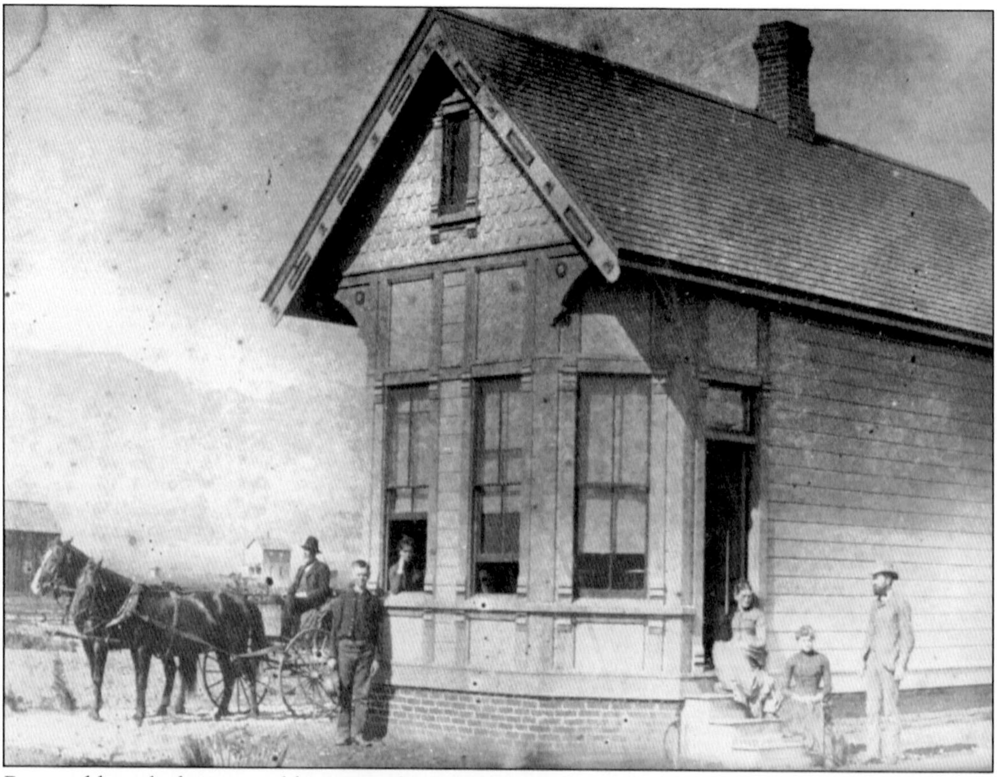

Pictured here before any additions is the original McCoy house, built in 1885. John J. McCoy's father and brother came to California from the East Coast and settled in Westminster, California. John's father, Josiah, is in the carriage at left and John J. is standing at right. John built this house in Beaumont at 668 Edgar Street, now known as the McCoy House. (Courtesy of Donald and Susan Echlin.)

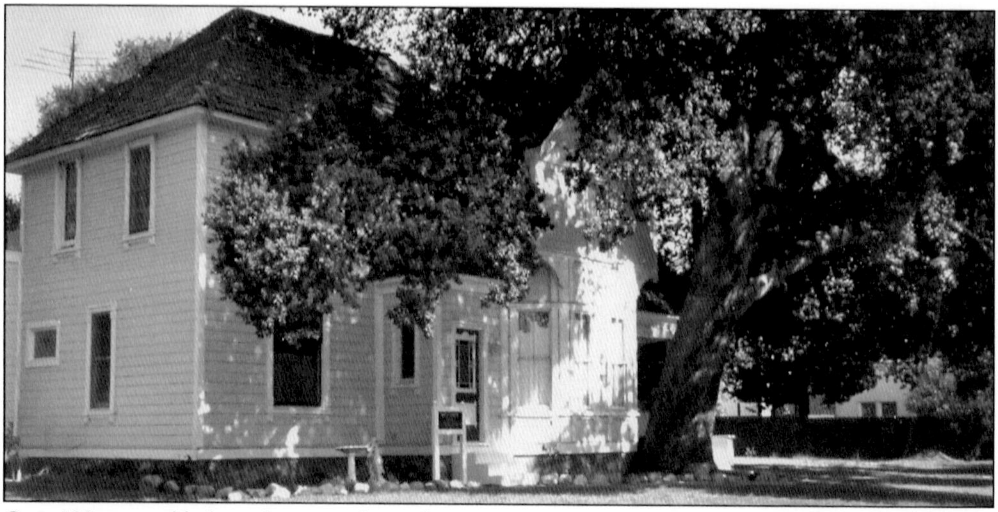

Over 100-years-old, this oak towers above the McCoy House today. The McCoy house was dedicated in 2001 as a historical site by the Native Daughters of the Golden West. In 1976, it was bought by Donald Echlin and is home to Donald, his wife, Susan, and their son Jeffrey. Donald's mother, June Velma McCoy Echlin, once lived here as well. (Courtesy of Donald and Susan Echlin.)

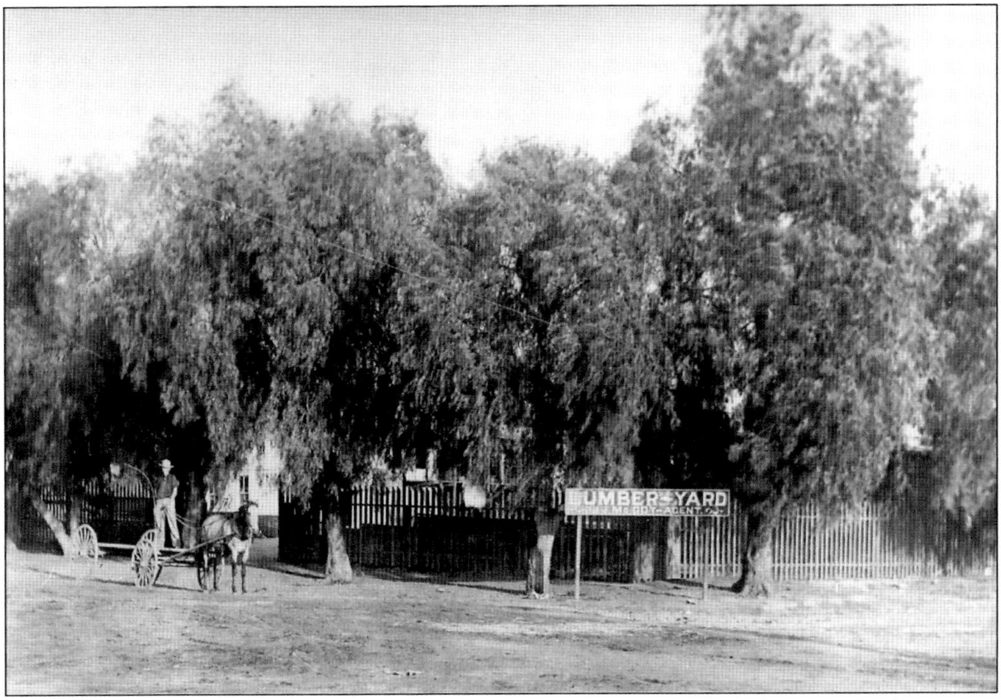

Allegedly this lumberyard was owned by John J. McCoy and was located next to his house. He was the first mayor of Beaumont and active in many ventures. He was a builder, having built his own home in Beaumont, his brother's house in Cherry Valley, and the old stone church on Egan and Seventh Streets. His son Horace built the historic Hilltop House in Banning. (Courtesy of Donald and Susan Echlin.)

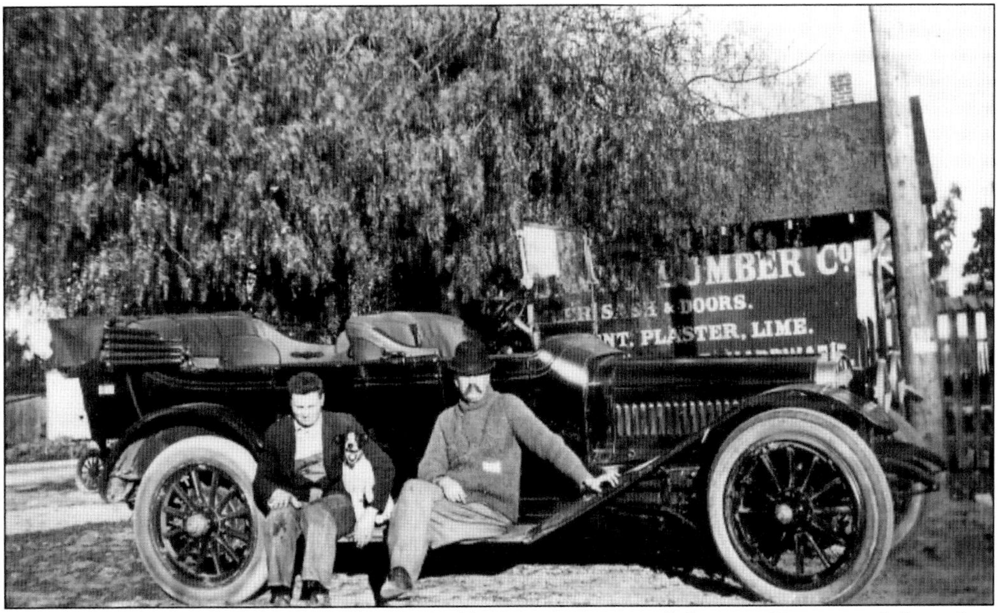

John J. McCoy sits on the running board of his touring car with his son Horace and their dog. Cars during this era were a status symbol and owners were often photographed with their prized possession. (Courtesy of Donald and Susan Echlin.)

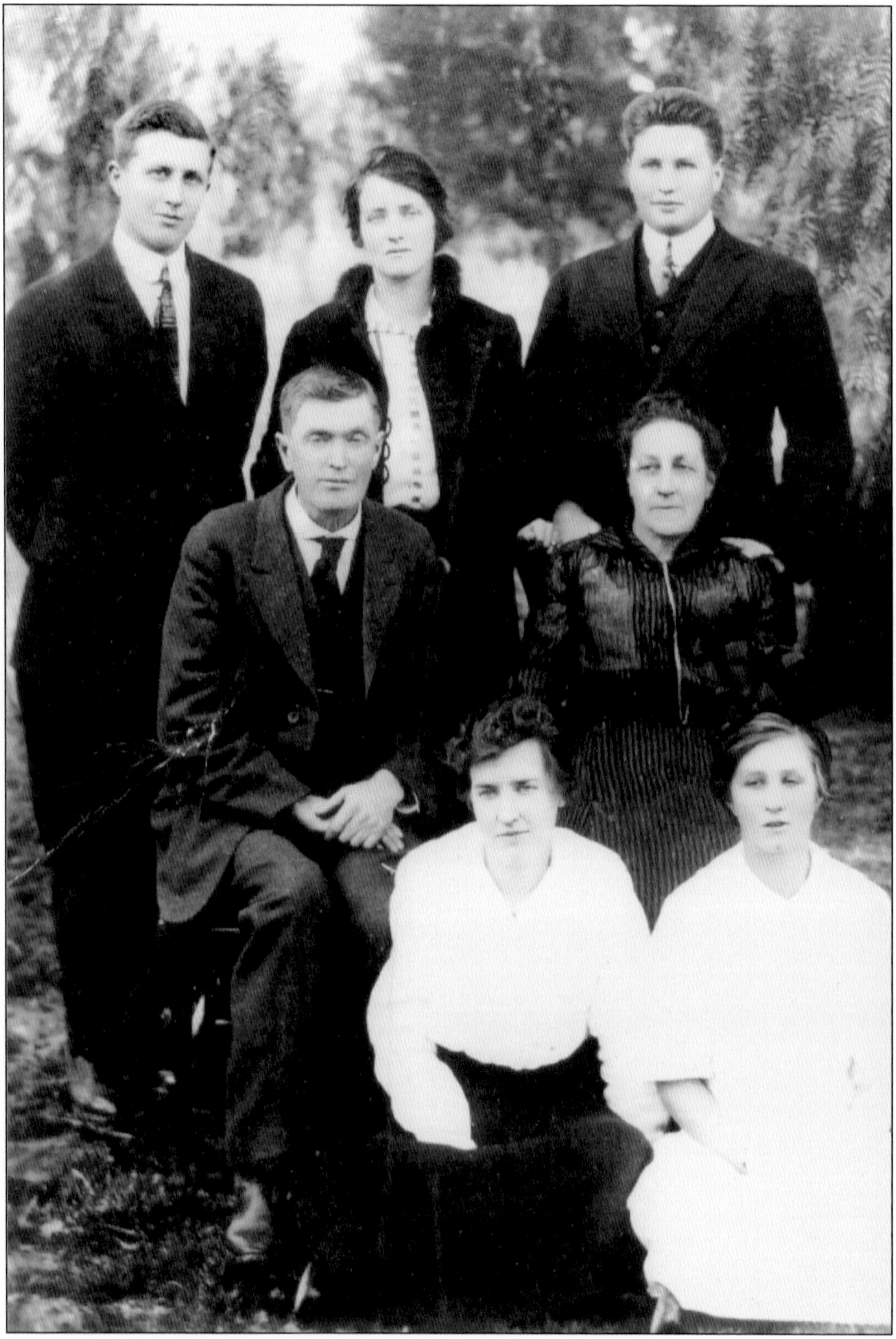

Shown here is a family photograph, years after John J. came to Beaumont and built his home. He is pictured sitting in the center of the photograph, with his wife, Mary, beside him. All five children grew up to be prominent citizens of Beaumont and served their community well. One of his sons, Horace, an orthopedic surgeon, built the historic Hilltop House in Banning. (Courtesy of Donald and Susan Echlin.)

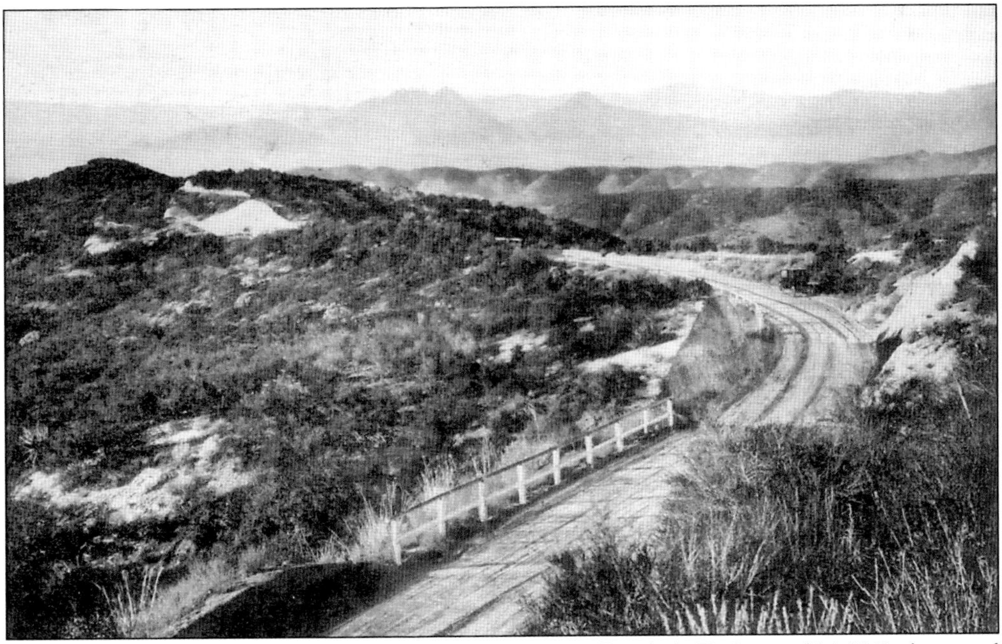

Jackrabbit Trail had a humble beginning. John. J. McCoy, Frank A. Tatley, and M. V. Park, armed with a bundle of lath, some white cloth, two axes, a carpenter's level, and a grading pole, laid out the road and light travel was established in 1895. It was first called San Gorgonio Drive, later dubbed Jackrabbit Trail. In 1935, it was paved. (Courtesy of Steve Lech.)

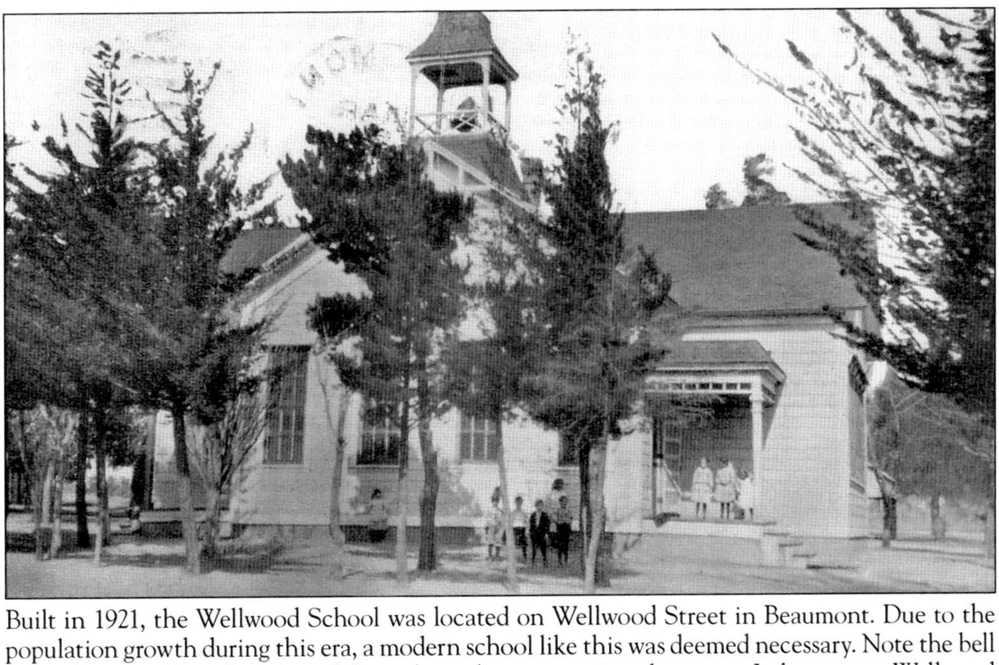

Built in 1921, the Wellwood School was located on Wellwood Street in Beaumont. Due to the population growth during this era, a modern school like this was deemed necessary. Note the bell tower that must have been heard throughout the community when rung. In later years, Wellwood School was demolished because it was thought to be unsafe if threatened by earthquake. (Courtesy of Donald and Susan Echlin.)

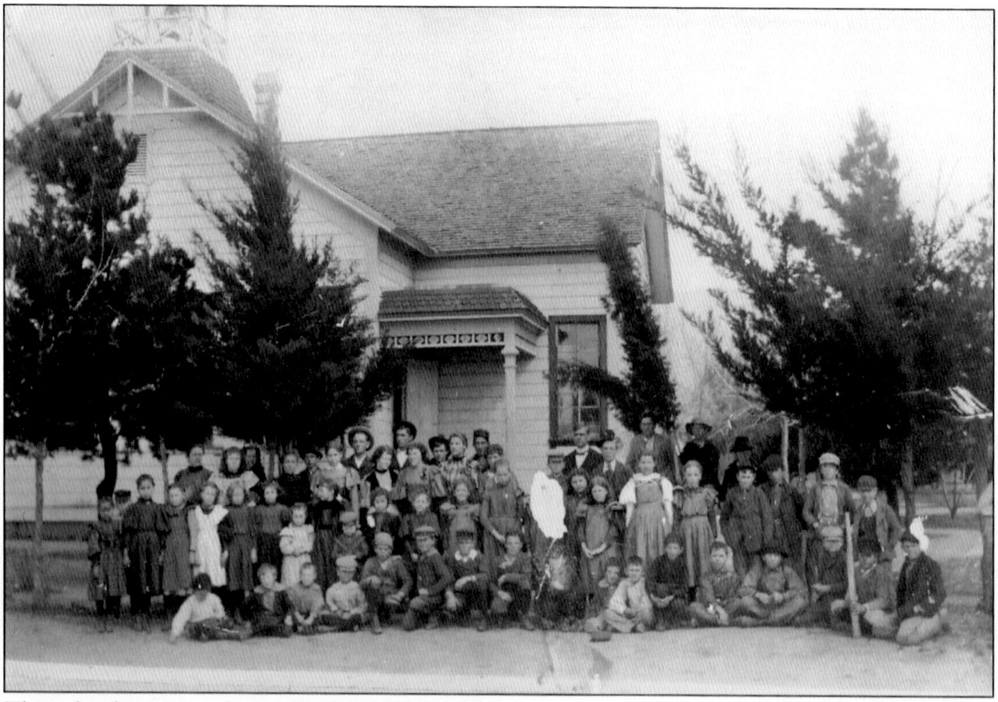

This school picture, taken at Wellwood School, represents a group of around 60, including teachers. Pictures like this were a highlight for both students and teachers. The year this photograph was taken is unknown, but it was sometime after construction based upon the mature landscape. (Courtesy of Donald and Susan Echlin.)

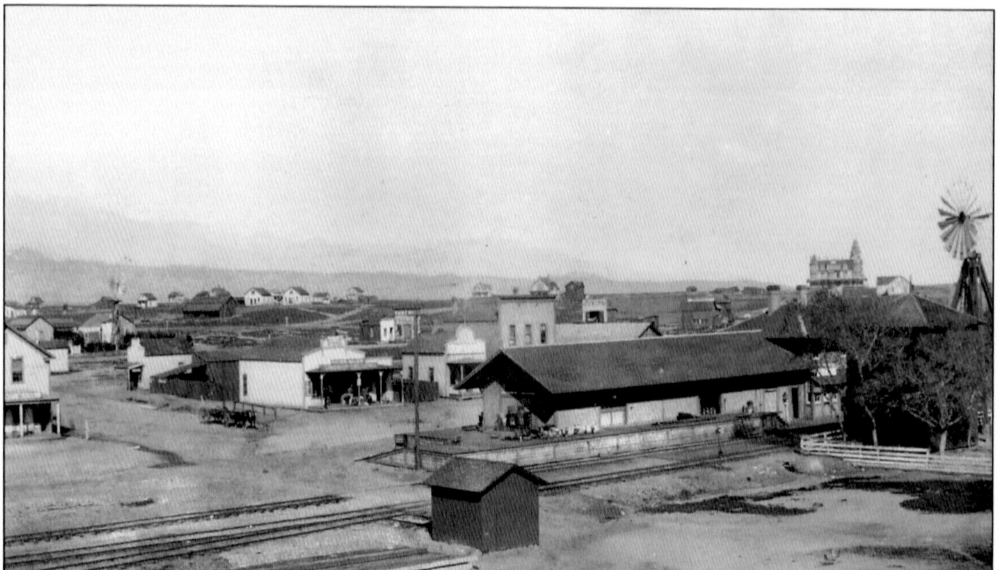

This early panoramic view of Beaumont tells a lot about its inception. The Summit House, with its sign, is at left center, minus the trees that later surrounded it. The luxurious Beaumont Hotel, seen right center, stands at the corner of Fifth Street and Beaumont Avenue. The SP Railroad station site later gave way to I-10. (Courtesy of Donald and Susan Echlin.)

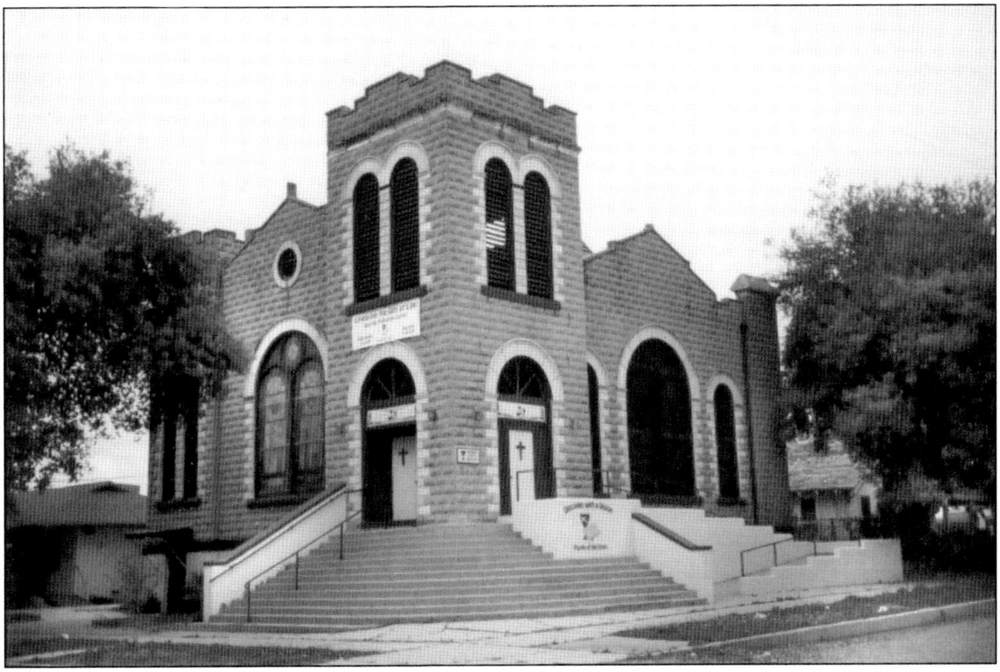

This is a current photograph of the ornate block church on the corner of Egan and Seventh Streets, built by John J. McCoy around 1885, the era of his construction ventures in and around Beaumont. Today it serves as the Disciples Fellowship Center and is a Beaumont landmark. (Courtesy of the author.)

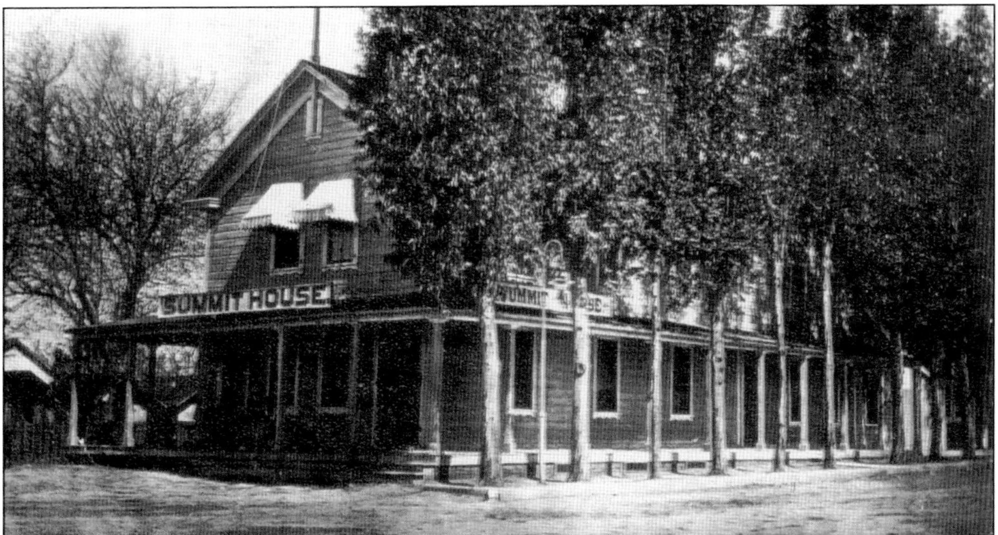

Beaumont's first hotel served the community well when it was built in 1884. It became a popular stopover for travelers through the San Gorgonio Pass and catered to large groups that desired a meeting place. Much to the regret of Beaumont citizens, it burned to the ground May 1925. (Courtesy of Steve Lech.)

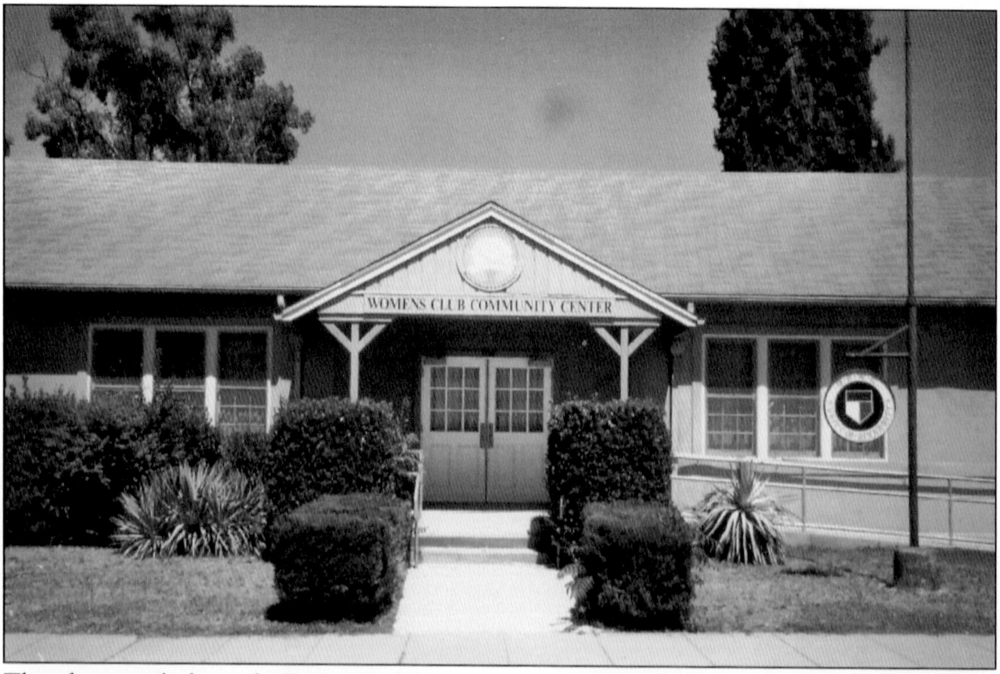

This photograph shows the Beaumont Woman's Club as seen today on Sixth Street in Beaumont. It was founded in 1916 in the home of Mrs. J. W. Elder and meetings were held there for some time. Since the inauguration of the club's building, it has for years been home to many functions. It continues to serve the community well. (Courtesy of the author.)

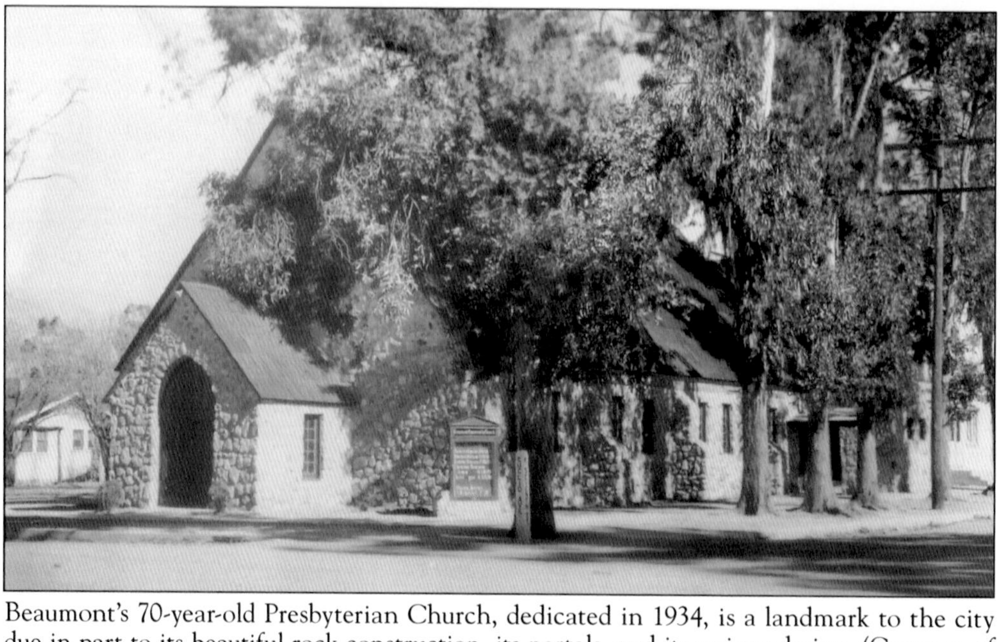

Beaumont's 70-year-old Presbyterian Church, dedicated in 1934, is a landmark to the city due in part to its beautiful rock construction, its portals, and its unique design. (Courtesy of Steve Lech.)

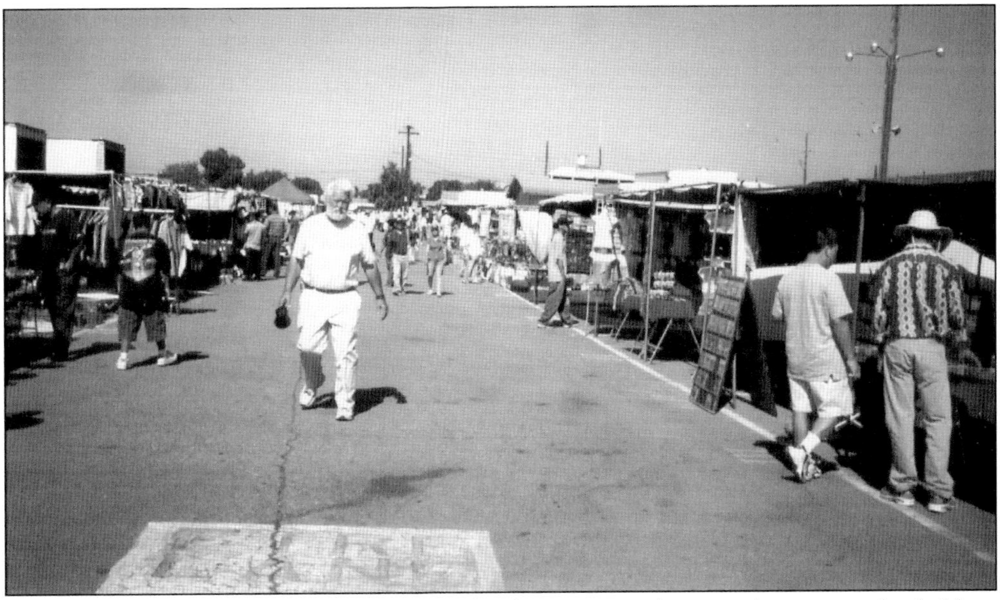

The Beaumont Swap Meet on Sixth Street has become popular over the years and is held on Saturday, Sunday, and Wednesday throughout the year. Sellers gather here en masse on its large grounds to sell both new and used items, and buyers converge from surrounding communities. (Courtesy of the author.)

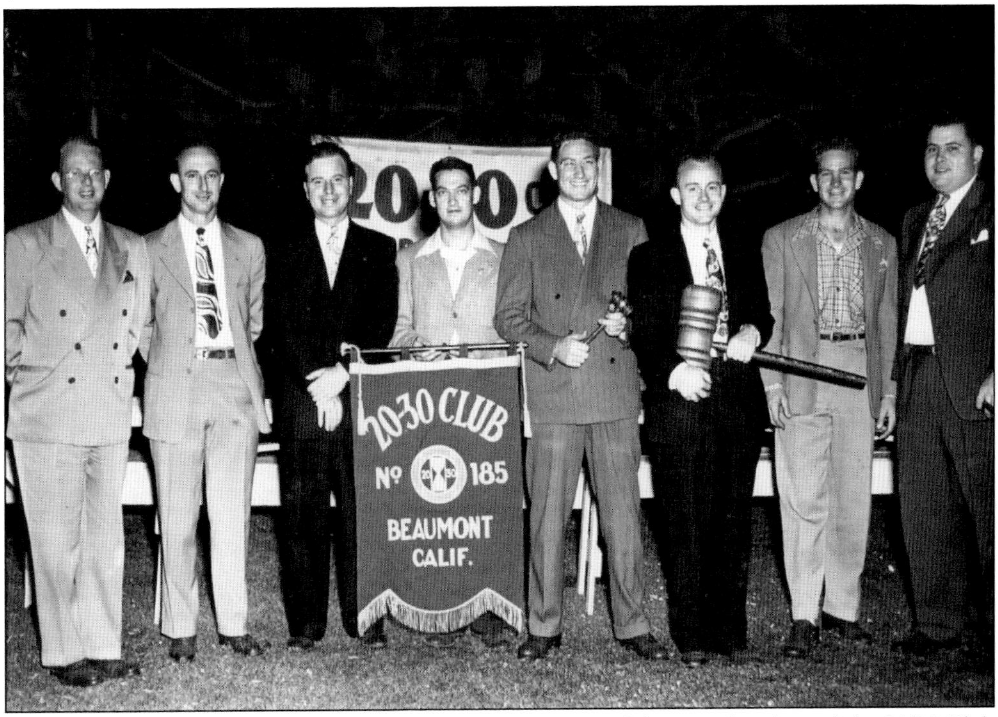

Pictured here are eight of Beaumont's leading businessmen of the past that formed the 20/30 Club of Beaumont, composed of men from ages 20 to 30. Banning also had a 20/30 Club and once sponsored Bob Hope's live radio show, broadcast from the Banning Theatre, now known as the Fox Cineplex Theater. (Courtesy of Beverly Lewis.)

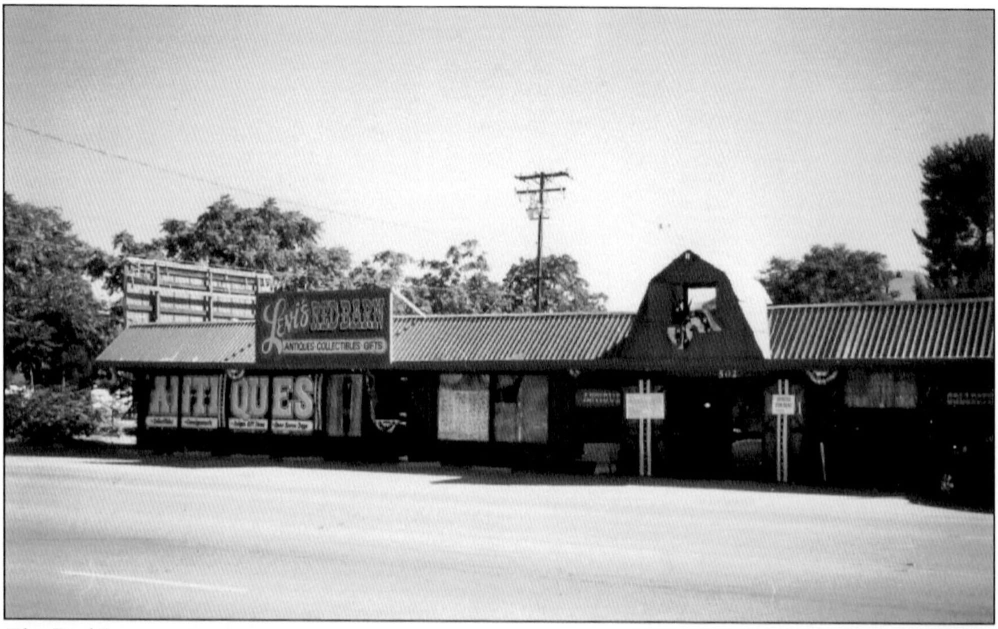

The Red Barn Antique Shop in Beaumont, more than half a century old, was recently bought by Debra Rapstine, a direct descendent of Wyatt Earp. It started as a dirt-floor fruit and vegetable stand, then a shed for horses, and later an antique barn with old farm implements and antiques. It has recently been remodeled. (Courtesy of Debra Rapstine.)

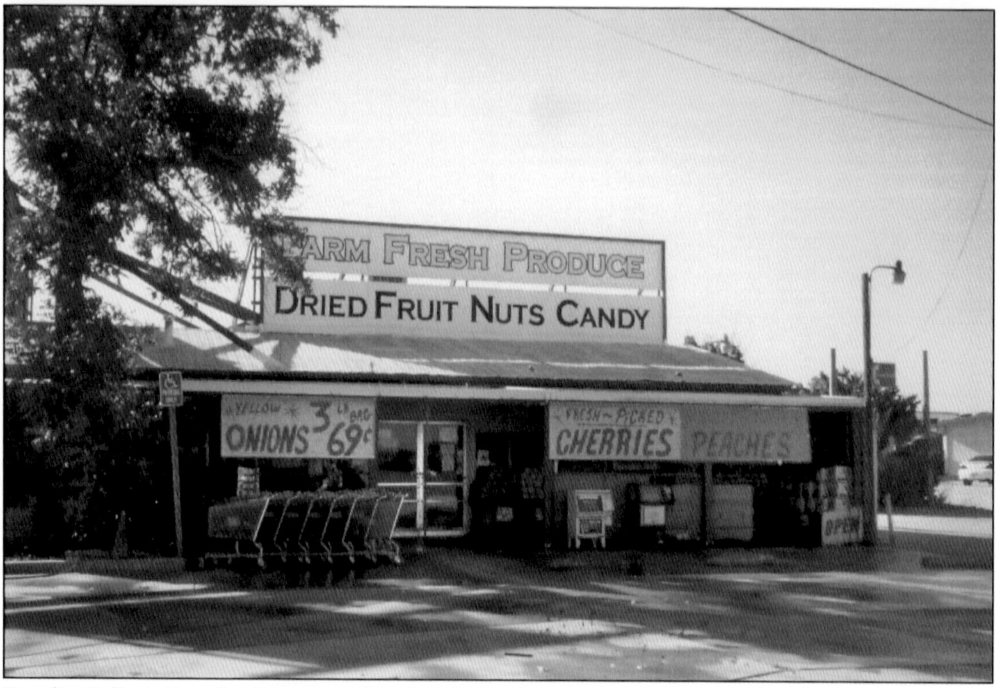

Dowling's Fruit Stand, a Beaumont landmark, has been around for over a half century. Its owner is Francis Dowling, a pioneer fruit grower in Beaumont, who lives on his fruit ranch. Dowling grows peaches, plums, cherries, and apricots. Several truckers, who often buy his fruit, are usually seen in the parking lot. (Courtesy of the author.)

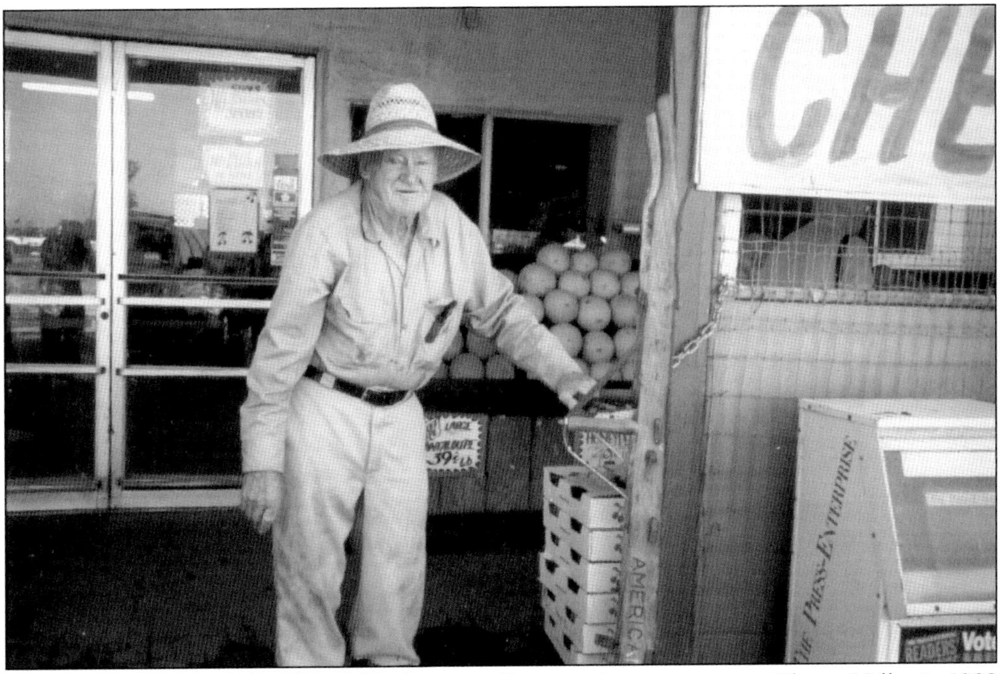

Francis Dowling stands beside a dolly. One set of his grandparents came to Cherry Valley in 1908 and planted some of the first cherry trees grown there. Dowling was born in Cherry Valley in 1925 and moved to Beaumont in 1951. Here he established his fruit orchards and fruit stand on a 61-acre site. (Courtesy of the author.)

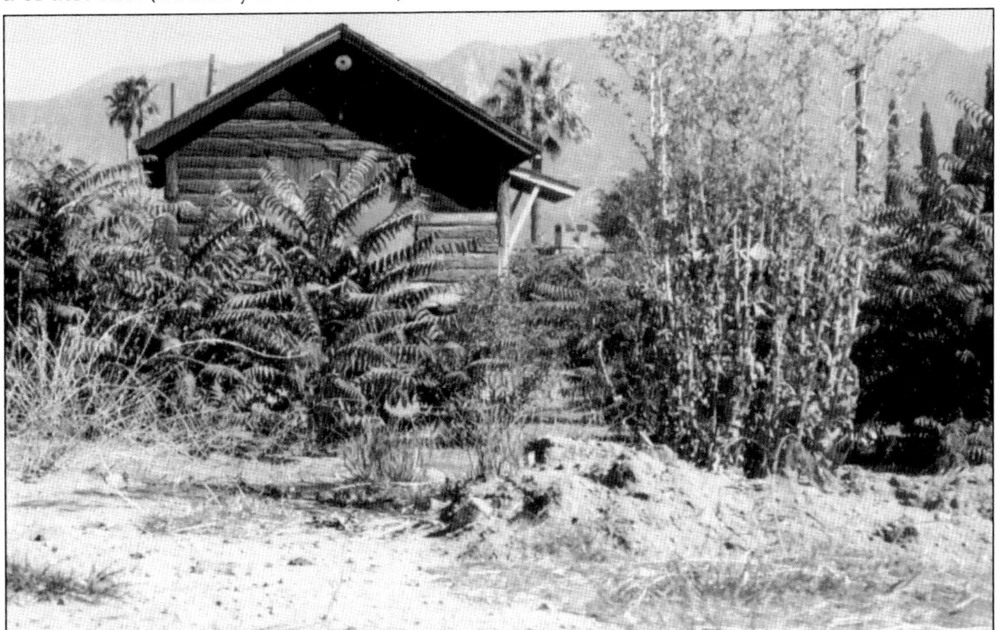

Pictured here is the historical Hall City schoolhouse, moved from historic Hall City and used for years in Cabazon. Recently it was purchased by the San Gorgonio Pass Historical Society and moved to Beaumont from Cabazon, currently awaiting installation on the Noble Creek Park grounds of the Beaumont-Cherry Valley Recreation and Park District. (Courtesy of the author.)

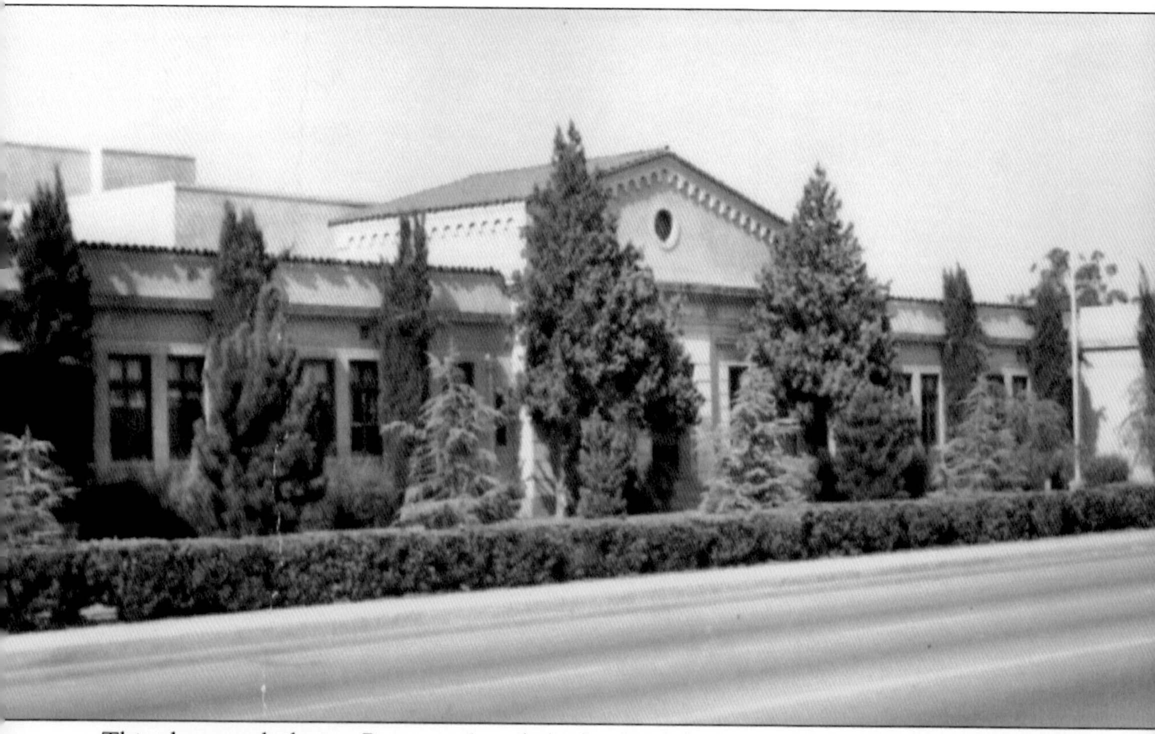

This photograph depicts Beaumont's early high school, built in 1935. It served in that capacity until it was relocated, at which time it became the home of a grammar school. The grammar school was later moved elsewhere and the school structure was converted to the Beaumont Civic Center, housing all city offices. (Courtesy of Nara Haskell.)

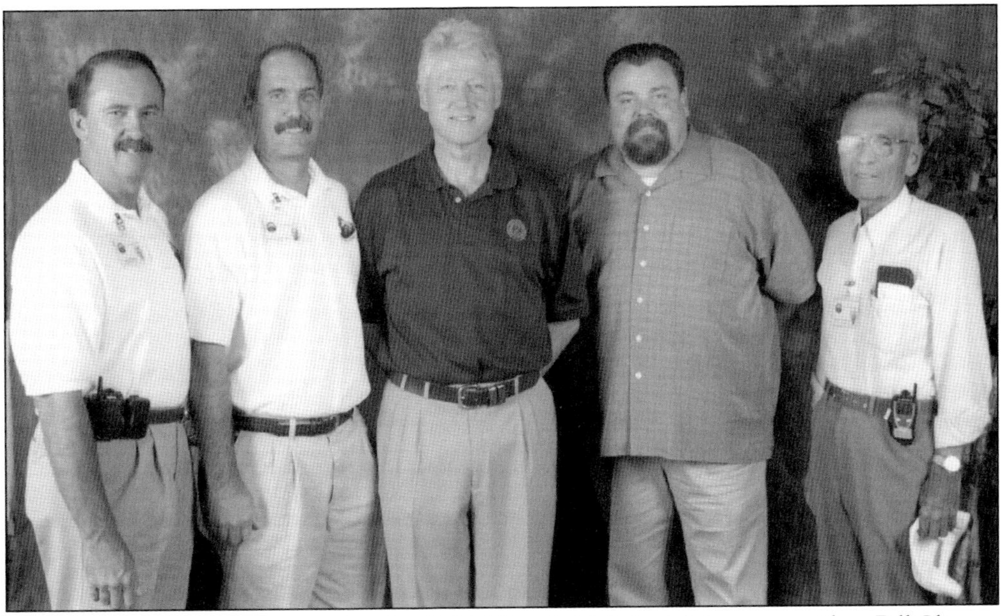

A group from Beaumont gathered at the Oak Valley Golf Club with former president Bill Clinton during his recent visit to the Southland. Pictured at a 2003 celebrity golf event, from left to right, are Larry Dressel, mayor of Beaumont, appointed January 2000; Brian DeForge, councilman; Bill Clinton; Jeff Fox, mayor pro tem of Beaumont; and Placido Valdivia, councilman. (Courtesy of Jeff Fox.)

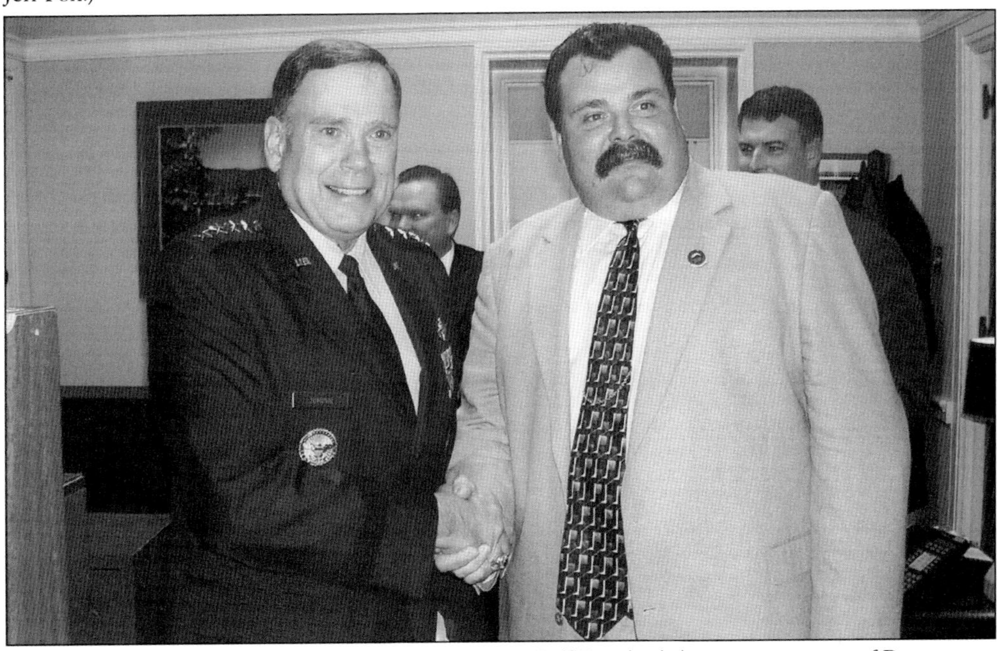

Pictured in the office of Congressman Jerry Lewis, Jeff Fox (right), pro tem mayor of Beaumont, shakes hands with Gen. John P. Jumper, chief of staff of the U.S. Air Force. On an official group tour from Beaumont to Washington D.C., in April 2004, Fox sought funding for further transportation projects. The effort was successful, netting $3 million for the Oak Valley Bridge. Fox is slated to serve as mayor of Beaumont in 2006. (Courtesy of Jeff Fox.)

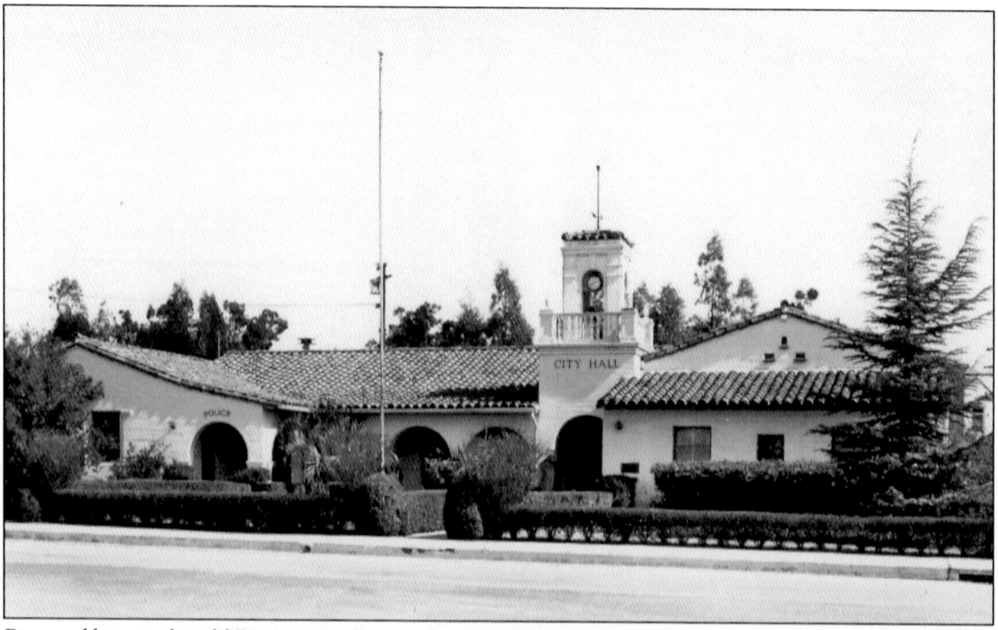

Pictured here is the old Beaumont City Hall at 500 Grace Street, before its relocation to Beaumont's Sixth Street grammar school building in the mid-1980s. City hall originally shared the building with the Beaumont police station. Since the city's offices were moved to Sixth Street, this structure has housed the school district offices. (Courtesy of Nara Haskell.)

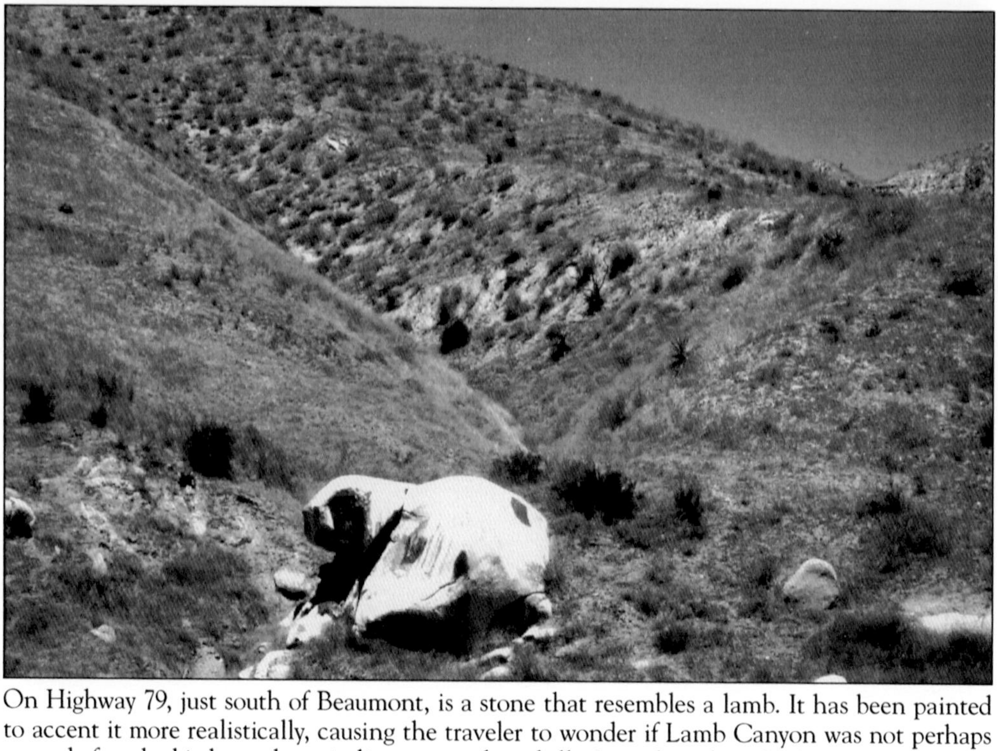

On Highway 79, just south of Beaumont, is a stone that resembles a lamb. It has been painted to accent it more realistically, causing the traveler to wonder if Lamb Canyon was not perhaps named after the big horn sheep indigenous to these hills. In reality, though, the name is derived from canyon homesteader, Mr. Lamb. (Courtesy of the author.)

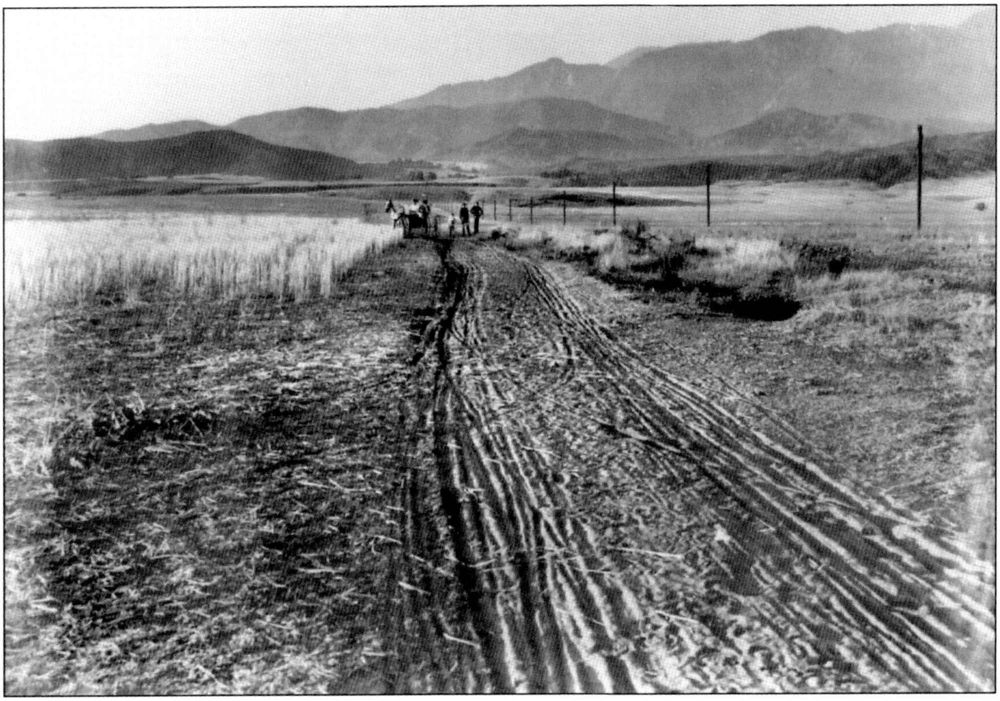

The view in this photograph of north Beaumont Avenue looks in a northerly direction. Dr. H. C. Singler and Associates bought the San Gorgonio town site in 1887, changed the name to Beaumont, and planted the street's first trees. Previously, in 1884, George C. Egan had laid out the San Gorgonio town site and this view represents some of his initial endeavor. (Courtesy of Nara Haskell.)

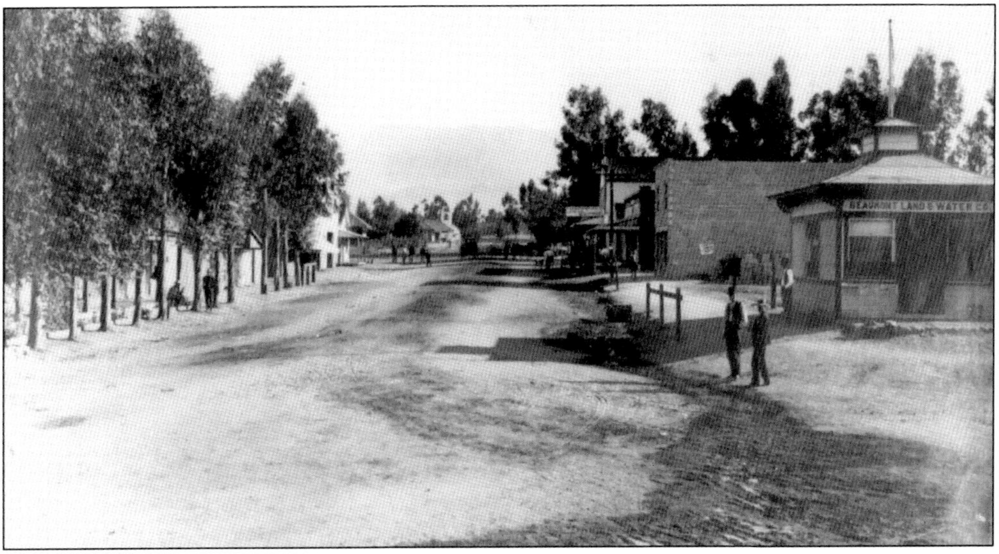

Egan Street is shown here in an early stage of development, c. 1910, only a number of years after it was laid out by George Egan. The Beaumont Land and Water Company had already been firmly established, as witnessed by its office building to the right of the photograph. Availability of water was an important prerequisite when bringing land buyers to the area. (Courtesy of Nara Haskell.)

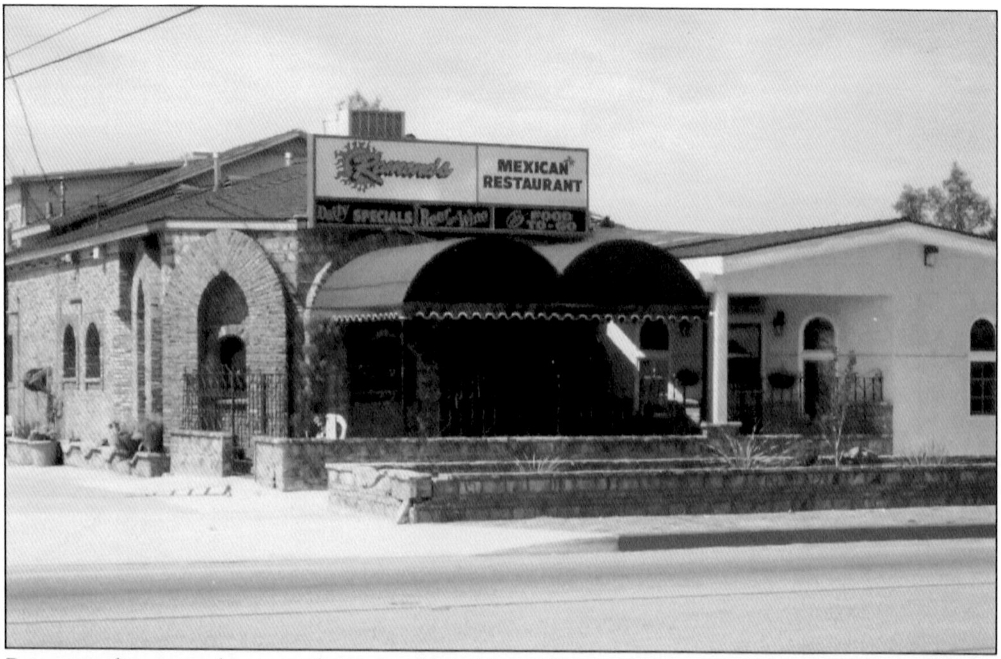

Beaumont has several eateries, but one of the oldest is Ramon's Mexican Restaurant on west Sixth Street. Its proprietors are Gill and Christina Vargas. The structure is a renovation of a smaller building that was the oldest Mexican restaurant in Beaumont. Ramon's Restaurant is often filled with locals and also with passersby. (Courtesy of the author.)

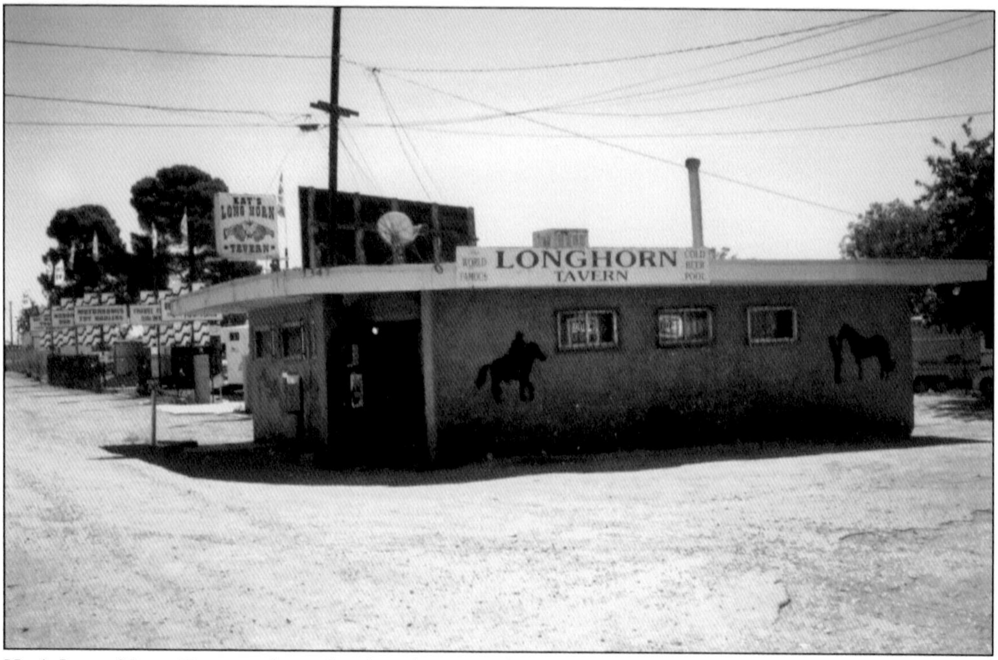

Kat's Long Horn Tavern, the red-colored tavern that stood on the south side of Sixth Street, was a landmark that vivified the street for many years. Recently, though, it has lost its illustrious red glow—it has been painted another color. It is interesting to note the jocular sign on the building's fascia that states the restaurant is word famous. (Courtesy of the author.)

Four

Cherry Valley and Oak Glen

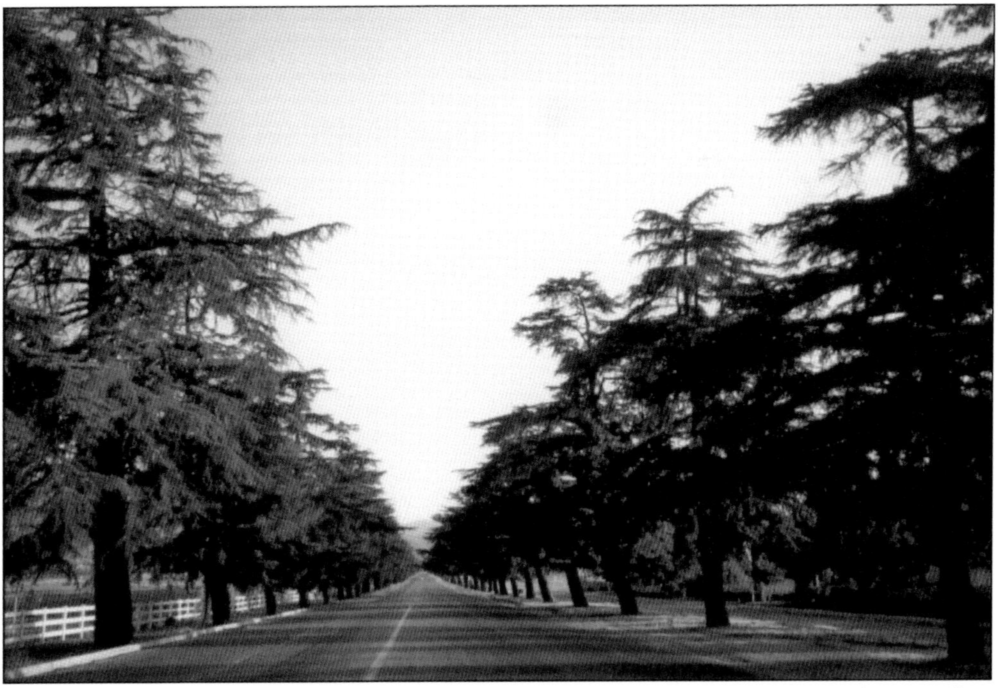

East Indian cedars, known as deodar trees, align Beaumont Avenue leading into Cherry Valley. It is often referred to as Christmas Tree Lane. It serves as a corridor for travel and a pathway for parades. Old-timers can remember a pink painted donkey parading this route on roller skates. (Courtesy of the author.)

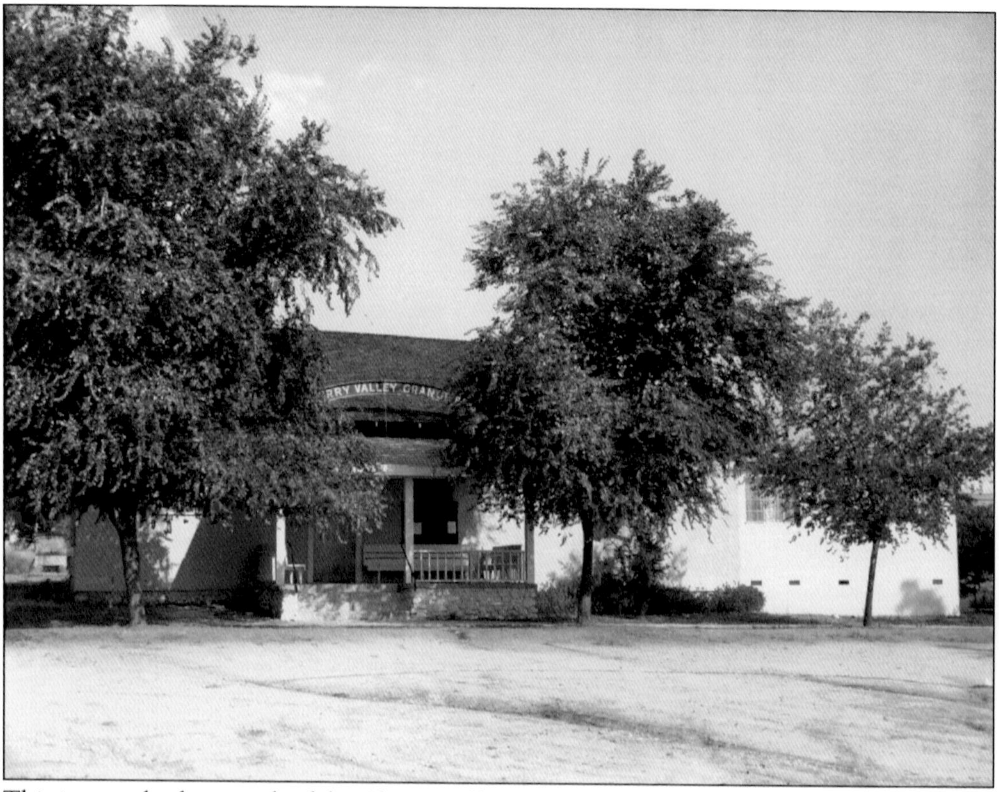

This is an early photograph of the Cherry Valley Grange No. 586 building, constructed in 1905 as a small schoolhouse with outside restrooms. According to local historians, it once had a bell tower. The grange was begun after the Civil War in 1867 to protect against dangers on the Western frontier. By 1950,it had bought the vintage schoolhouse, and the building became its meeting hall. (Courtesy of Ros Otero.)

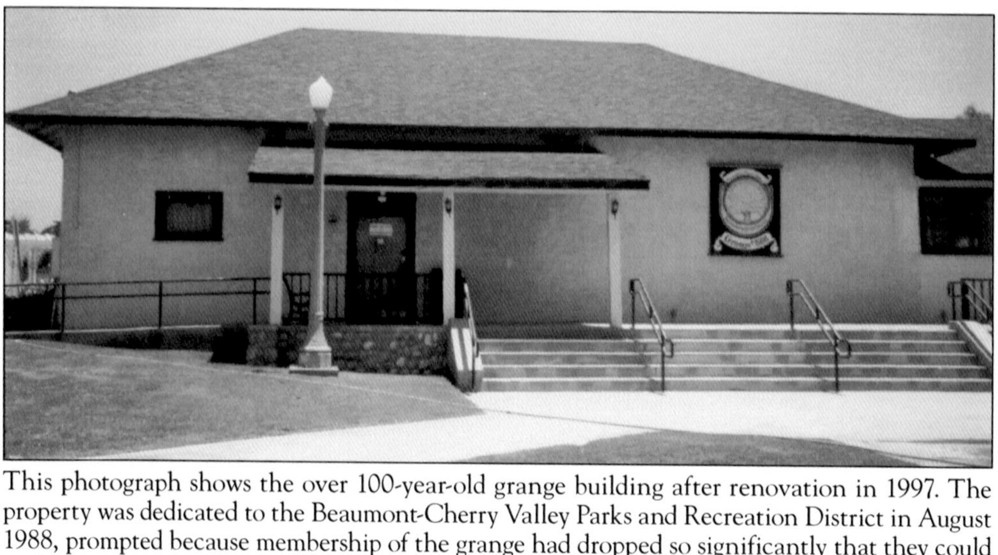

This photograph shows the over 100-year-old grange building after renovation in 1997. The property was dedicated to the Beaumont-Cherry Valley Parks and Recreation District in August 1988, prompted because membership of the grange had dropped so significantly that they could no longer maintain the building. It is still known as Cherry Valley Grange and still functions as a meeting hall for various activities. (Courtesy of the author.)

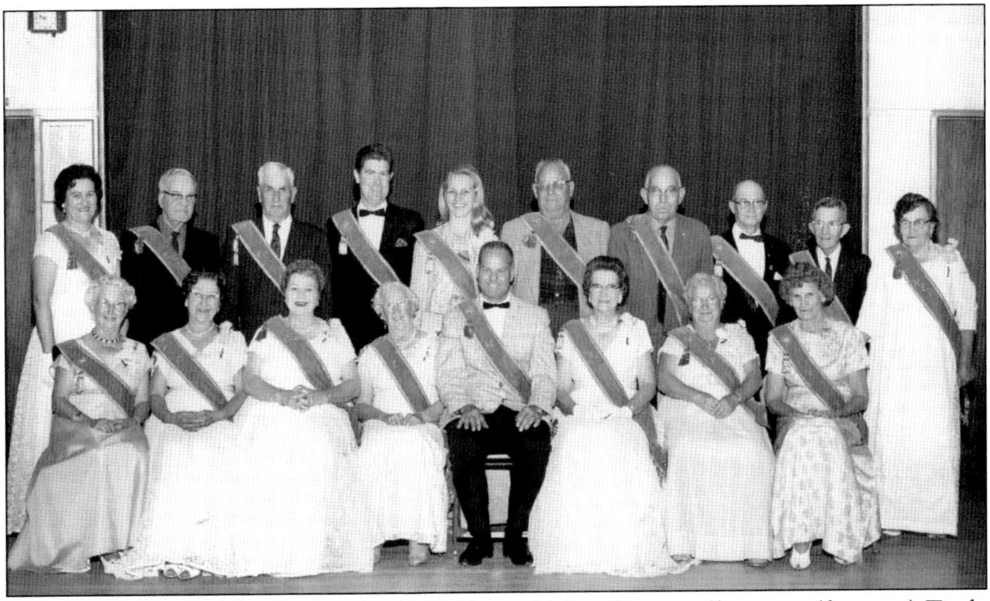

Pictured here, from left to right, the 1968 Cherry Valley Grange officers are (first row) Trudy Haueter, treasurer; Florence Walker, ceres; Ivy Nelson, chaplain; Berth Vlasek, lecturer; Chick Hoover, master; Anna Schmidt, lady assistant steward; Martha Engel, flora; and Mayme Hayes, pianist; (second row) Annie Endres, pomona; John Vlasek, one-year executive; Jack Stark, two-year executive; Terry Speers, overseer; Linda Hoover, secretary; Oscar Huckfeldt, gatekeeper; Chuck Wacker, three-year executive; Luther Ward, assistant steward; Clarence Hurt, steward; and Stella Hammer, WAC chairman. (Courtesy of Ros Otero.)

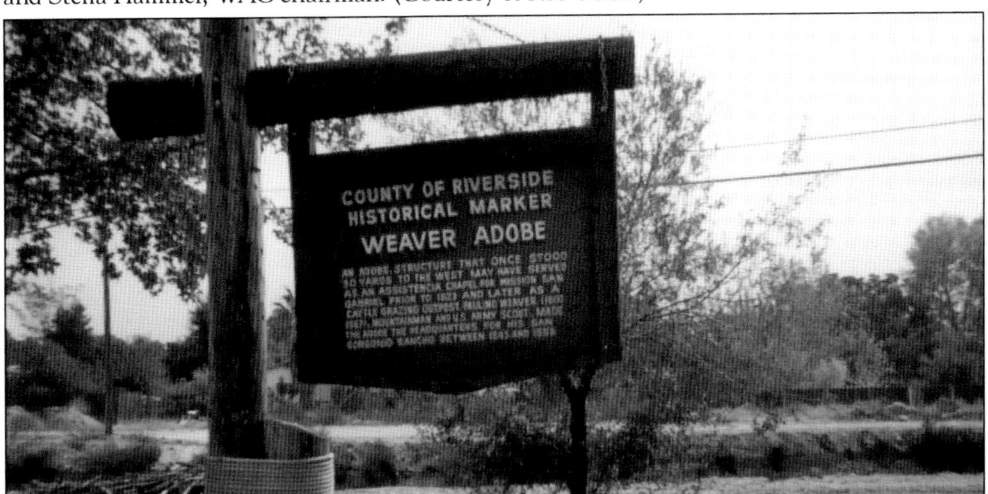

Pictured here is the marker of the Weaver Adobe. Paulino Weaver became a naturalized Mexican citizen and a man of some standing, witnessed by the fact he was one of two grantees upon which Gov. Pio Pico bestowed the deserted San Gorgonio Rancho. He was in the U.S. Army during the Civil War. In 1862, he discovered gold on the Colorado River. (Courtesy of the author.)

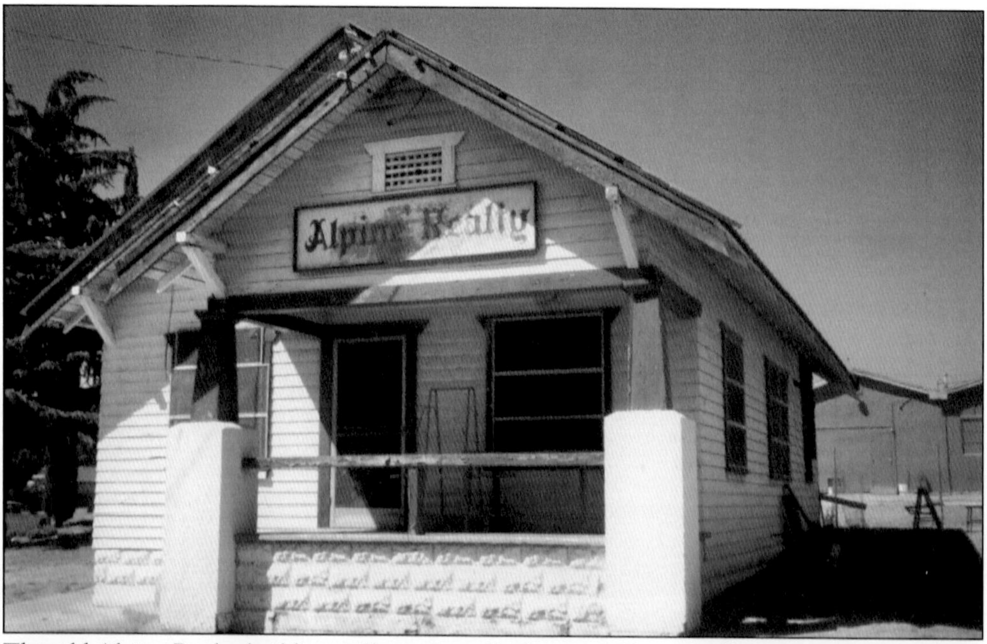

This old Alpine Realty building still stands in the heart of Cherry Valley. It is alleged to be the first prominent real estate business to come upon this scene and can boast of many past land sales. Note the building at the right rear of the photograph. This Ace Hardware was built from two of General Patton's old hospital barracks once standing nearby. (Courtesy of the author.)

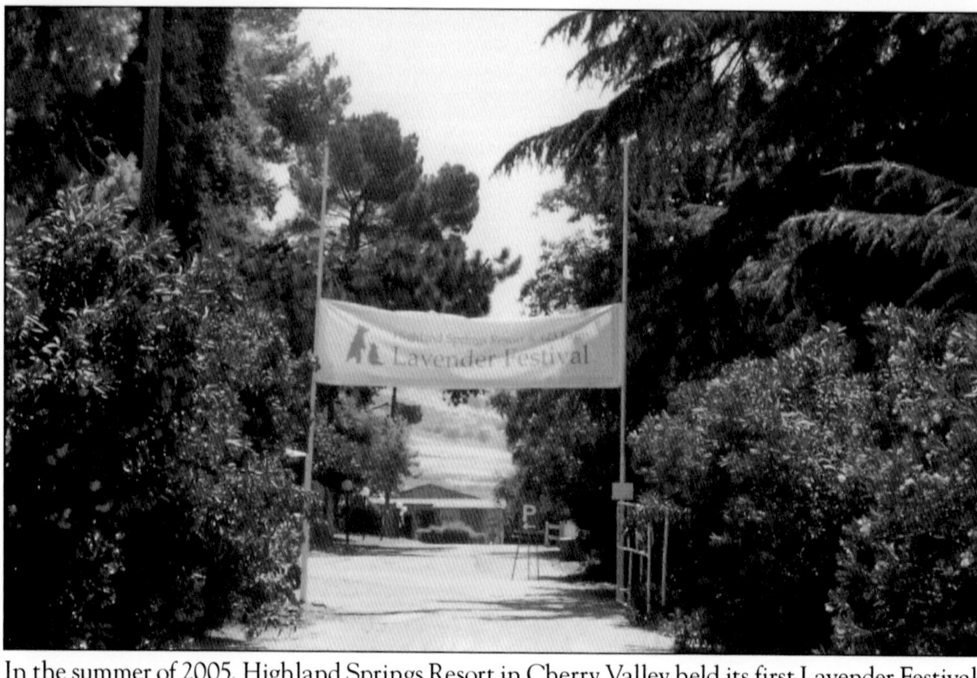

In the summer of 2005, Highland Springs Resort in Cherry Valley held its first Lavender Festival. Shown here is the banner leading to the festival grounds. Guests toured the lavender farm and were introduced to the many lavender varieties. Products derived from lavender were displayed under the nearby tall trees. Plans have been enacted for a yearly festival. (Courtesy of the author.)

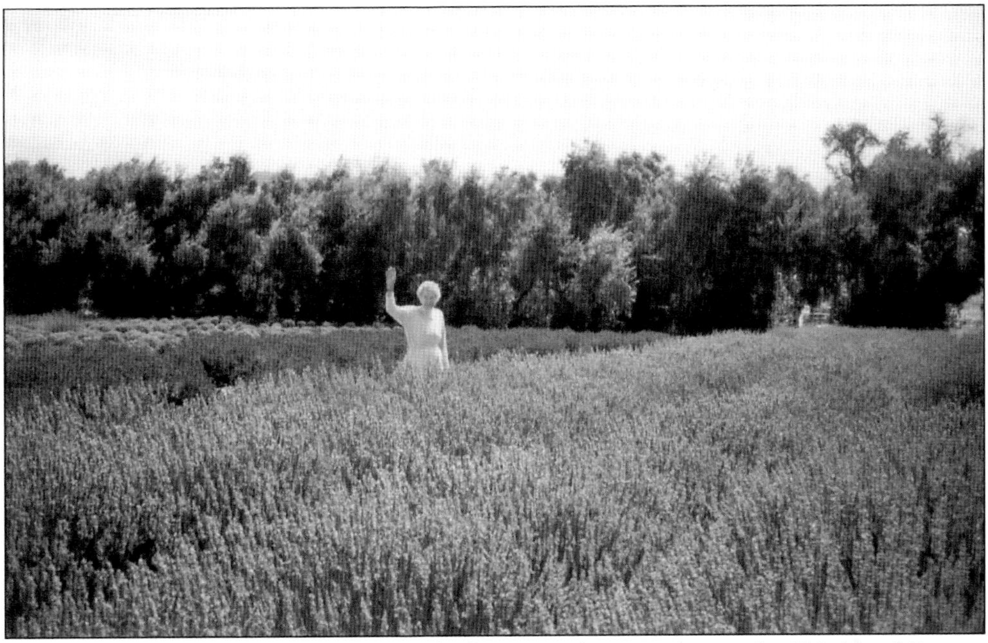

A sea of blue lavender grows on the lavender farm near the central grounds of Highland Springs Resort. The author's wife, Margaret, is engulfed in this canopy of lush lavender. It meshes well with the sprawling olive groves, rolling green lawns, and tall pines. It is a treat for visitors to come and witness the colorful beauty that abounds. (Courtesy of the author.)

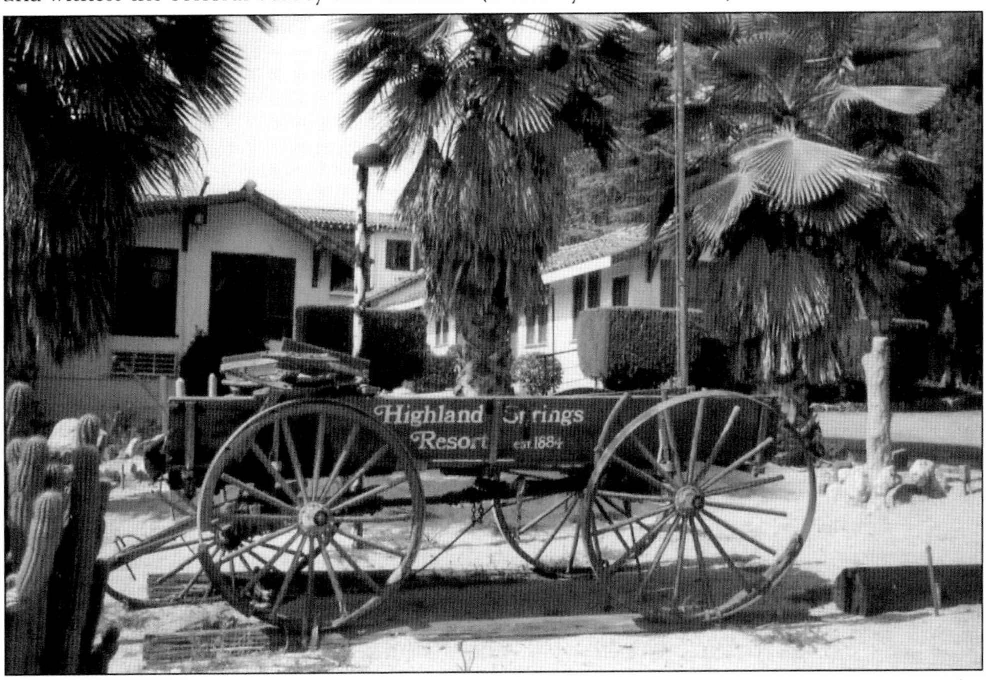

This old buggy, advertising the Highland Springs Resort, shows several of the bungalows on the resort's grounds. Tourists come here to visit and vacation and others come to attend the conferences that are sometimes held at the resort's facilities. The essence of the park is its splendor, 100-year-old pines, and history revolving back to 1884. (Courtesy of the author.)

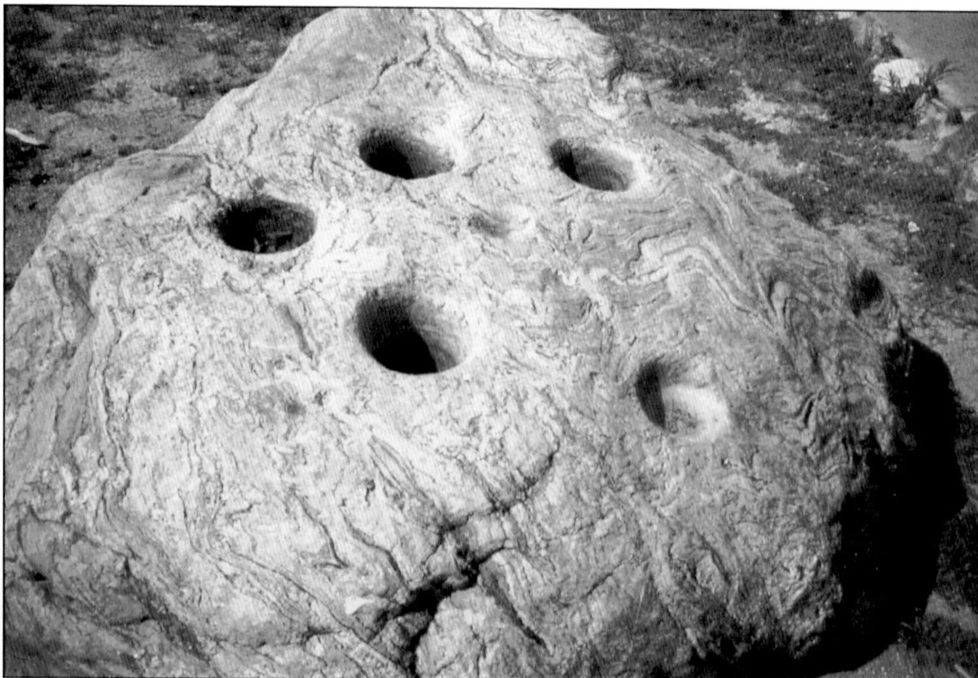

This slab of stone was brought in from nearby mountains and placed on the grounds of Highland Springs Resort as a display. It was these kinds of mortars that Native Americans used so successfully. Using a pestle, they ground acorns, seeds, and plant material in these mortars. Other sites found in the hill contain multiple mortars in large granite outcrops. (Courtesy of the author.)

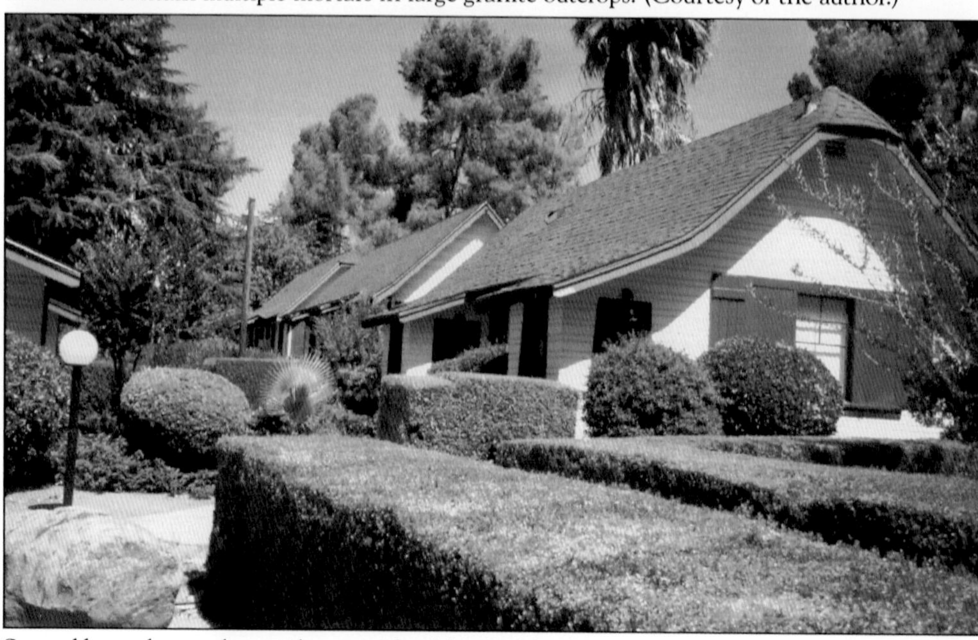

Several bungalows enhance the grounds of the Highland Springs Resort and Convention Center. There are numerous ones on the premises, some dating back many years, but all providing a fanciful atmosphere at the resort. Tourists and convention members always enjoy staying in these remote, quaint accommodations. (Courtesy of the author.)

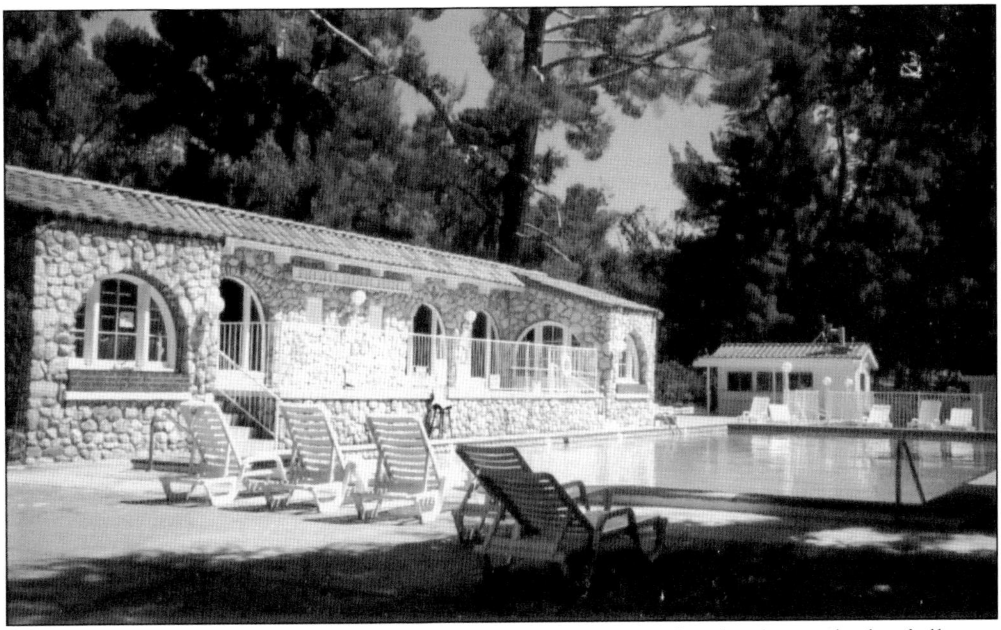

One of the highlights of the Highlands Springs Resort is its pool, a slumbering body of alluring blue water set under a canopy of tall pines and cool greenery. The pool's clubhouse and lockers are in a rock building, which adds a pleasant aura to the pool's surroundings. The resort's pool has become a favorite retreat for many during the summer months. (Courtesy of the author.)

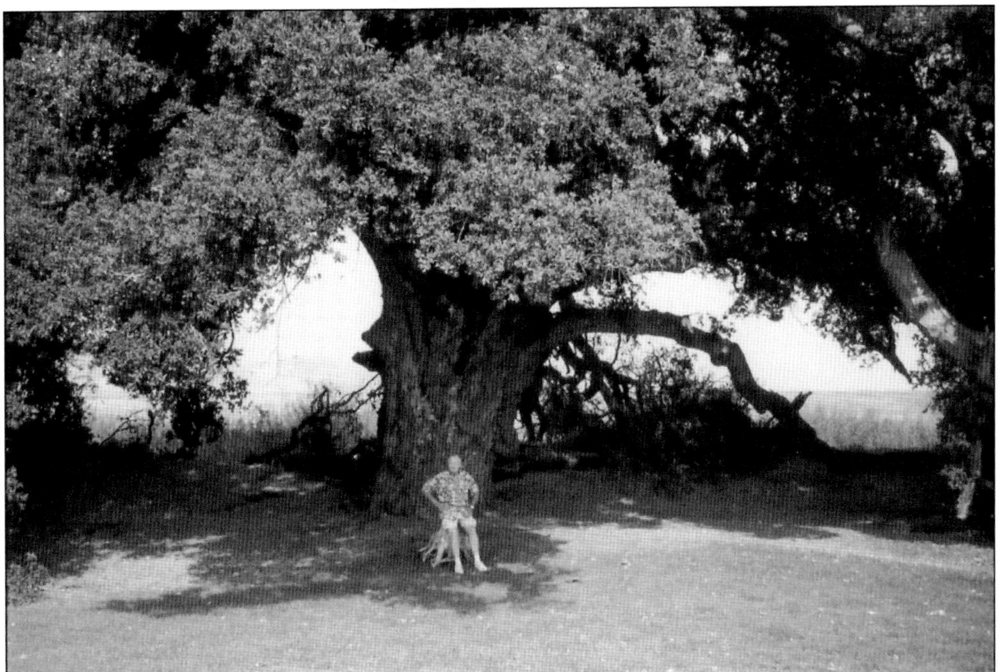

The author pictured here sitting on a stump at Highland Springs Resort. It is used as a marker against the old oak tree behind it that is over 1,000 years old. The author rounded the big oak with six out-reached arm lengths, circling the circumference of the tree, which calculated to be around 30 feet. It is considered the oldest oak tree in California. (Courtesy of the author.)

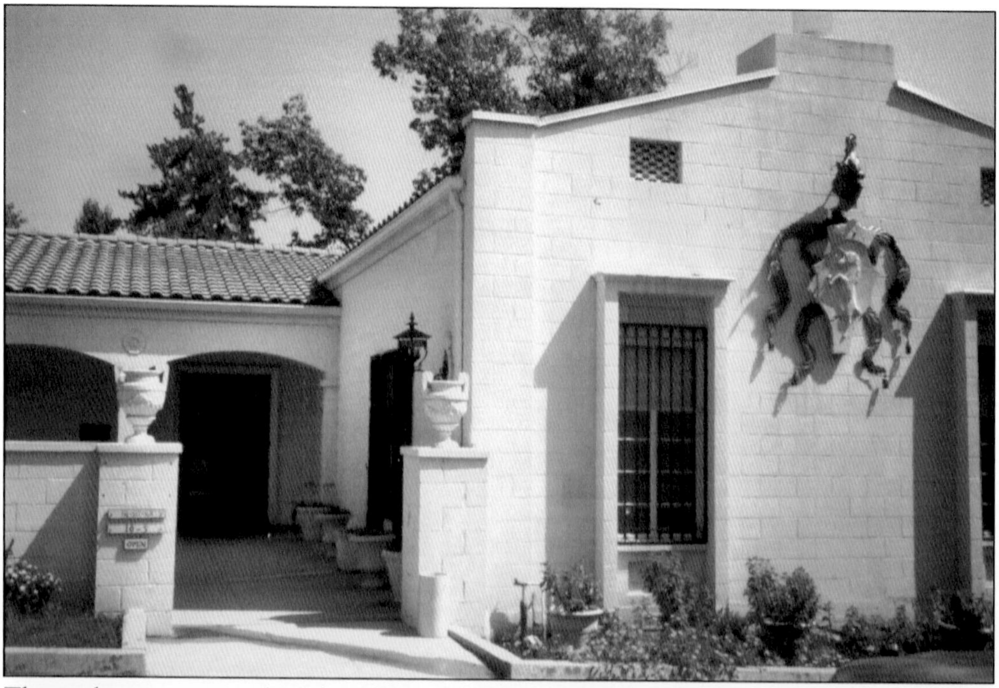

This is the entrance to the Edward-Dean Museum of Decorative Arts, enhanced by a formal garden and pool to the left. The museum is situated on 16 beautifully landscaped acres that contain a group of other buildings. It was originally purchased by J. Edward Eberle and Dean W. Stout, who built a gallery for their huge collection of antiques. It was deeded to the County of Riverside to become a cultural center. (Courtesy of the author.)

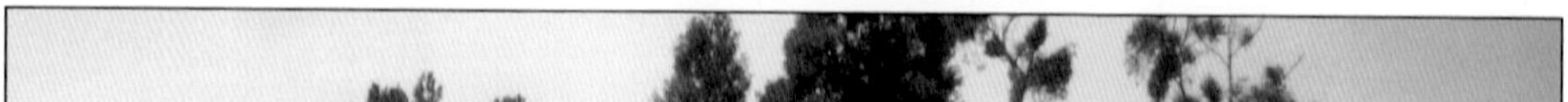

The Kay Ceniceros Cultural Arts Center is located on the grounds of the Edward-Dean Museum. It is an inviting concert hall where entertainment is presented routinely during the concert season. It serves many people of the San Gorgonio Pass, as well as others from around the area. The center has added much to the popularity of the museum. (Courtesy of the author.)

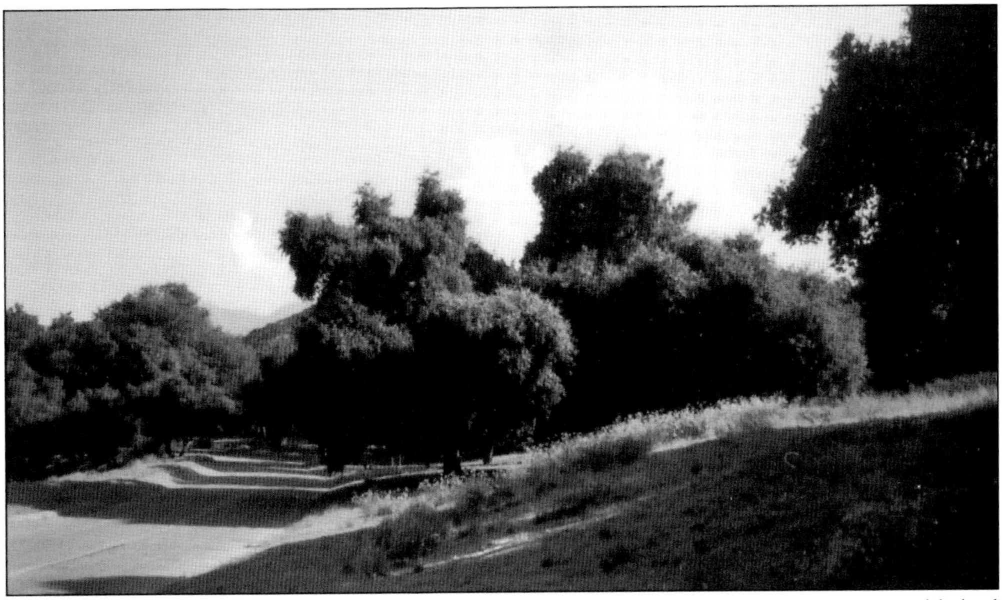

This photograph was taken on the grounds of Bogart Park in Cherry Valley. It was established in 1931, upon necessity of having a meeting place for large crowds, and named in honor of Dr. Guy Bogart, who initiated the establishment of the park. The park consists of 400 acres of open space, campsites, picnic areas, and an equestrian camp. It is operated and maintained by Riverside County Regional Park and Open-Space District. (Courtesy of the author.)

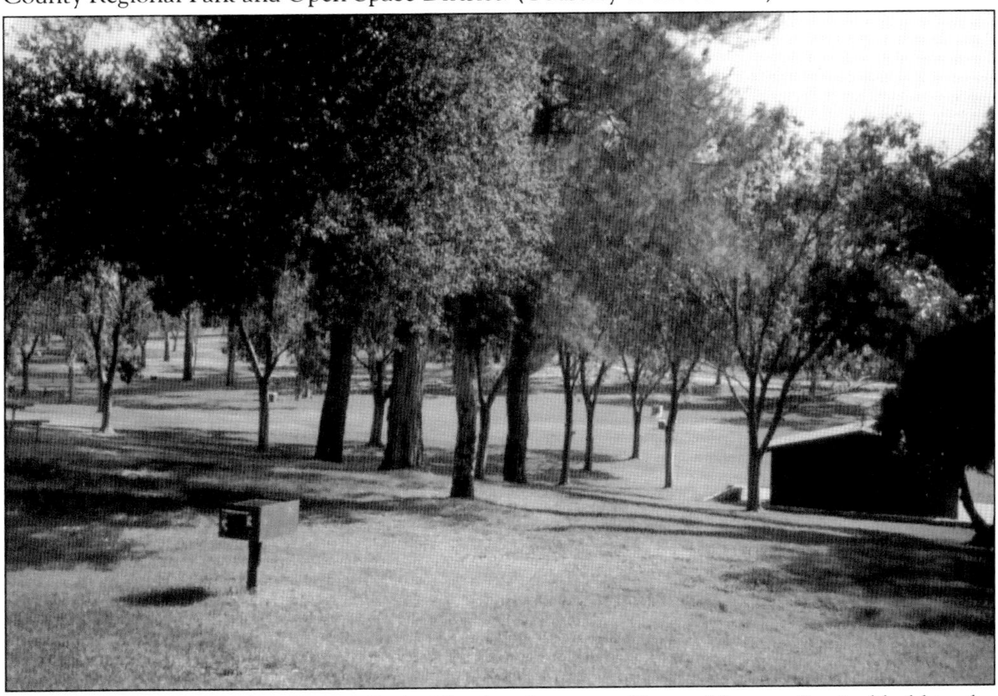

Here is the Bogart Bowl in Bogart Park. The first Japanese Cherry Blossom Festival held in the United States in 1930, drew a crowd of 32,000 people to tiny Beaumont, with a population of only 1,332 citizens. In view of this, Mayor Bogart of Beaumont promoted this park of roving live oak trees to accommodate large crowds. (Courtesy of the author.)

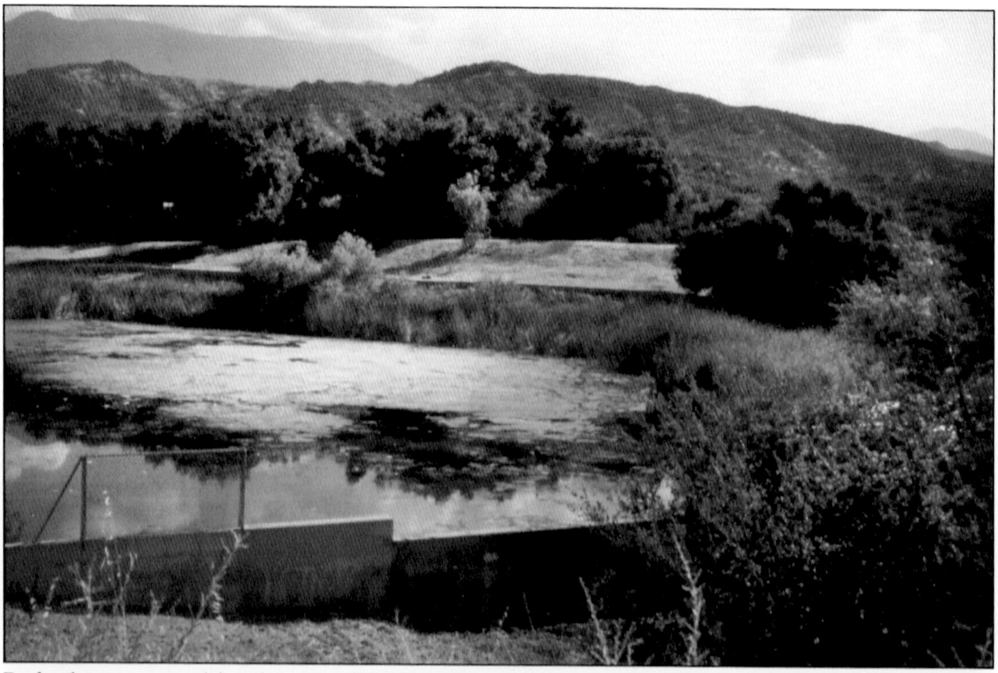

Refreshing scenes like the one shown here can be seen throughout Bogart Park, originally named International Park. Dr. Bogart, founder of the Japanese Cherry Festival and the prime mover behind the purchase of the park acreage, was appointed first superintendent of the park. In October 1931, dedication of the park was held in the Bogart Bowl, the park's amphitheater. In 1959, the park name was changed to Bogart Park at the request of the Beaumont Chamber of Commerce. (Courtesy of the author.)

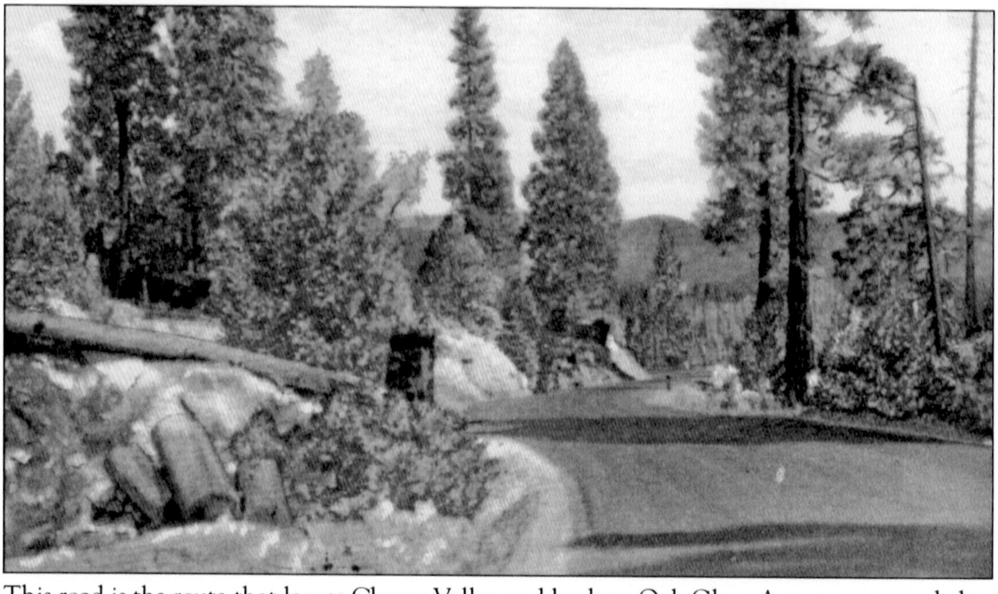

This road is the route that leaves Cherry Valley and leads to Oak Glen. A route was needed to transport oak lumber from Oak Glen to the wood-burning trains passing through Beaumont. The road is a scenic drive from Cherry Valley in route to Oak Glen, the hillside community that is only around nine miles away. (Courtesy of the author.)

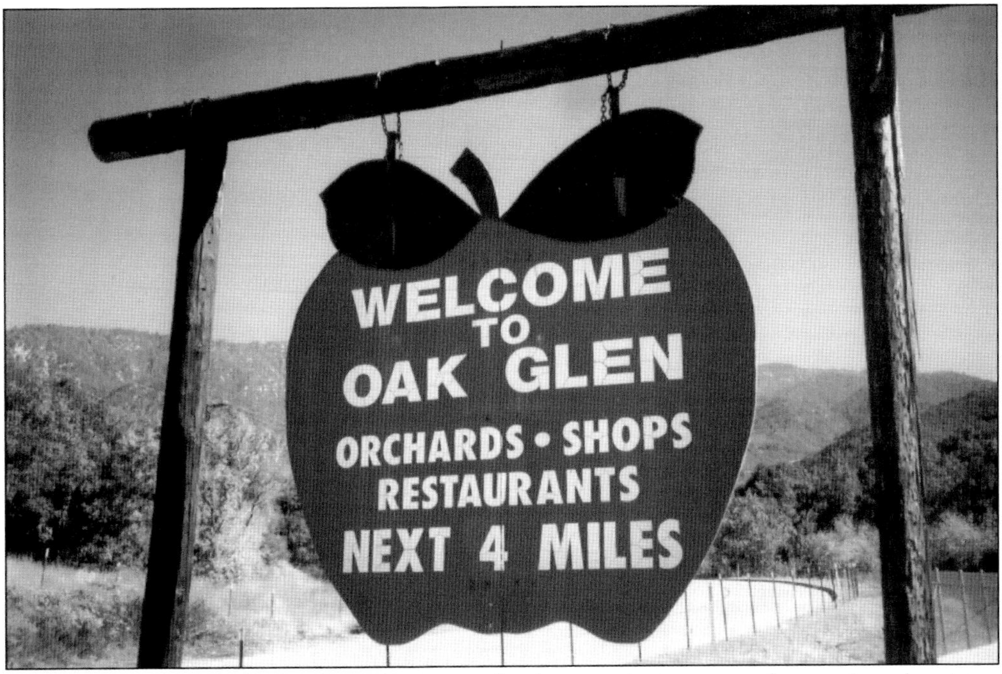

Just before reaching Oak Glen from Beaumont, this large apple sign greets the traveler, advertising that apple country is nearby. Oak Glen was originally called Potato Canyon, but when apple production replaced potato farming, the potato icon was replaced by the apple. Apple season brings many from near and far to Oak Glen. (Courtesy of the author.)

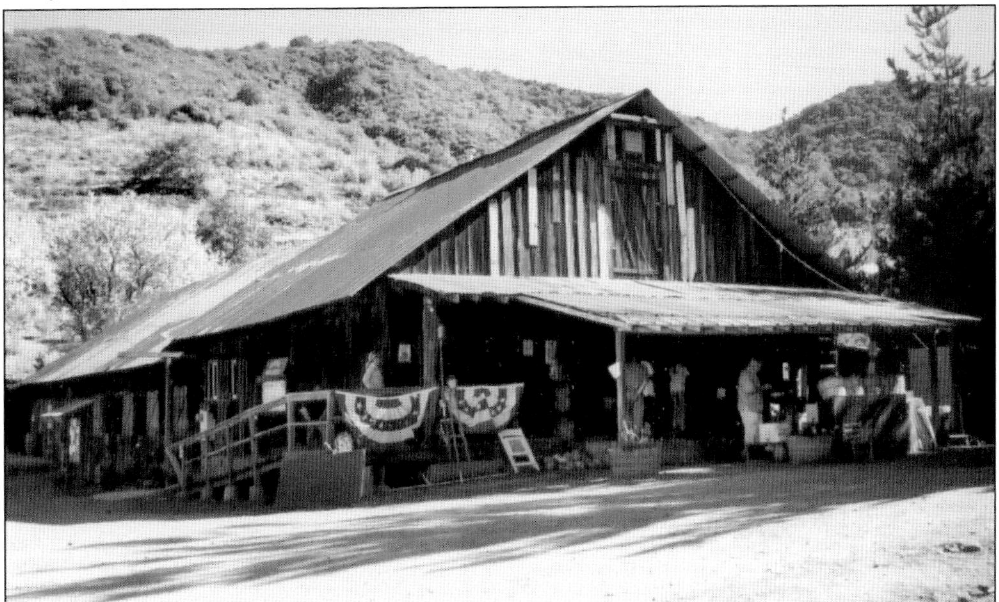

This large packing shed was built by the Wilshire family, pioneers in Oak Glen. It provided for its flourishing apple and fruit production. Originally, brothers Ed, Will, Fred, and Bert Wilshire homesteaded acreage here to form their large ranch. Today Grandpa Ray and Grandma Bea Riley own and operate 760 acres. (Courtesy of the author.)

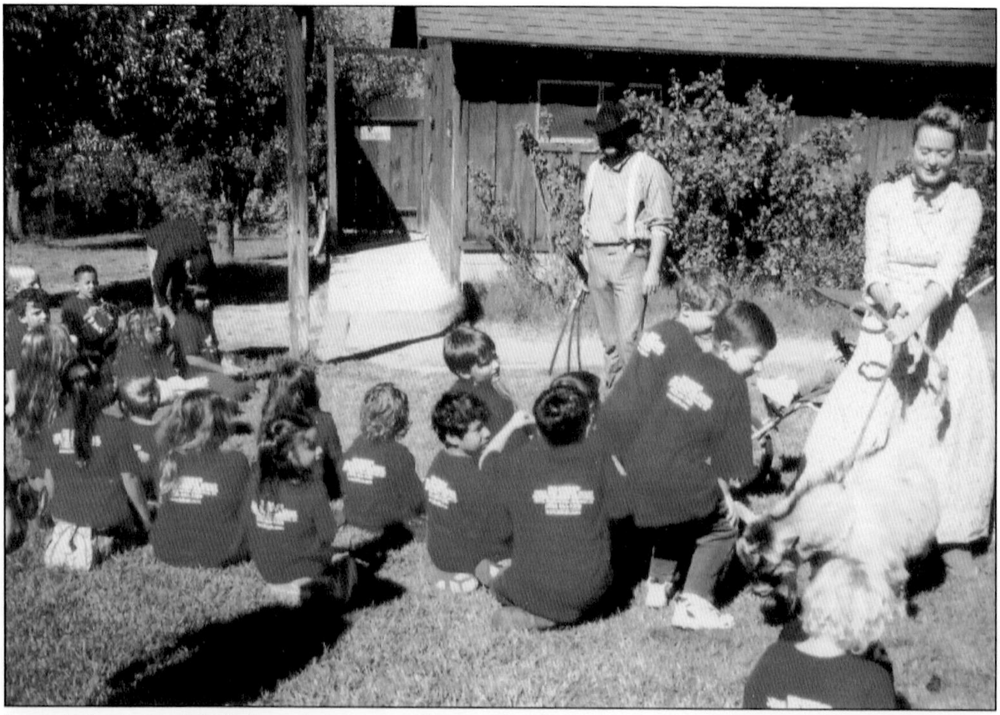

Jessie Riley, one of 36 Riley relatives, conducts a children's tour of one of the Serrano and Yucaipa Indian trails around Oak Glen's Riley Ranch. Field trips, hayrides, dances, and barbecues are frequent at the ranch. (Courtesy of Jessie Riley.)

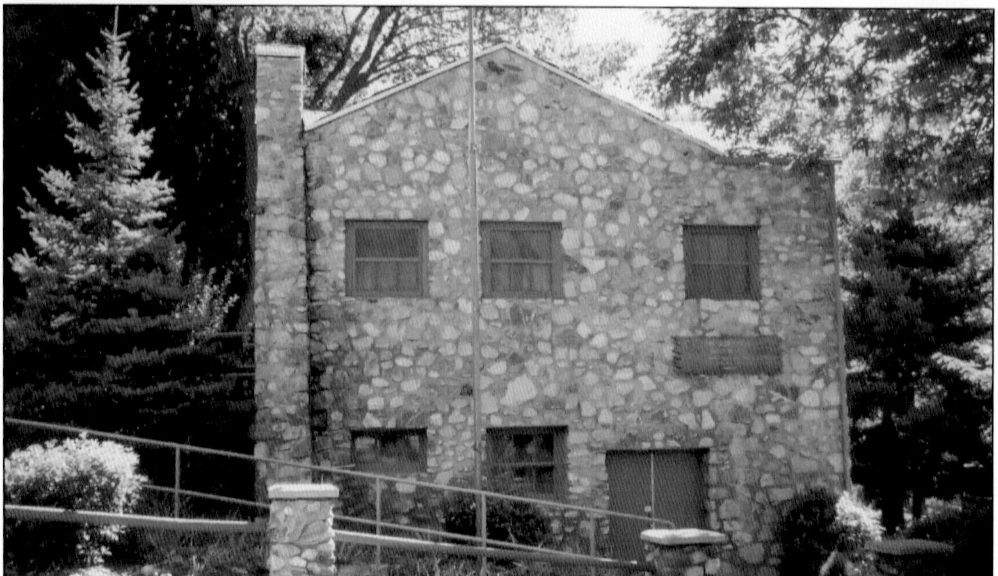

This is a recent photograph of Oak Glen's greatest historical treasure, the old rock schoolhouse. Prior to 1927, a small wooden school, built in 1888, was used. A few times, the wooden school was moved from one side of the glen to the other to accommodate students. In 1928, a new stone school was built. Twenty-seven years later, it closed due to the Field Act of 1965, enforcing stringent earthquake standards. However, it remained as a museum.

Five

Stewart Ranch and Family

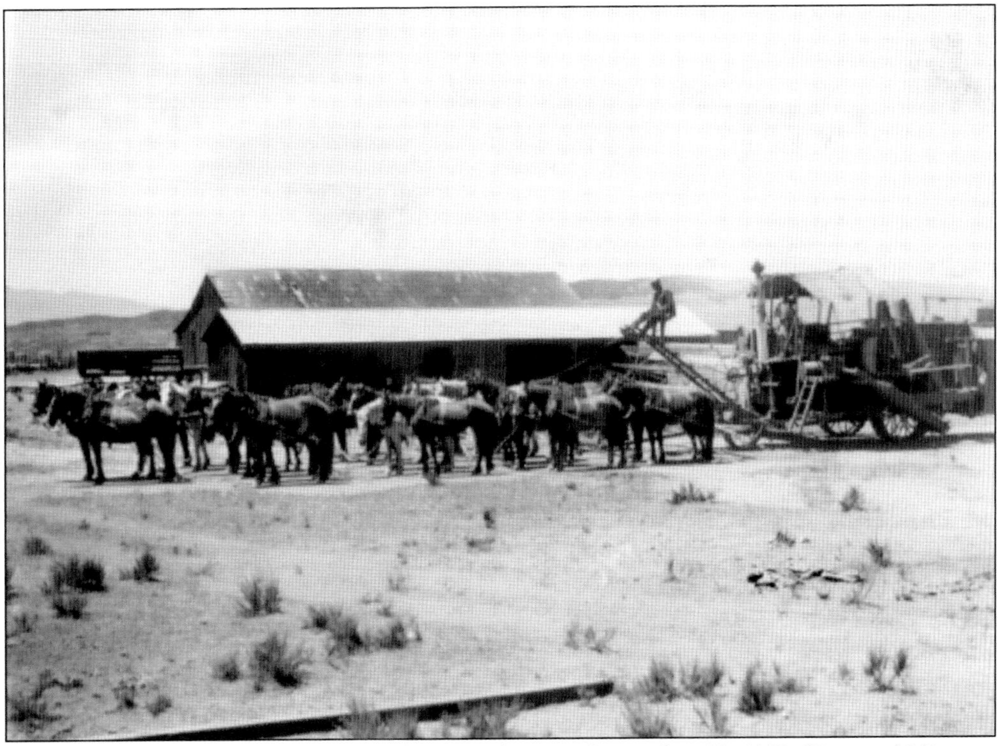

The San Gorgonio Pass was not well known when on September 18, 1878, 33-year-old Renzor Perry Stewart and several of his friends drove in from Yolo County. He brought in two train carloads of horses and soon set his hand to the plow on the Banning Bench. Later he built a large barn on a homestead south of Banning. (Courtesy of Marilyn Vonderheide and Laura Mae Stewart Foundation.)

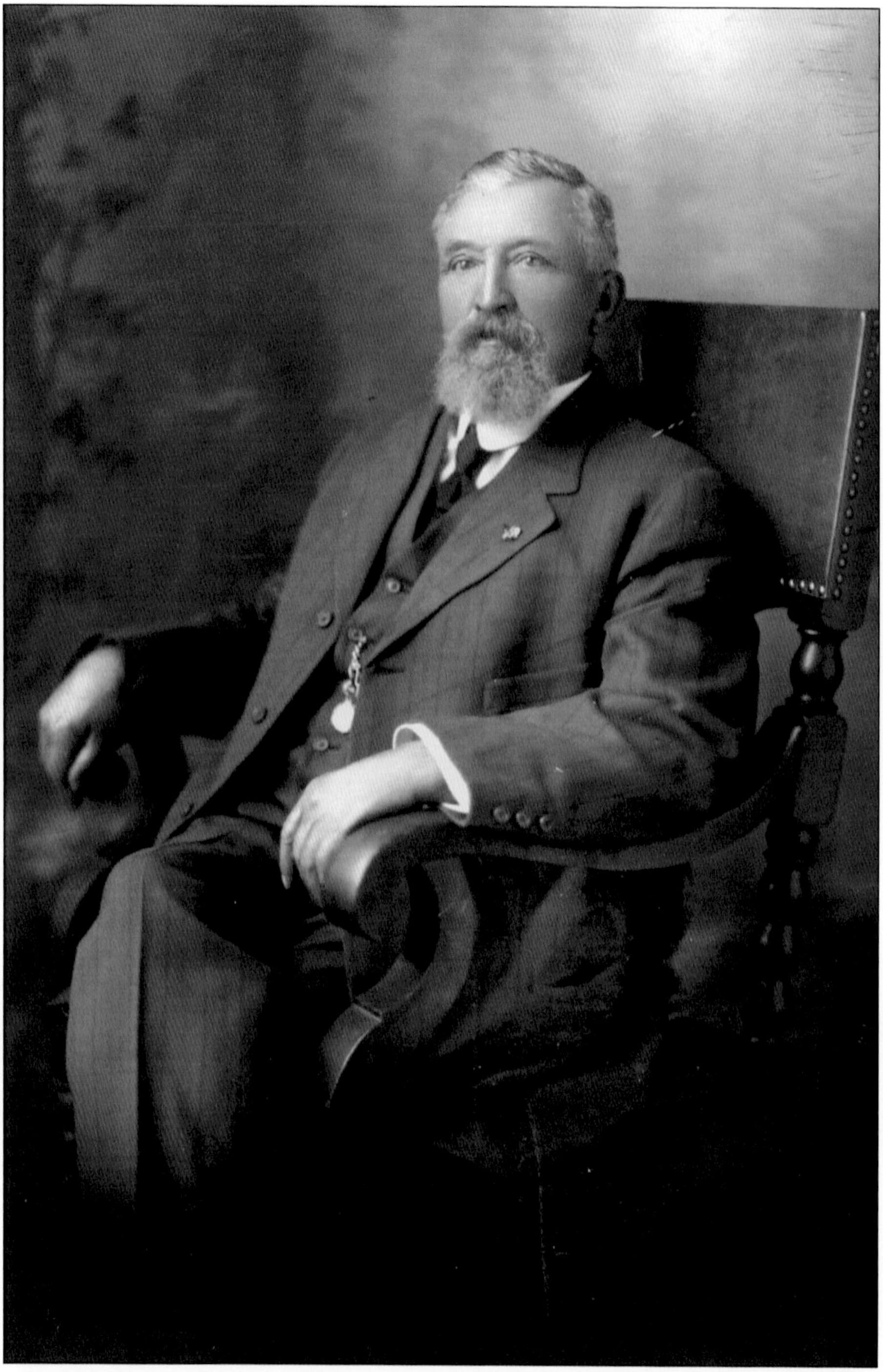

This picture of Renzor Perry was taken years after the Stewart Ranch was firmly established. In 1883, he took up a homestead four miles southwest of Banning. Patents to this land were issued by Presidents Grover Cleveland and Benjamin Harrison. Perry bought 1,800 acres more from the railroad and began dry farming and hay growing on a great scale. (Courtesy of Marilyn Vonderheide and Laura Mae Stewart Foundation.)

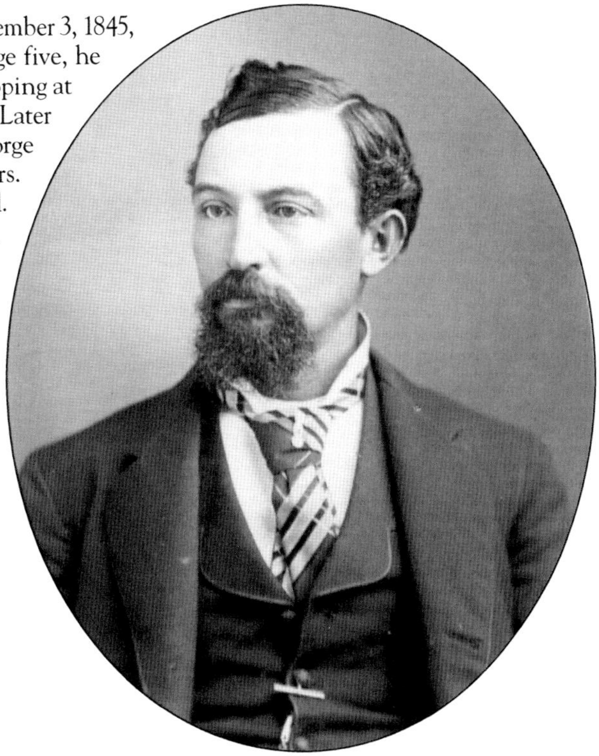

Renzor Stewart, born in Illinois on November 3, 1845, is pictured here as a young man. At age five, he and his mother crossed the plains, stopping at Hangtown, California, now Placerville. Later Renzor became foreman of the vast George Scott ranches, remaining there 21 years. Here he met Kit Carson and Buffalo Bill. (Courtesy of Marilyn Vonderheide and Laura Mae Stewart Foundation.)

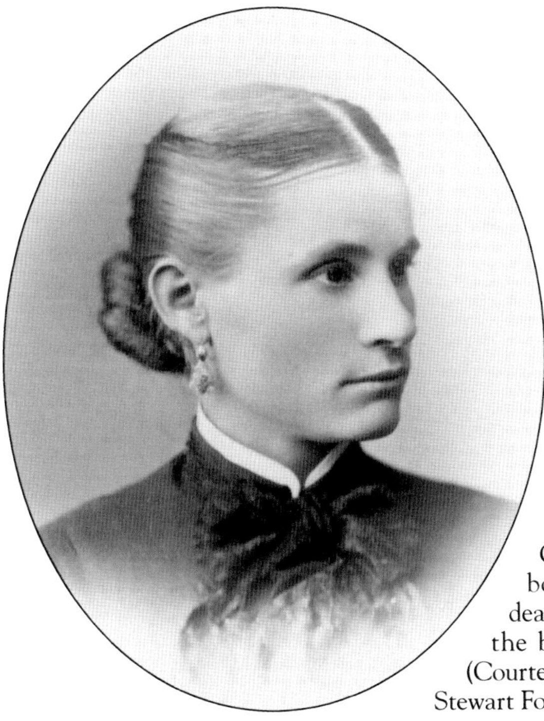

Pictured here is Renzor's wife, Mary Christensen, whom he married on December 30, 1880. She was the step-daughter of prominent Banning resident, C. F. Jost. Three boys and two girls were born to her. She succumbed to an early death on August 30, 1890, a few months after the birth of her fifth child, Renzor Perry Jr. (Courtesy of Marilyn Vonderheide and Laura Mae Stewart Foundation.)

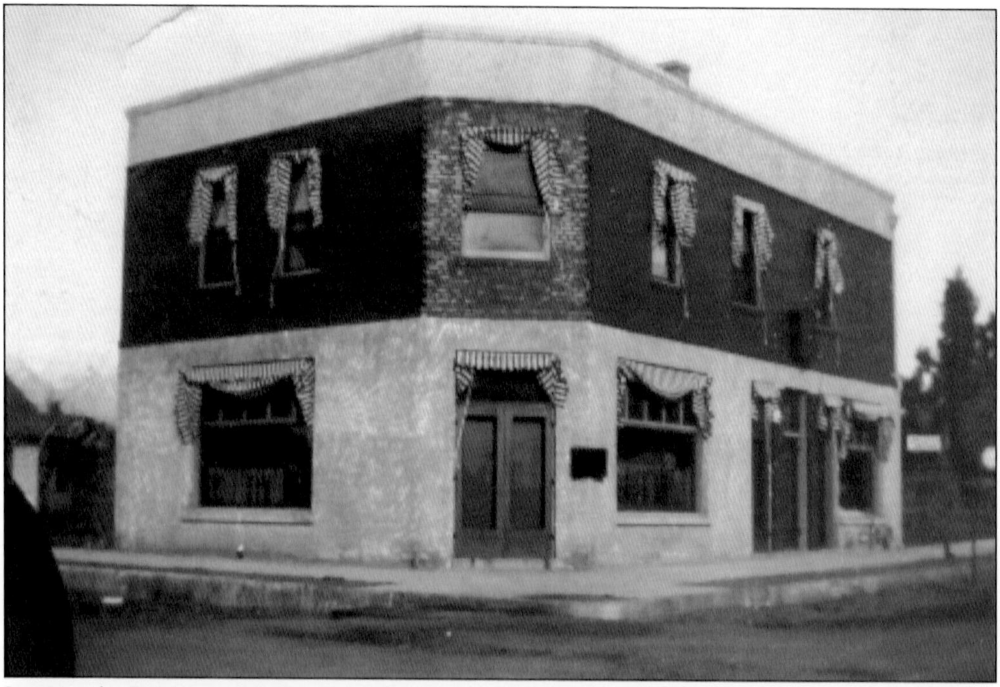

In 1911, the Beaumont Bank, pictured here, was built. Renzor Stewart was one of its founders and its president for several years. During the war, he heavily bought Liberty Bonds. With the large farming that was beginning to occur, the plentiful water, and the real estate boom in progress in the San Gorgonio Pass, establishment of a bank was inevitable. (Courtesy of Marilyn Vonderheide and Laura Mae Stewart Foundation.)

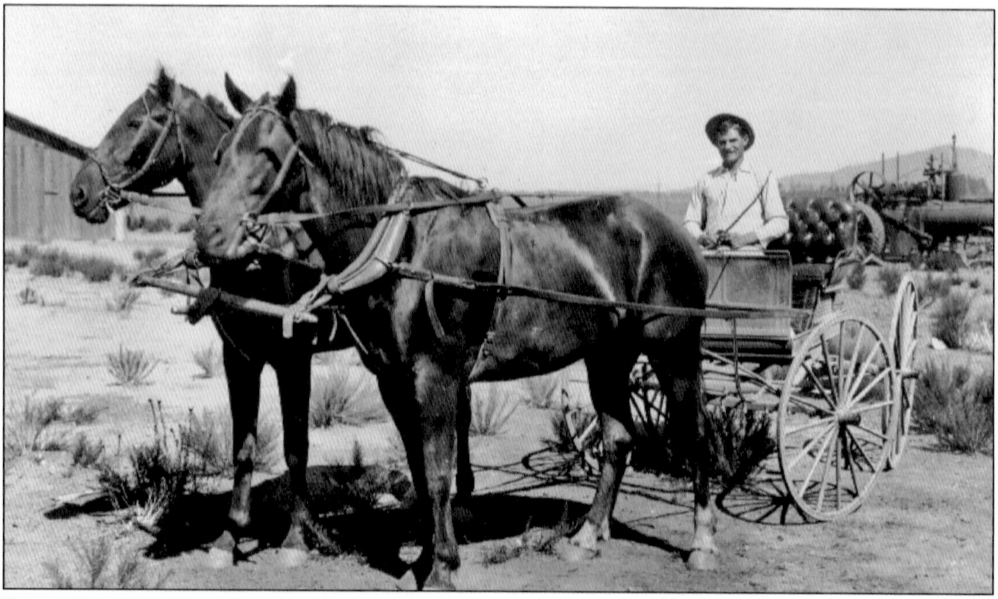

Emery Ross Stewart, the oldest son of Renzor and Mary Stewart, adapted well to farming and enjoyed working with his father. Here he has harnessed the horses and made ready the carriage, perhaps for a trip to town for shopping or some business event. (Courtesy of Marilyn Vonderheide and Laura Mae Stewart Foundation.)

The Stewart family, pictured here, from left to right, are (first row) Arthur, Reznor Perry Jr., Clara, and Laura; (second row) Emery. Emery and Laura were both born at the Banning Bench home and Arthur, Clara, and Renzor Perry Jr. at the ranch home southwest of Banning. Emery died at sea in 1925, Arthur in Lima, Peru, in 1913, and Renzor Perry Jr. in San Francisco in 1906. (Courtesy of Marilyn Vonderheide and Laura Mae Stewart Foundation.)

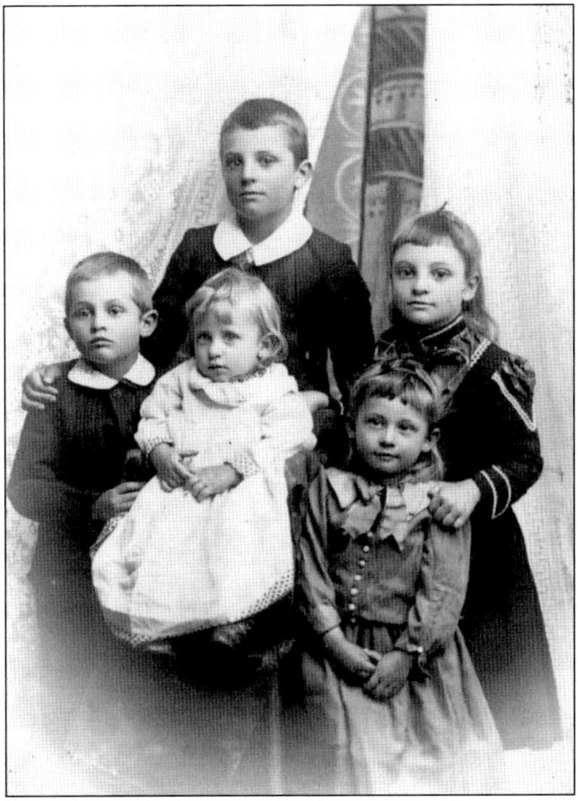

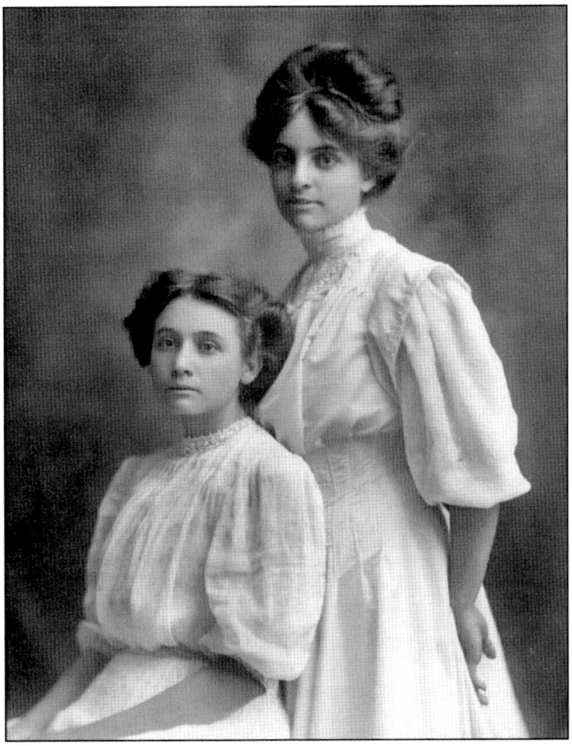

This photograph depicts Laura, right, and her sister Clara, all grown up. After the girls' mother died, they helped on the ranch with vigor, often hitching up a buggy and heading to the grain fields to deliver lunch and cold water to the crew. On one Fourth of July celebration, Laura was chosen Beaumont's carnival queen. (Courtesy of Marilyn Vonderheide and Laura Mae Stewart Foundation.)

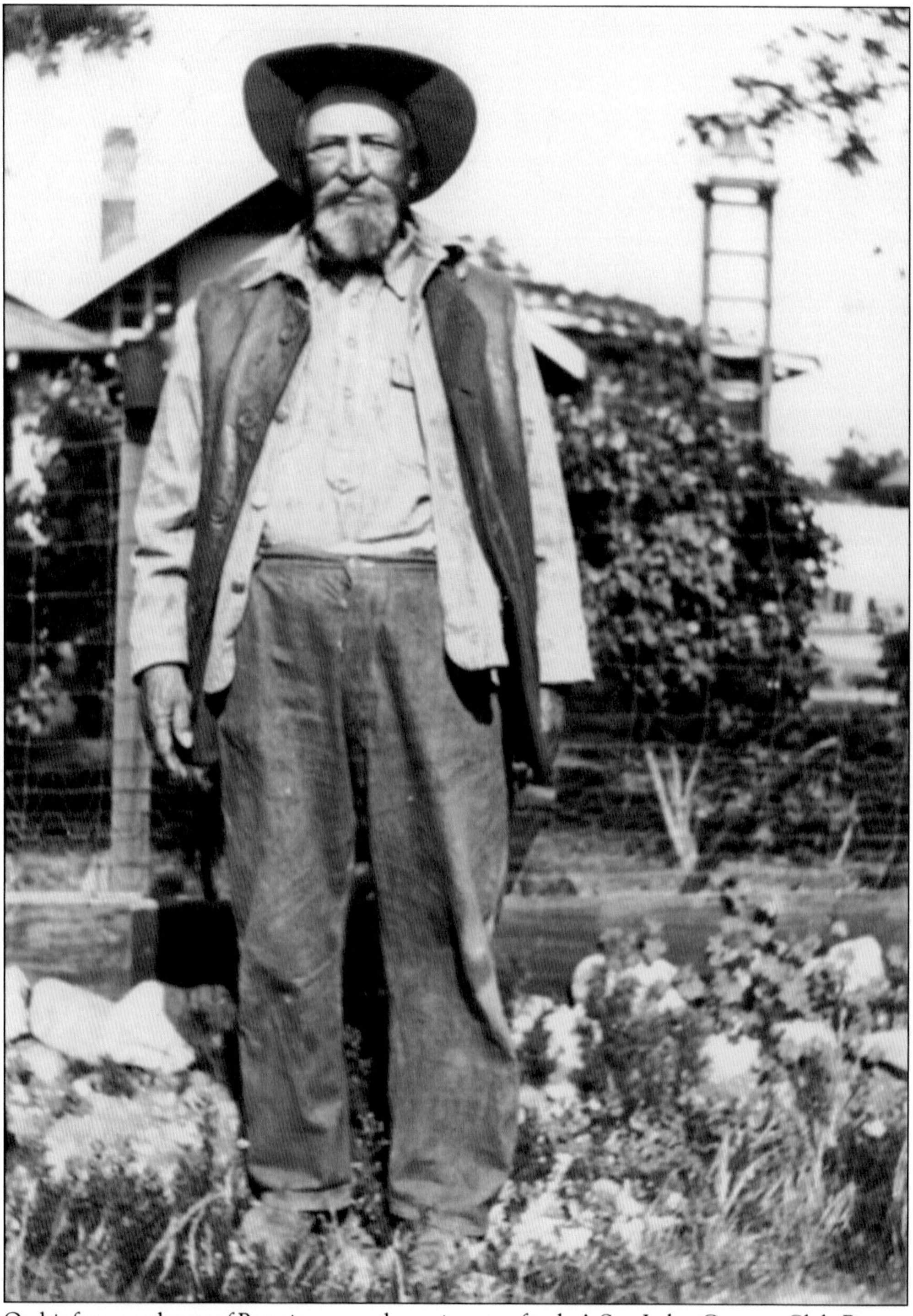

On his farm southwest of Banning, near the main gate of today's Sun Lakes Country Club, Reznor Stewart stands in front of the ranch house that he moved from his farm on the Banning Bench by Water Canyon. When the house was moved away, it left behind the great rock chimney, which was long a landmark. (Courtesy of Marilyn Vonderheide and Laura Mae Stewart Foundation.)

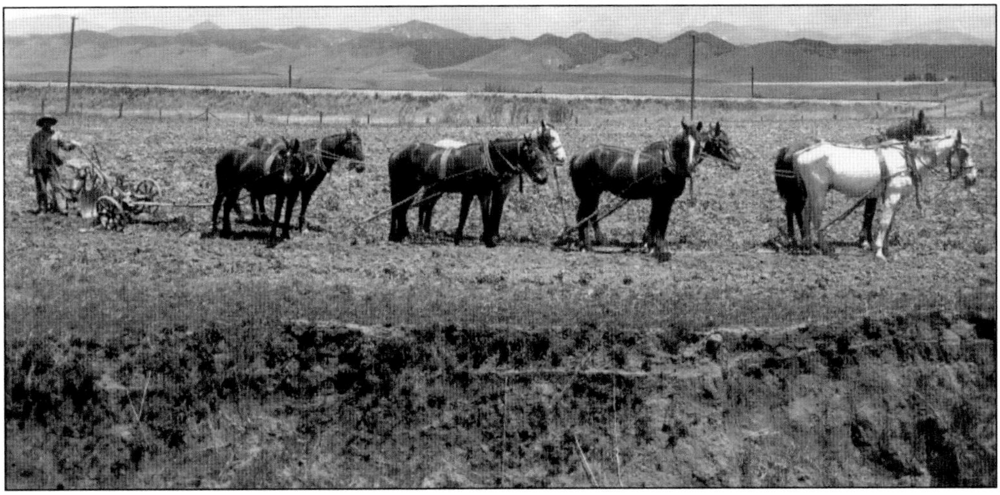

A team of horses is ready to begin plowing a field on the Stewart Ranch, south of the railroad. Much horsepower was required to pull the large plow blade through the hard-packed soil that was often encountered in some areas on the farm. Behind the plow is ranch hand Carl Beaseley, who married Clara Stewart. (Courtesy of Marilyn Vonderheide and Laura Mae Stewart Foundation.)

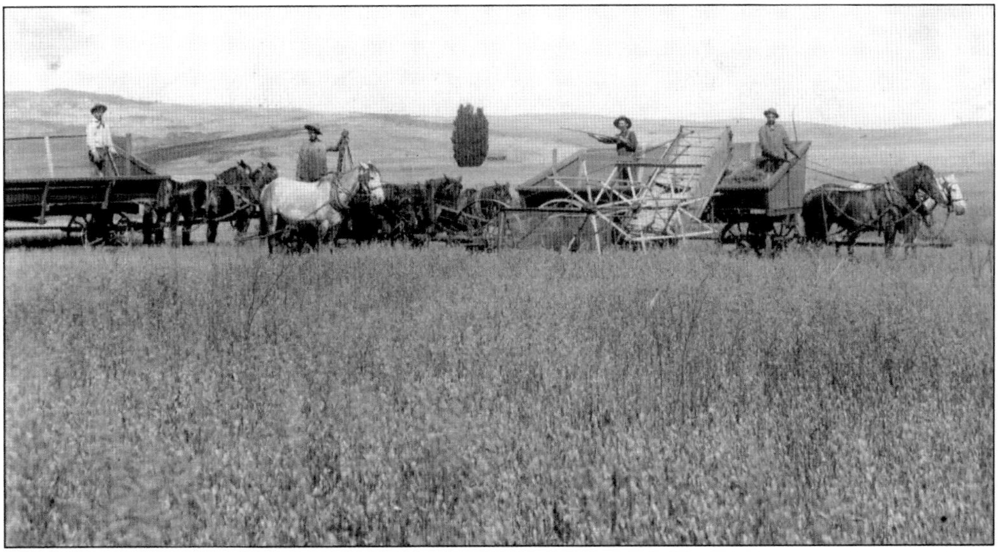

Oats were the second largest grain crop grown on the Stewart Ranch. Pictured here is a farm crew in the field cutting and loading oats. It was quite a task to cut the oats, haul the seeds and rubble to the thresher to be threshed, and then sack and remove them from the field. During this era, the market was good and the incentive to raise oats was strong. (Courtesy of the Laura Mae Stewart Foundation.)

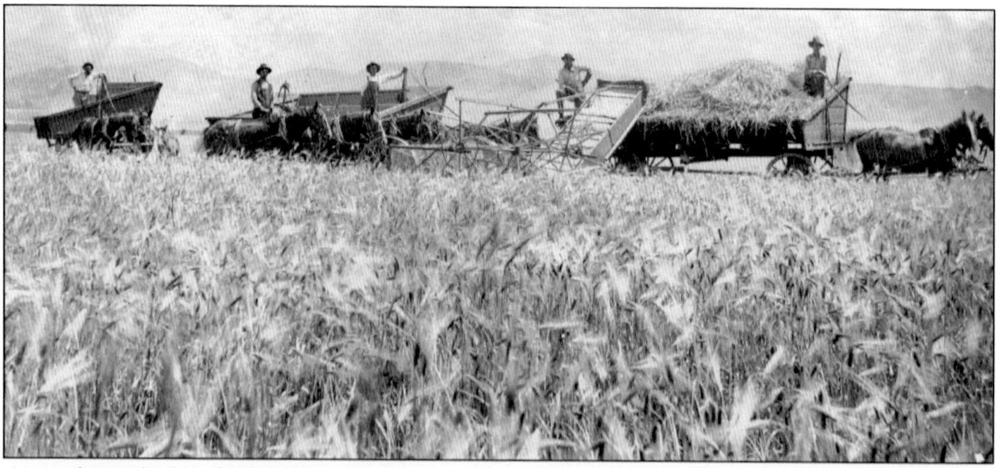

A good stand of barley, the largest grain crop grown on the Stewart Ranch, is being cut and loaded to be hauled to the thresher. This was a tedious task, for the thresher was usually remote and not moved often. Grain yields at the Stewart Ranch produced 10,000 sacks of grain a year and 200 tons of hay. Among the 57 consecutive crops, there has not been one failure. (Courtesy of Marilyn Vonderheide and Laura Mae Stewart Foundation.)

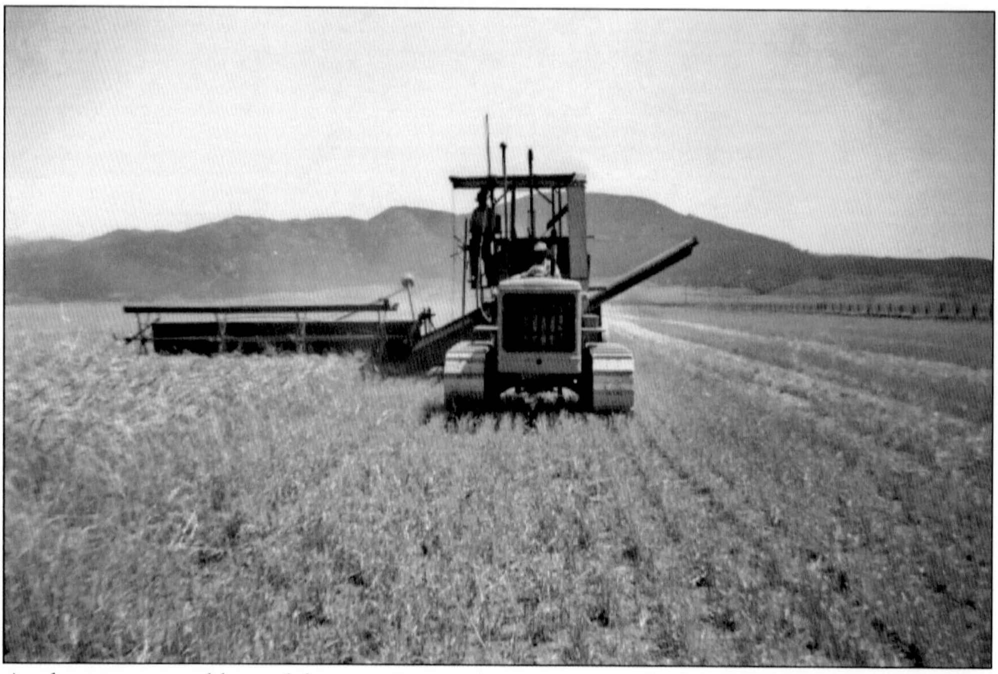

As the years passed by and farm equipment became more advanced, new tractors and other machinery were incorporated. This Caterpillar cleat tractor worked on the Stewart Ranch cutting barley. Farming on this level alleviated many hours of labor and expense involved in equipping and caring for horses, previously used for this type of work. (Courtesy of Marilyn Vonderheide and Laura Mae Stewart Foundation.)

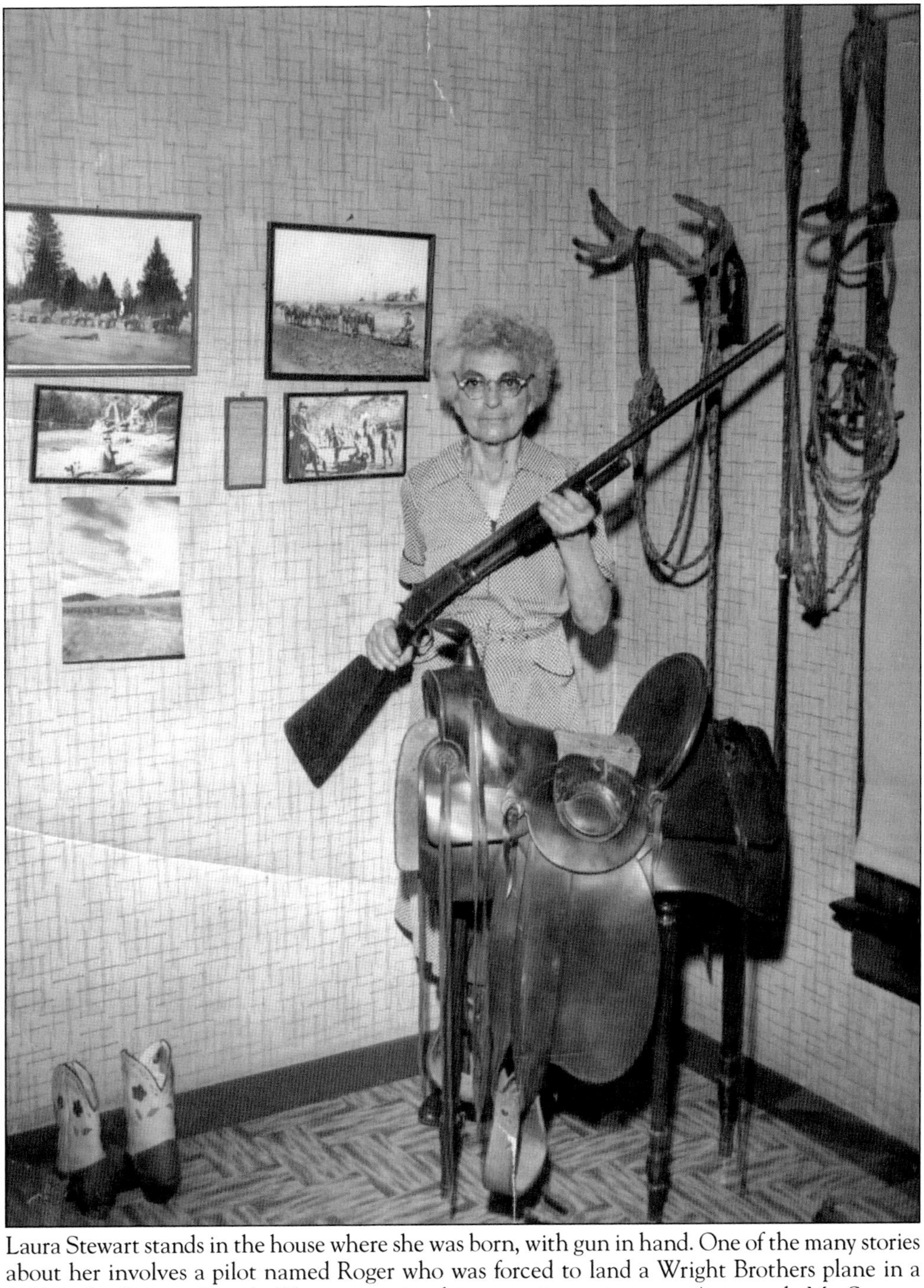

Laura Stewart stands in the house where she was born, with gun in hand. One of the many stories about her involves a pilot named Roger who was forced to land a Wright Brothers plane in a field at the Stewart Ranch. The event stirred some major excitement. Apparently Mr. Stewart rushed into the house and jovially yelled, "Get your gun, Laura. The biggest hawk I have ever seen just landed out in our barley field!" (Courtesy of Marilyn Vonderheide and Laura Mae Stewart Foundation.)

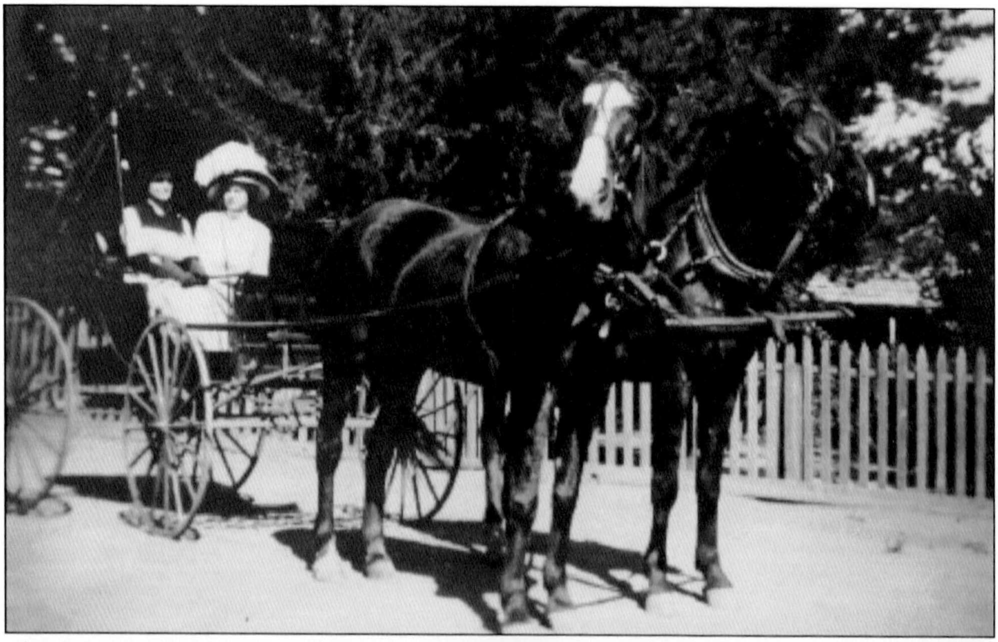

This June 15, 1911, photograph shows Laura and her friend Blanch sitting in a buggy with the horses harnessed, perhaps en route to church or some special event. Laura is seated at left with reins in her hand. The scene is near the Stewart Ranch house, which was located near the corner of today's Highland Springs Boulevard and Sun Lakes Avenue. (Courtesy of Marilyn Vonderheide and Laura Mae Stewart Foundation.)

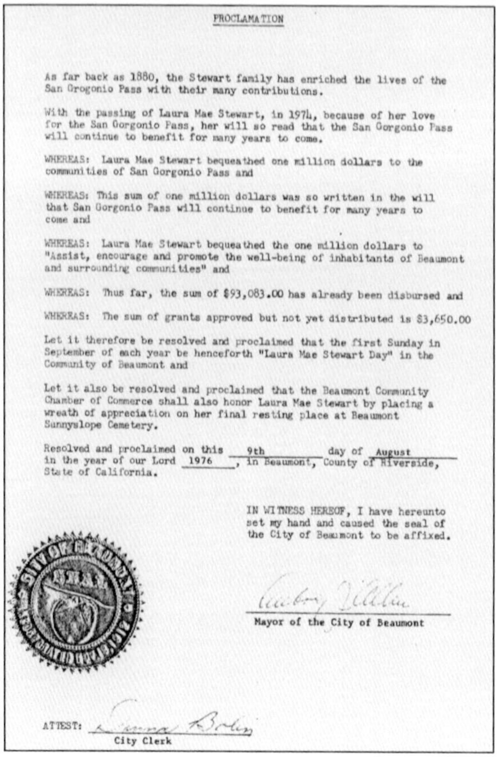

PROCLAMATION

As far back as 1880, the Stewart family has enriched the lives of the San Grogonio Pass with their many contributions.

With the passing of Laura Mae Stewart, in 1974, because of her love for the San Gorgonio Pass, her will so read that the San Gorgonio Pass will continue to benefit for many years to come.

WHEREAS: Laura Mae Stewart bequeathed one million dollars to the communities of San Gorgonio Pass and

WHEREAS: This sum of one million dollars was so written in the will that San Gorgonio Pass will continue to benefit for many years to come and

WHEREAS: Laura Mae Stewart bequeathed the one million dollars to "Assist, encourage and promote the well-being of inhabitants of Beaumont and surrounding communities" and

WHEREAS: Thus far, the sum of $93,083.00 has already been disbursed and

WHEREAS: The sum of grants approved but not yet distributed is $3,650.00

Let it therefore be resolved and proclaimed that the first Sunday in September of each year be henceforth "Laura Mae Stewart Day" in the Community of Beaumont and

Let it also be resolved and proclaimed that the Beaumont Community Chamber of Commerce shall also honor Laura Mae Stewart by placing a wreath of appreciation on her final resting place at Beaumont Sunnyslope Cemetery.

Resolved and proclaimed on this 9th day of August in the year of our Lord 1976, in Beaumont, County of Riverside, State of California.

IN WITNESS HEREOF, I have hereunto set my hand and caused the seal of the City of Beaumont to be affixed.

Mayor of the City of Beaumont

ATTEST:
City Clerk

This proclamation decreed that Laura Mae Stewart has bequeathed $1 million to the communities of the San Gorgonio Pass upon her death. Because of Laura's endowment, this gracious action continues. Over time, this endowment has enlarged to around $2 million, with thousands of dollars gifted from it. (Courtesy of Marilyn Vonderheide and Laura Mae Stewart Foundation.)

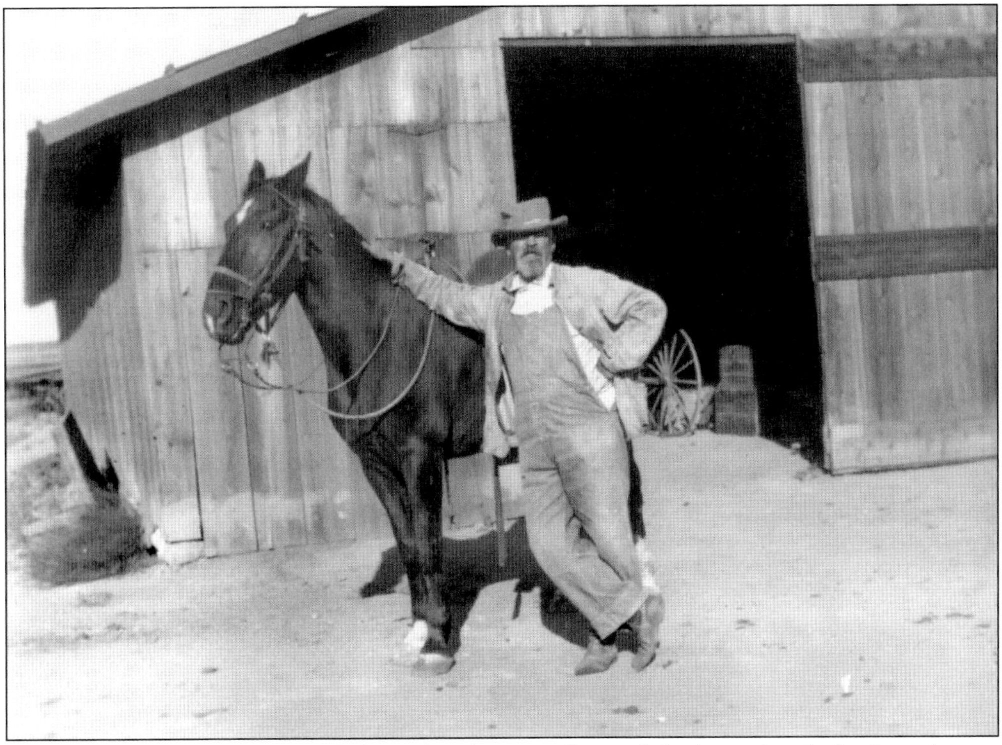

Renzor Perry Stewart poses with his riding horse in front of the barn that he built in August 1883, shortly after he homesteaded land south of Banning below today's I-10. He worked hard at farming his large acreage, becoming one of the most successful farmers in the San Gorgonio Pass. (Courtesy of Marilyn Vonderheide and Laura Mae Stewart Foundation.)

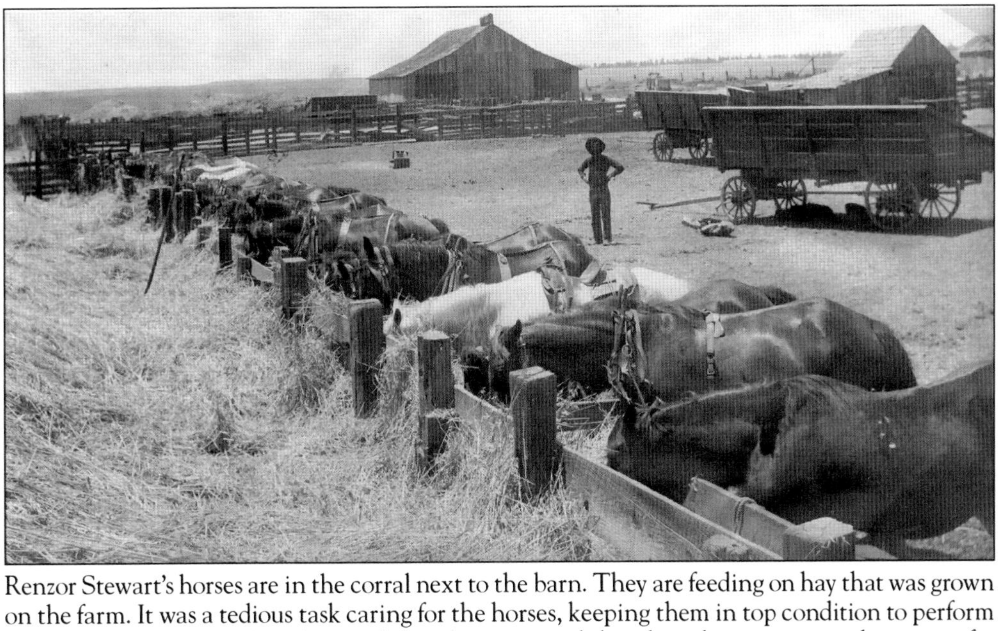

Renzor Stewart's horses are in the corral next to the barn. They are feeding on hay that was grown on the farm. It was a tedious task caring for the horses, keeping them in top condition to perform the numerous ranch tasks. The ranch hand, center, with hands on hips, is anxiously waiting for the feeding to finish. (Courtesy of Marilyn Vonderheide and Laura Mae Stewart Foundation.)

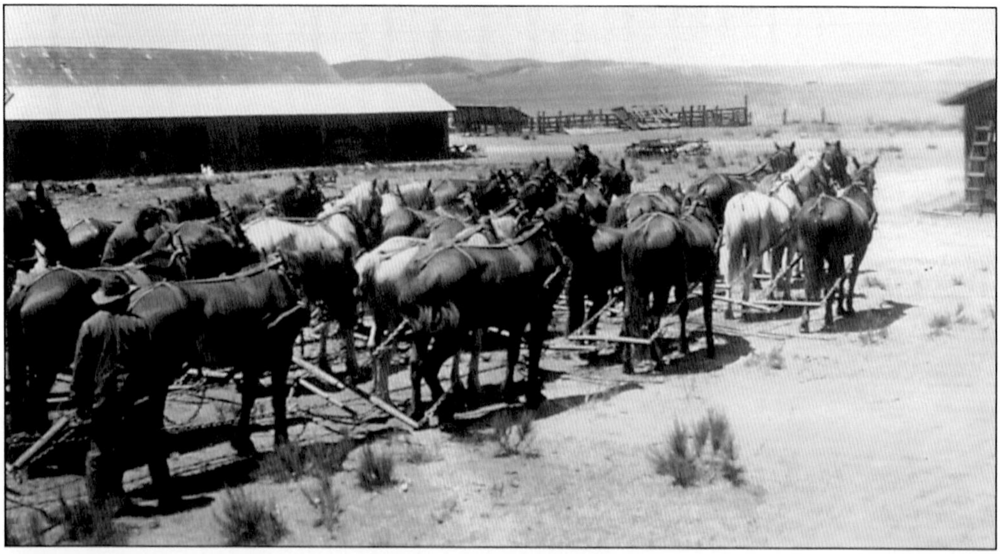

A team of horses is harnessed and ready for work in the field. Because dry farming on the Stewart ranch required getting the seeds planted before significant rains came, there was always a hurry to get the ground prepared and the grain planted. Teams like this were a pertinent requirement to meet this challenge. (Courtesy of Marilyn Vonderheide and Laura Mae Stewart Foundation.)

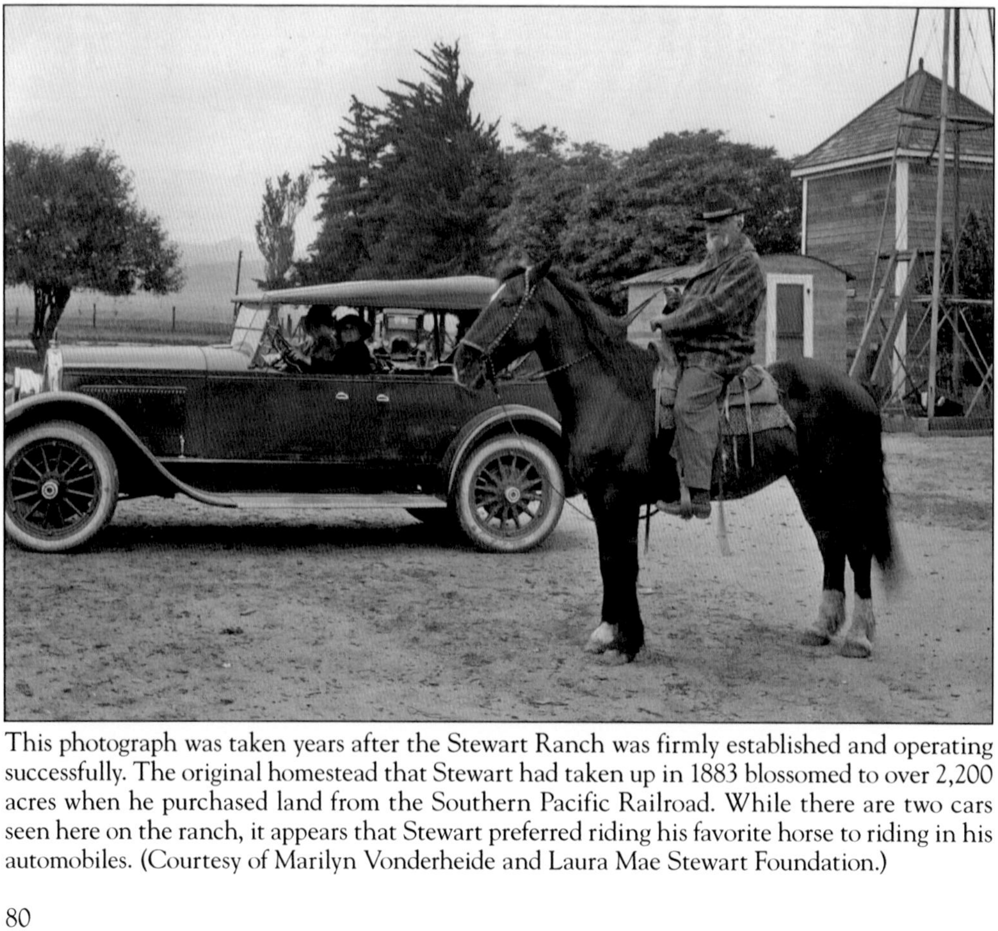

This photograph was taken years after the Stewart Ranch was firmly established and operating successfully. The original homestead that Stewart had taken up in 1883 blossomed to over 2,200 acres when he purchased land from the Southern Pacific Railroad. While there are two cars seen here on the ranch, it appears that Stewart preferred riding his favorite horse to riding in his automobiles. (Courtesy of Marilyn Vonderheide and Laura Mae Stewart Foundation.)

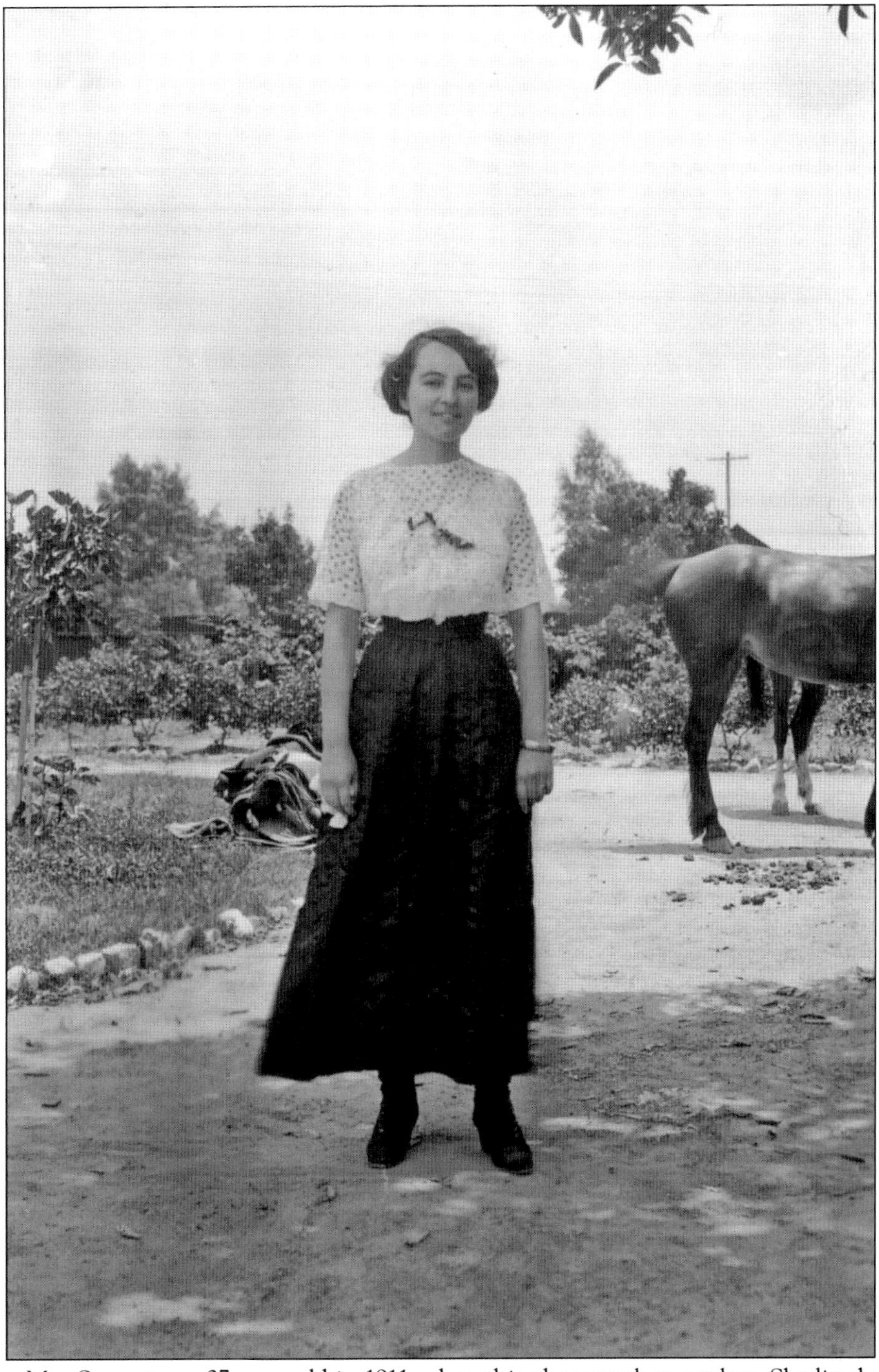

Laura Mae Stewart was 27 years old in 1911, when this photograph was taken. She lived to be 90 and was active much of that time, helping to run the large ranch with her sister for their father. Upon Laura's death in 1974, her assets were used to establish the Laura Mae Stewart Foundation, as previously designated by her. (Courtesy of Marilyn Vonderheide and Laura Mae Stewart Foundation.)

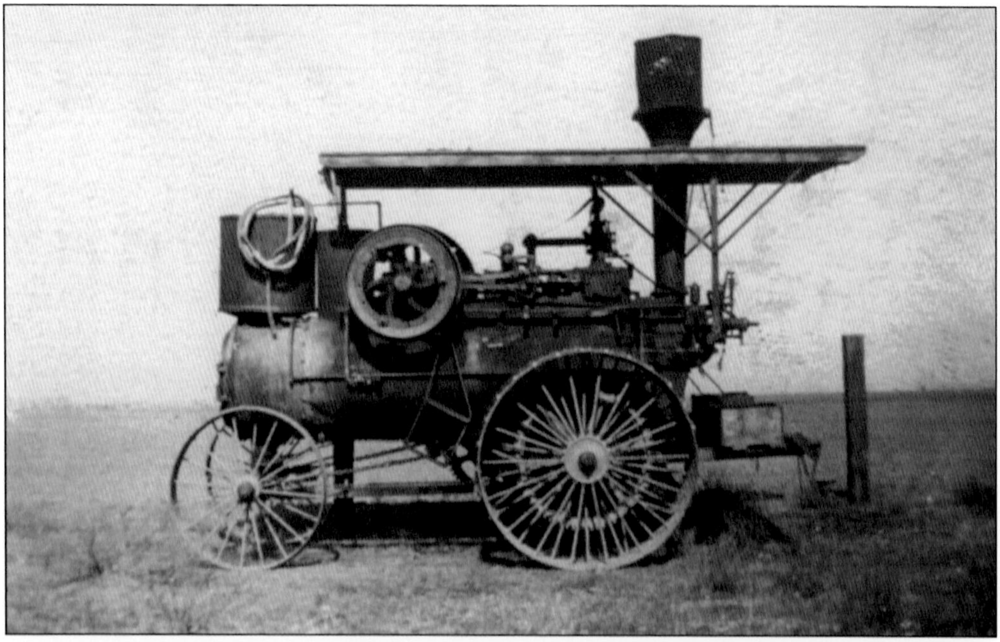

This is a photograph of the first threshing machine ever used in the San Gorgonio Pass area. It was originally purchased by Renzor Stewart and two of his neighbors, who jointly used it in their farming operations. After its purchase, Renzor's grain yield increased drastically, producing up to 10,000 sacks a year. (Courtesy of Marilyn Vonderheide and Laura Mae Stewart Foundation.)

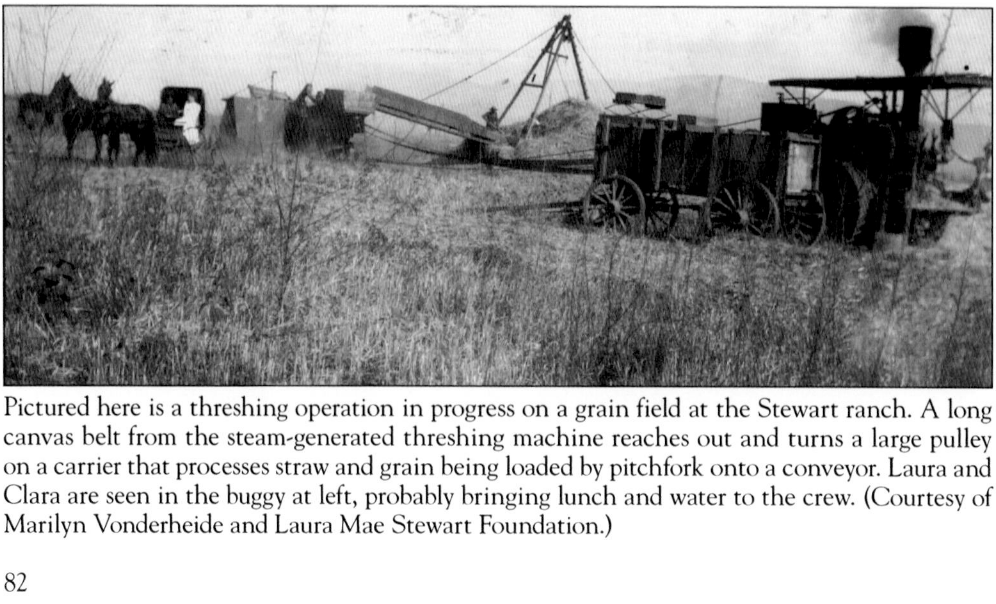

Pictured here is a threshing operation in progress on a grain field at the Stewart ranch. A long canvas belt from the steam-generated threshing machine reaches out and turns a large pulley on a carrier that processes straw and grain being loaded by pitchfork onto a conveyor. Laura and Clara are seen in the buggy at left, probably bringing lunch and water to the crew. (Courtesy of Marilyn Vonderheide and Laura Mae Stewart Foundation.)

Six

Banning and Its Bench

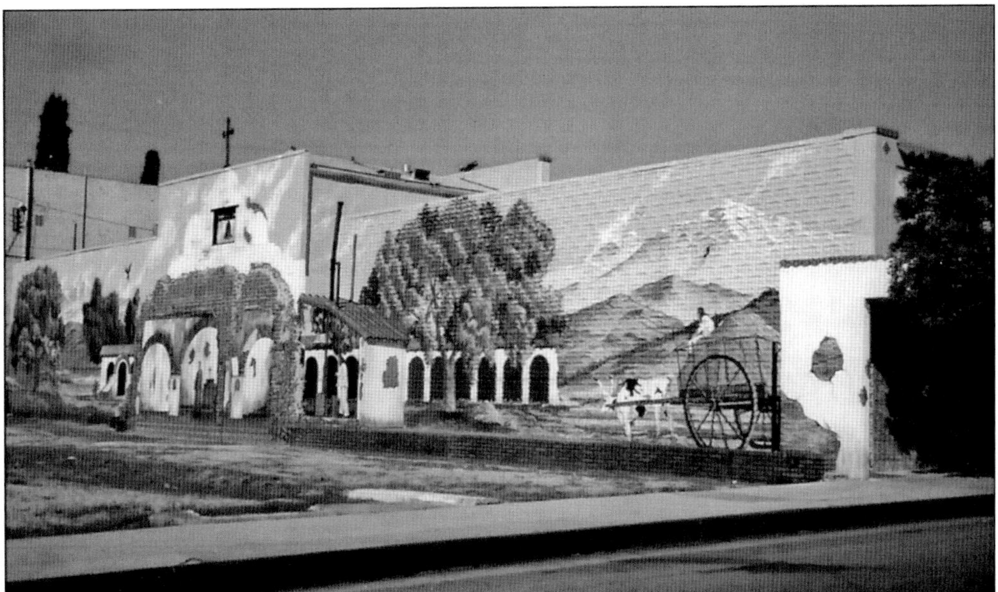

This remarkable rendition of a mission scene was painted by muralist William "Ironhand" Swick and perhaps has become the impetus that promoted exponential mural expansion. One planned mural is a collage of famous Hollywood entertainment caricatures painted on the east wall of the Fox Cineplex Theater. Could Banning soon be dubbed "Mural City," with tour buses stopping to see its murals? (Courtesy of the author.)

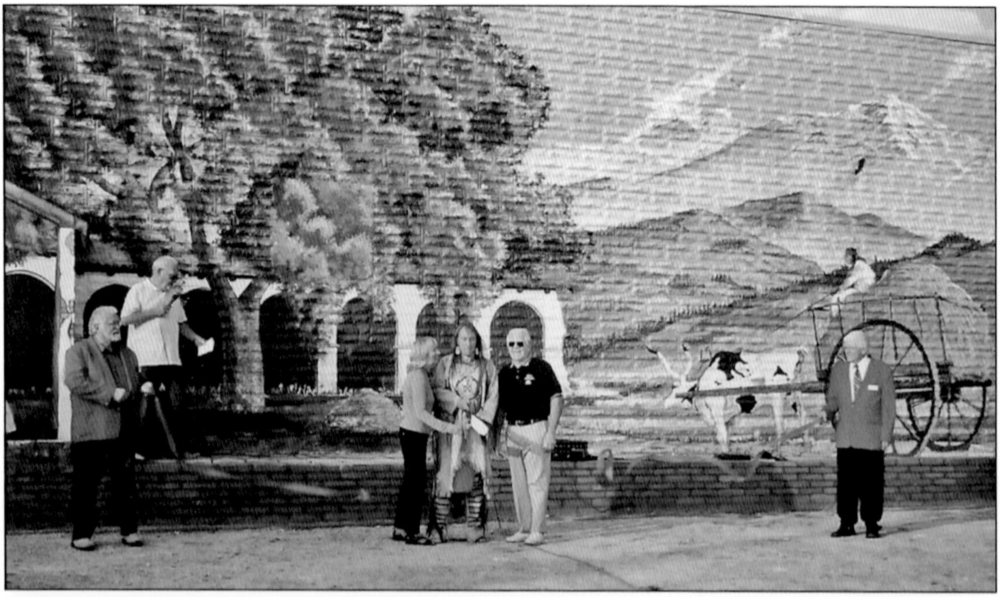

This photograph was taken during the ribbon-cutting ceremony of Banning's fifth mural. It was sponsored by the Banning Chamber of Commerce and brought forth by the Beautification and Mural Committee, chaired by Claudia Keeling. Participants, from left to right, are BCC ambassador Bill Dickerson; Jack Holden, Banning Chamber of Commerce executive director; Claudia Keeling; William "Ironhand" Swick, mural artist; Banning mayor John Machisic, and BCC ambassador Buddy Cunningham. (Courtesy of the author.)

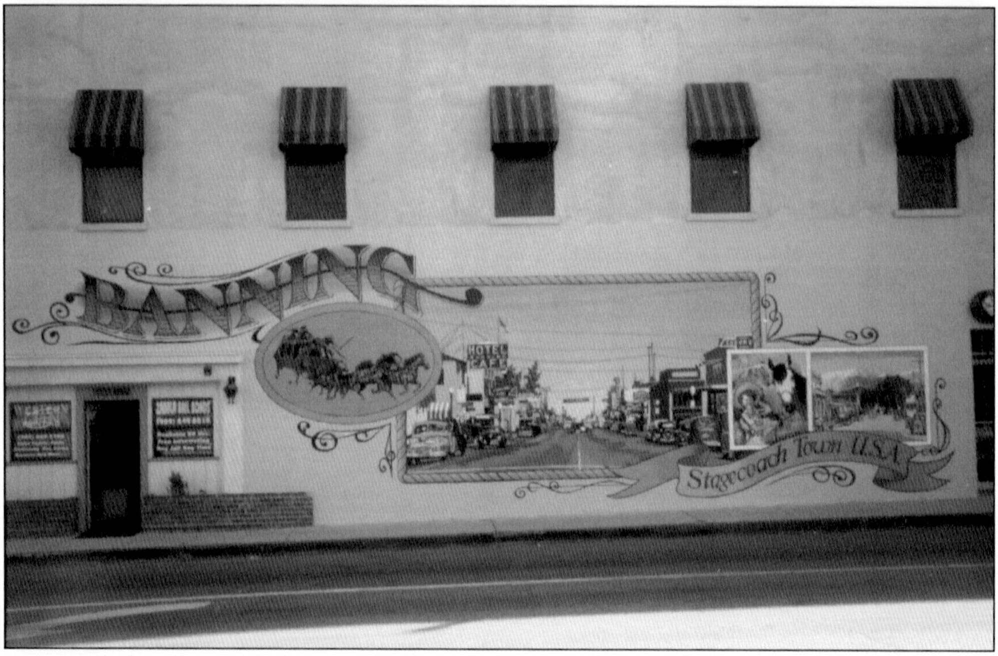

Banning's fourth mural, *Stagecoach Town U.S.A.*, was painted during the "mural in a day project," done by 20 local artists and supervised by artist Art Mortimer. Located at West Ramsey Street and San Gorgonio Avenue, it adds much excitement to the intersection. (Courtesy of the author.)

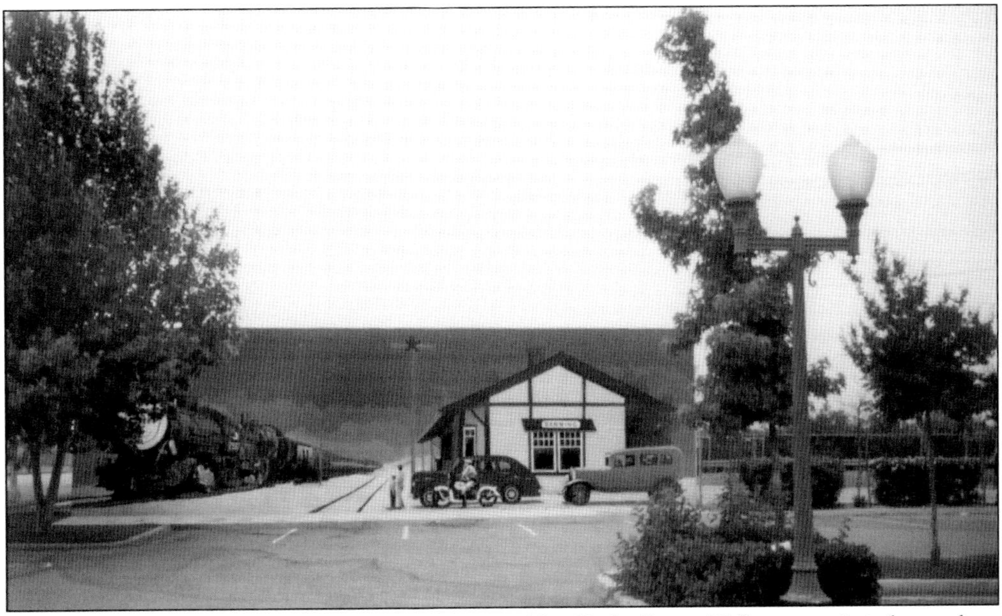

Banning's third mural, pictured here, was painted by Kathy Boyer Talkington. It is located on the north side of the building housing the Lithopass Printing Company, on the west side of San Gorgonio Avenue. It was painted from an actual photograph that was taken in Banning near the train station that no longer exists. Both the photograph and mural are well known today. (Courtesy of the author.)

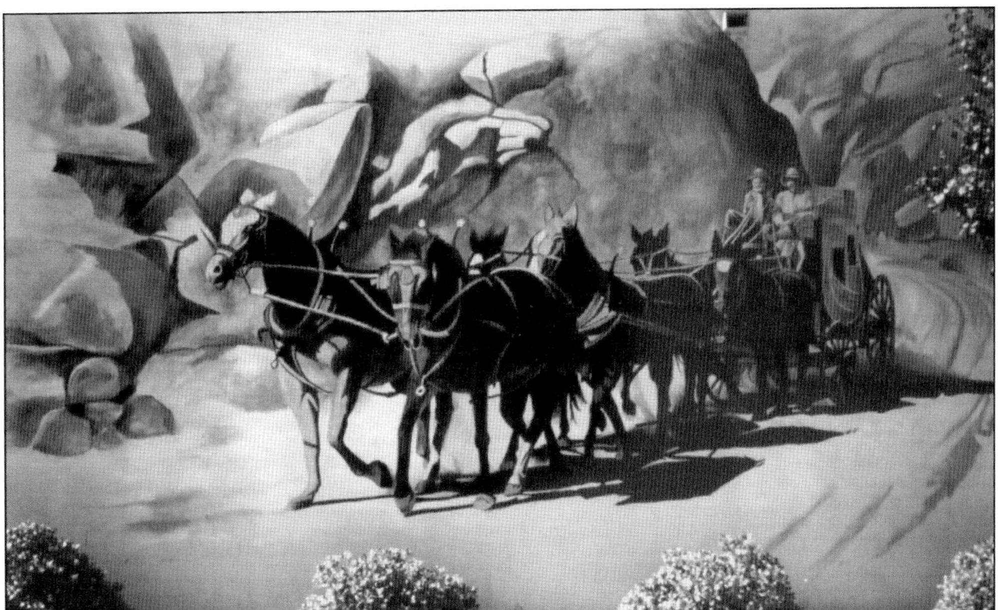

This is Banning's first mural, *Stagecoach*, painted by Butch Murphy on the east wall of the Stagecoach Tavern, across from the Fox Cineplex Theater. The Stagecoach Tavern was recently renamed by its new owner, Paddy O'Reilly, and the sign now reflects the new restaurant name—Paddy O'Reilly's. It is a popular eatery and tavern in the heart of Banning. (Courtesy of the author.)

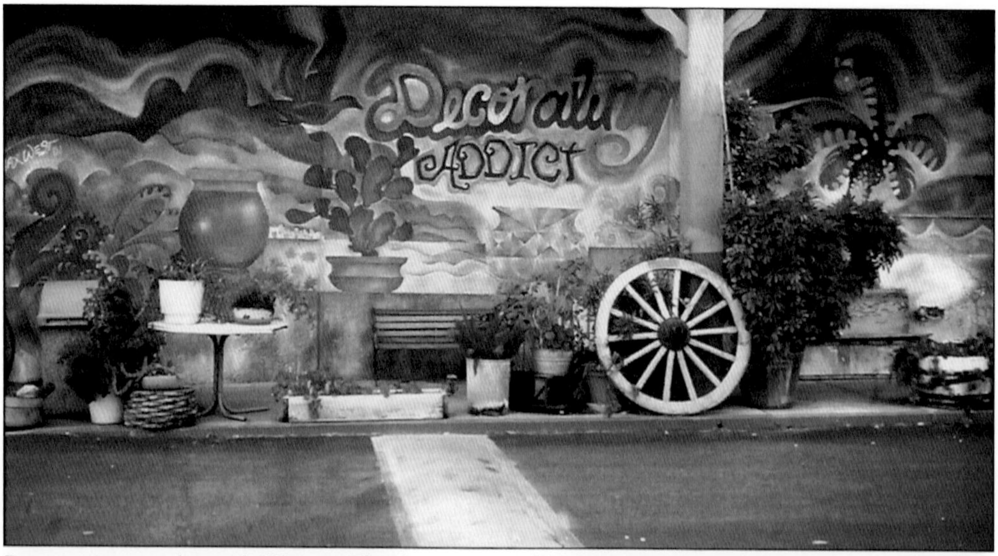

Banning's second mural, *Western Floral*, was created by Max West. It is located on the front wall of the Antique Attic, a popular antique store on Ramsey Street. Murals had only just come into play in Banning at this time, but this one sparked further interest. The wagon wheels and pottery appear to be part of the mural, but are actually antique items. (Courtesy of the author.)

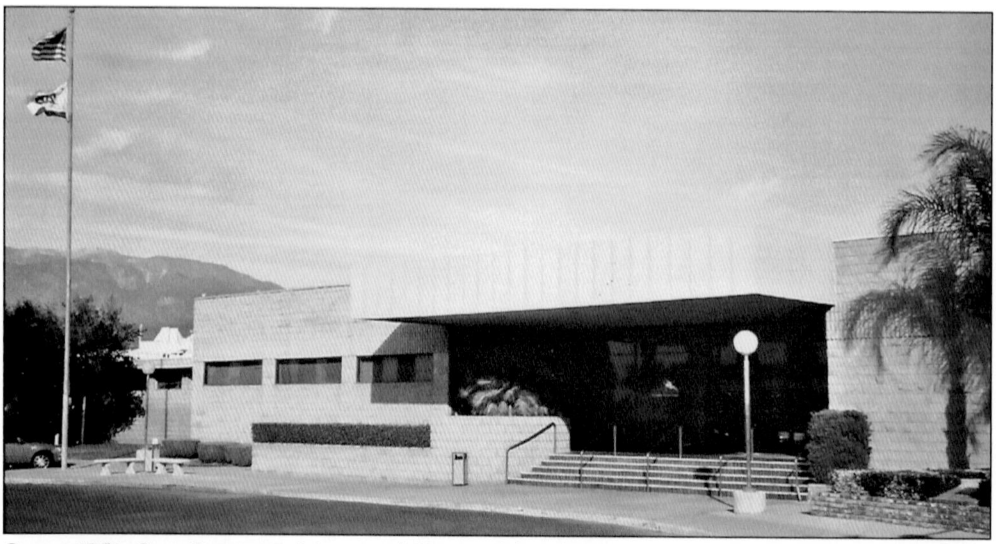

Since 1951, San Gorgonio Memorial Hospital has been meeting the health care needs of San Gorgonio area residents every day, 24 hours around the clock. By 2005, the hospital had delivered thousands of babies. Their outstanding emergency department has provided critical care for a wide range of patients, including victims rushed to them from the nearby I-10. (Courtesy of Gary Curto.)

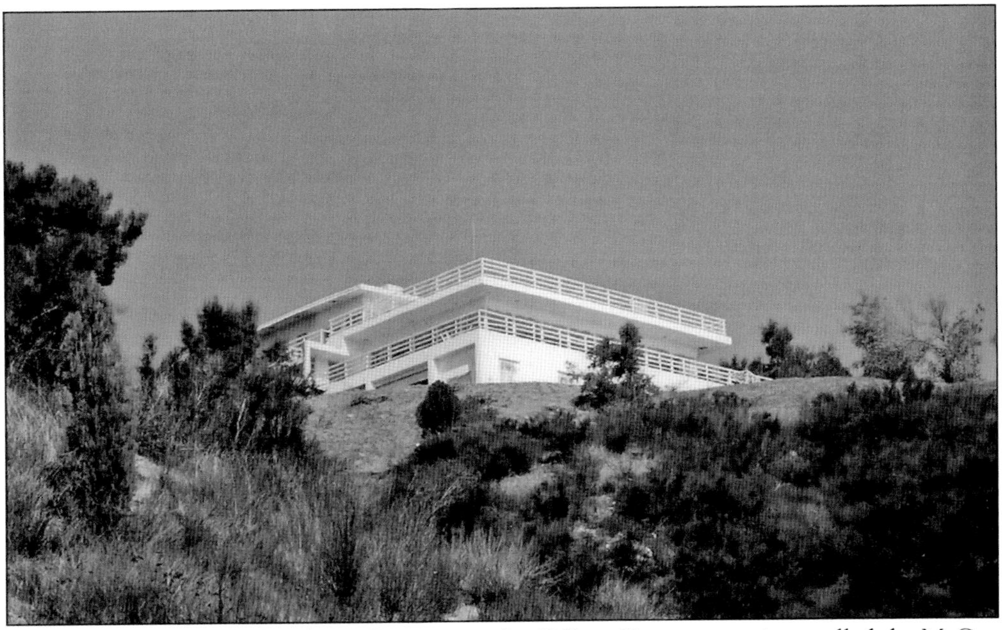

Pictured here, atop a high ridge in Banning, is the Hilltop House, sometimes called the McCoy House, because of its builder, Horace McCoy. His son dubbed it Father's Folly. Horace McCoy, always dreamed of living in a house on a hill as a boy and returned to fulfill that dream after a successful practice as an orthopedic surgeon in Long Beach. Bob Hope once looked at this house when it was up for sale. (Courtesy of the author.)

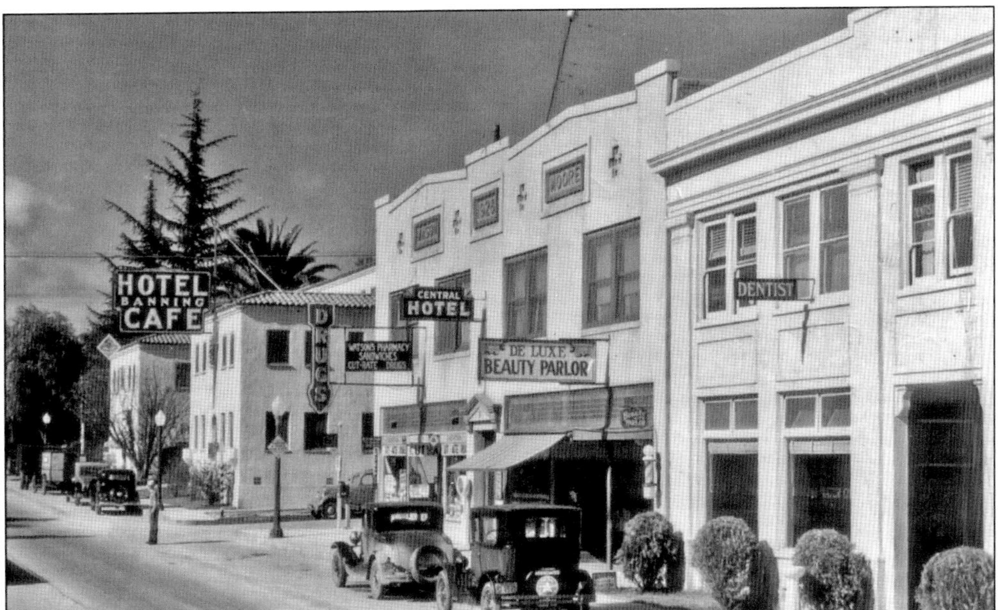

This close-up of Ramsey Street shows the Hotel Banning and the Central Hotel, separated by Second Street. Both hotels were popular and served the community well. The Banning Hotel outlasted the 1928 Wilson and Moore Building, leaving behind a vacant lot today. Note the drug and beauty parlor business below the Central Hotel. (Courtesy of Steve Lech.)

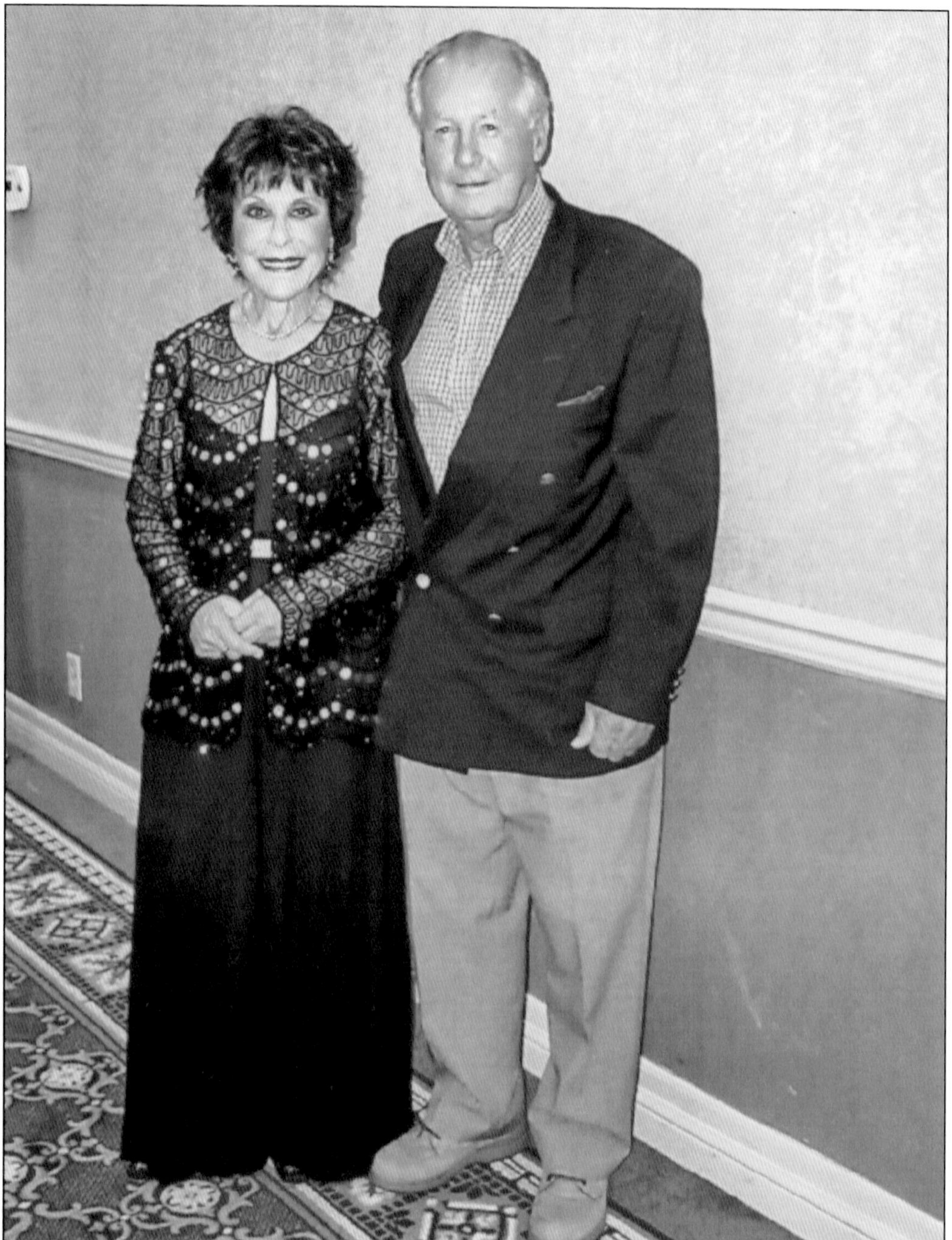

Pictured here on June 12, 2005, are Pearl Kaufman and the author, after her piano classics concert at the Friendship Club at Sun Lakes Country Club in Banning. Her performances are featured in over 200 films, such as *Doctor Zhivago* and *The Great Escape*. She has recorded music for film composers Henry Mancini, Elmer Bernstein, and others, and appeared as a soloist with the Los Angeles Philharmonic and numerous orchestras. (Courtesy of Roz Feldman.)

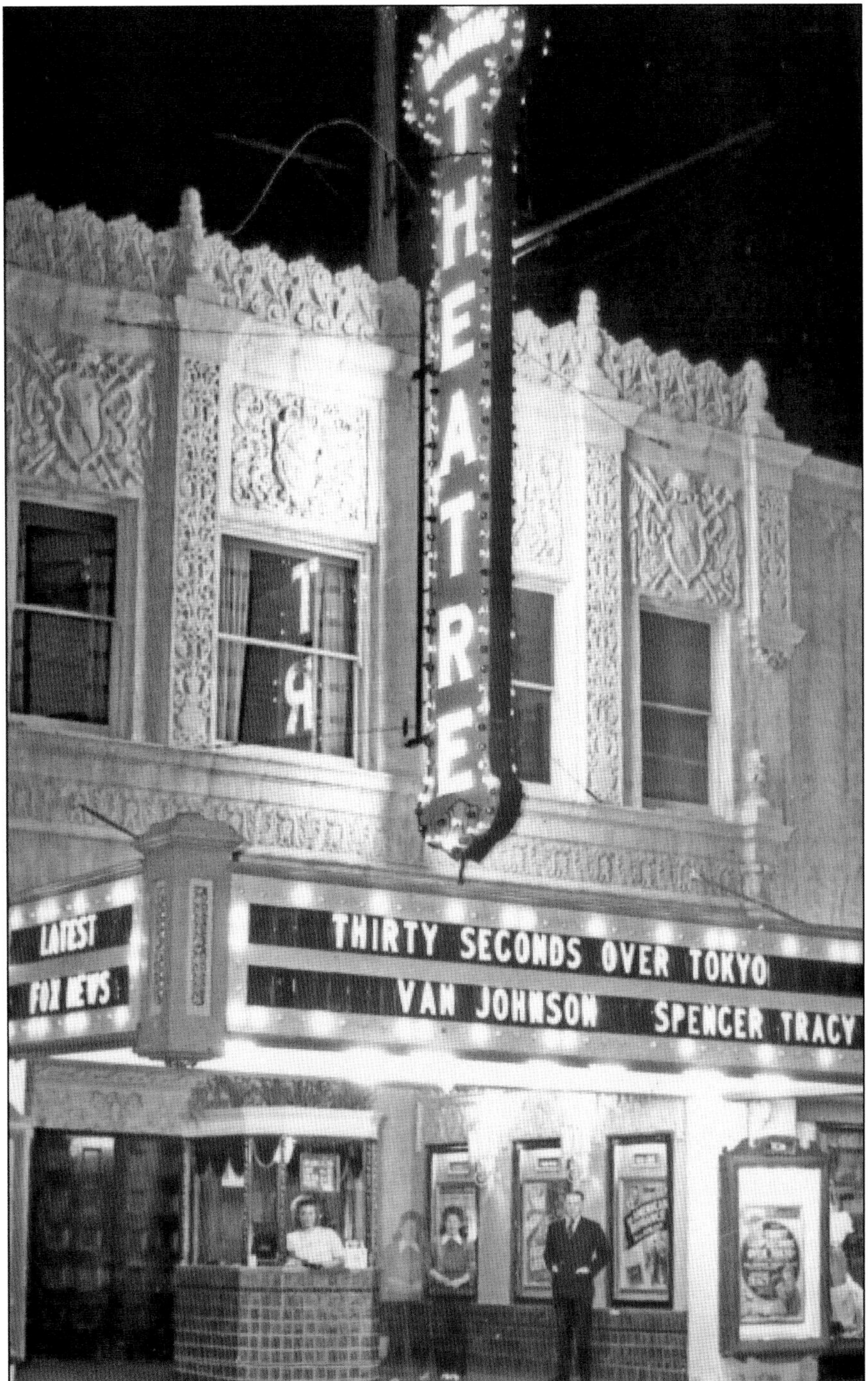

This 1944 photograph shows the Banning Theatre at night. It has Mervyn LeRoy's movie of that year, *Thirty Seconds over Tokyo*, posted on its marquee. The classic black-and-white movie was an amazingly detailed true story of the Doolittle raid, based on the novel of the same name. Interesting to note is the marquee's advertising of the "latest Fox news," at left. (Courtesy of Nara Haskell.)

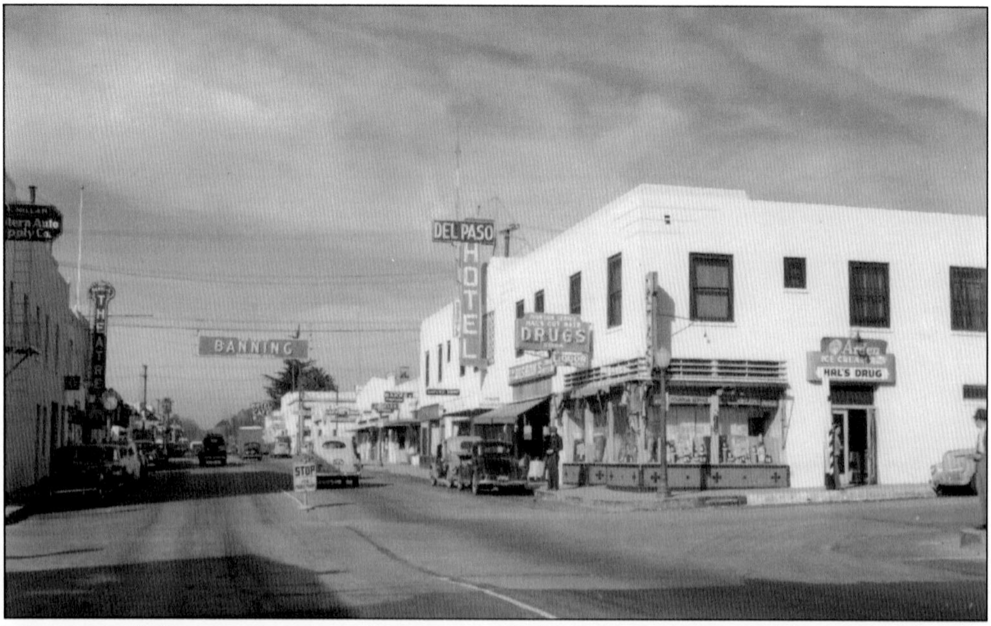

This early 1940s street scene in Banning, probably taken around midday, shows the Del Paso Hotel on the right, with Hal's Drug Store at the east end. This was a spot dear to the hearts of many of Banning's young crowd who lined the stools inside for cokes. To the extreme left is the large Franklin Building, with the Banning Theatre farther to its west. (Courtesy of Steve Lech.)

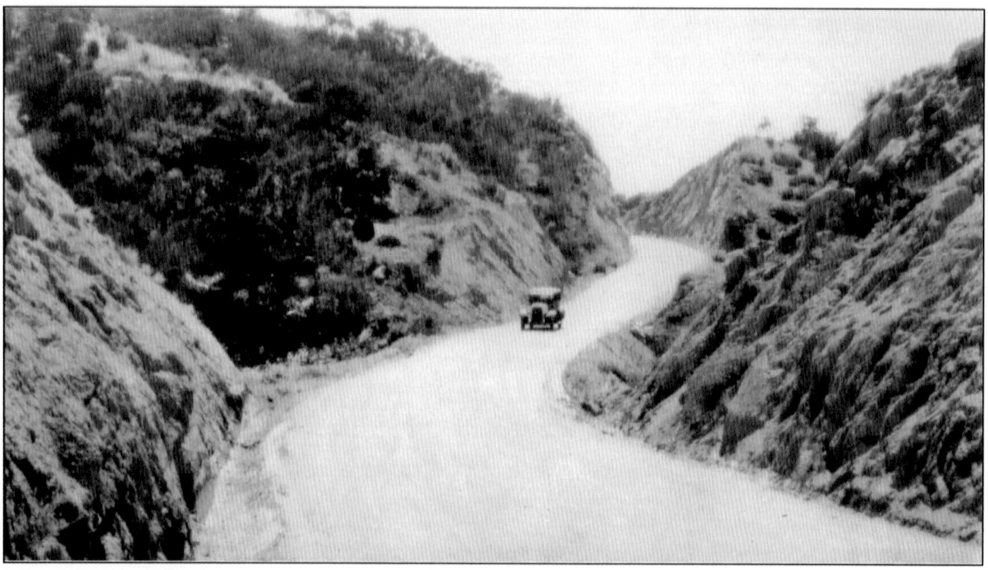

This photograph shows two curves on the early road that was constructed from Banning to Idyllwild. Its construction was a tedious task because of the antiquated equipment available at that time. The unpaved road was treacherous to drive during the winter months due to either rain or snow. Today the highway is paved, but the curves remain. (Courtesy of Steve Lech.)

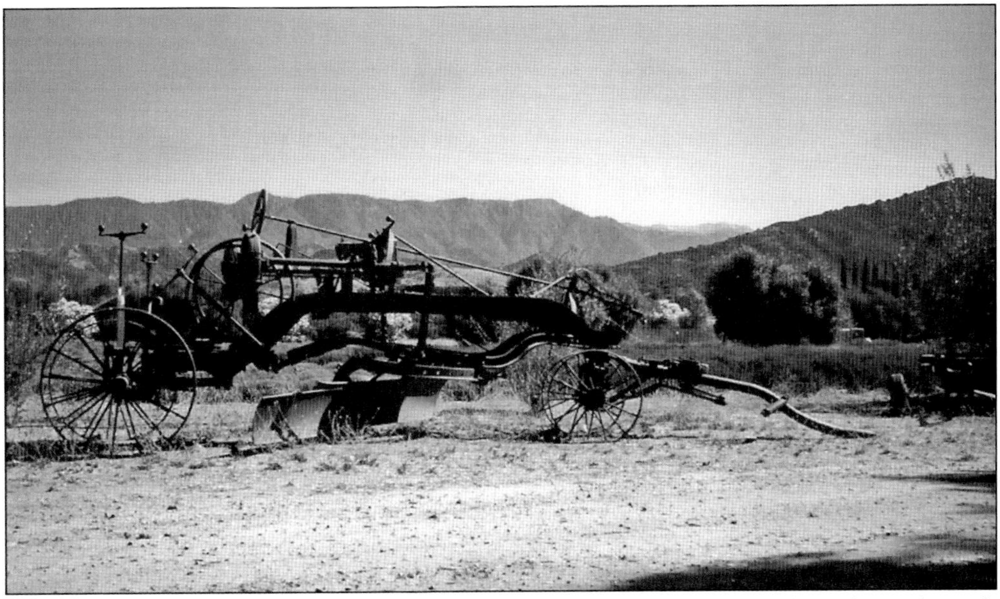

This horse-drawn grader was perhaps used to grade parts of the Idyllwild road or other early roads around the pass. Road construction was a tedious task, with graders like this one. In 1908, there began a struggle for completion of the Banning-Idyllwild road, which had stalled earlier due to a stalemate, one caused by difficult road construction. (Courtesy of the author.)

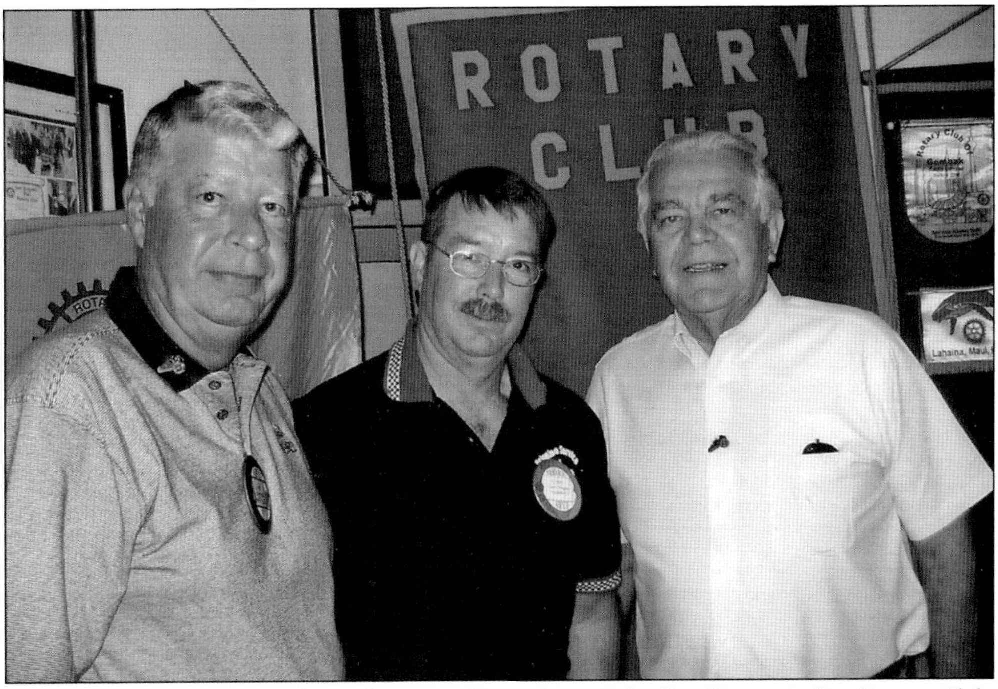

The three Banning mayors shown here are all members of the San Gorgonio Pass Rotary Club. Pictured, from left to right, are Art Welch, mayor in 2003–2004, who served the Banning community well and is still an active member on the Banning City Council; Larry Higgins, who was mayor in the 1980s; and John Machisic, who became Banning's mayor in 2005 after Art Welch. (Photograph by and courtesy of Charles G. Ferrell.)

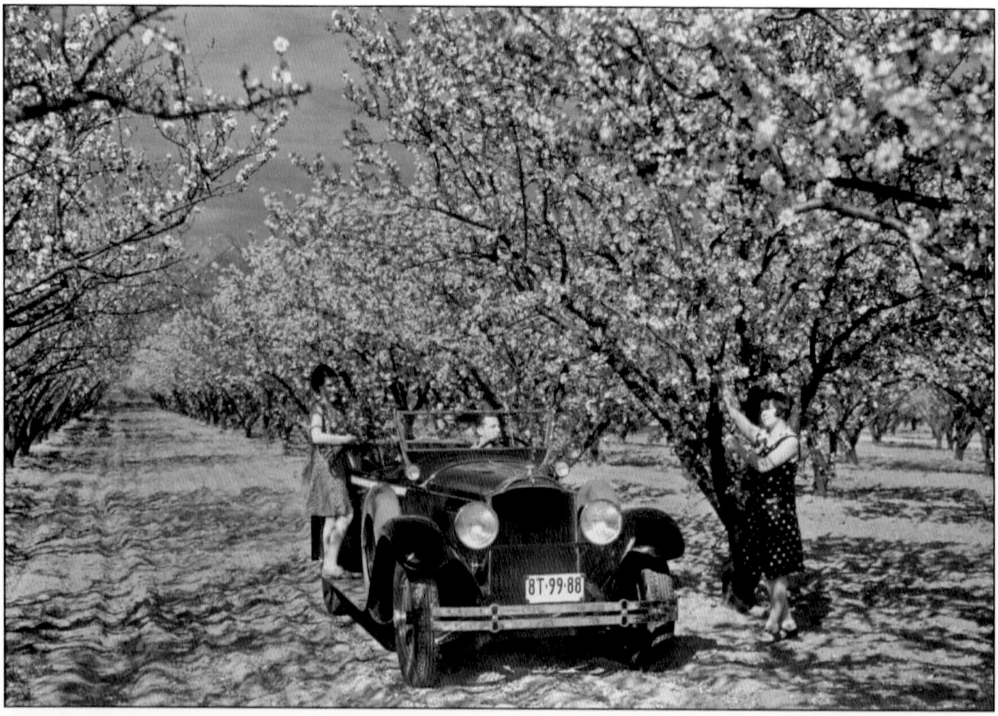

This large almond orchard was a beautiful view to behold when in full bloom. Almonds were a major crop in Banning and the farmers and owners of orchards had a reason to be proud. This picture is accentuated by those posing for the photograph with the great status symbol of that era—the car. (Courtesy of the author.)

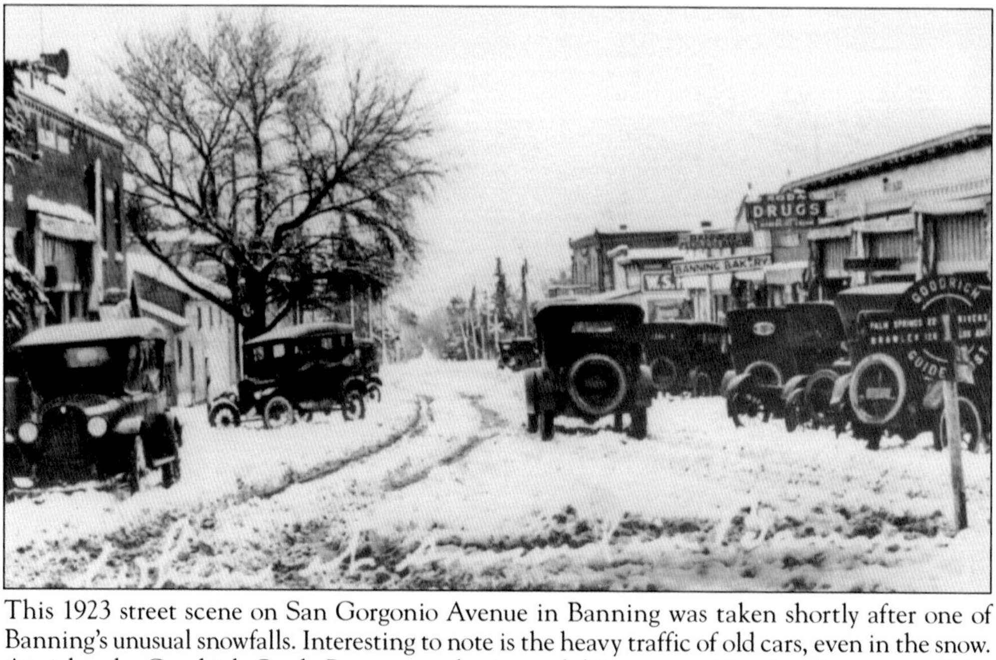

This 1923 street scene on San Gorgonio Avenue in Banning was taken shortly after one of Banning's unusual snowfalls. Interesting to note is the heavy traffic of old cars, even in the snow. At right, the Goodrich Guide Post, a popular icon of this era, provides the distances to Palm Springs, Brawley, Riverside, and Los Angeles. (Courtesy of Nara Haskell.)

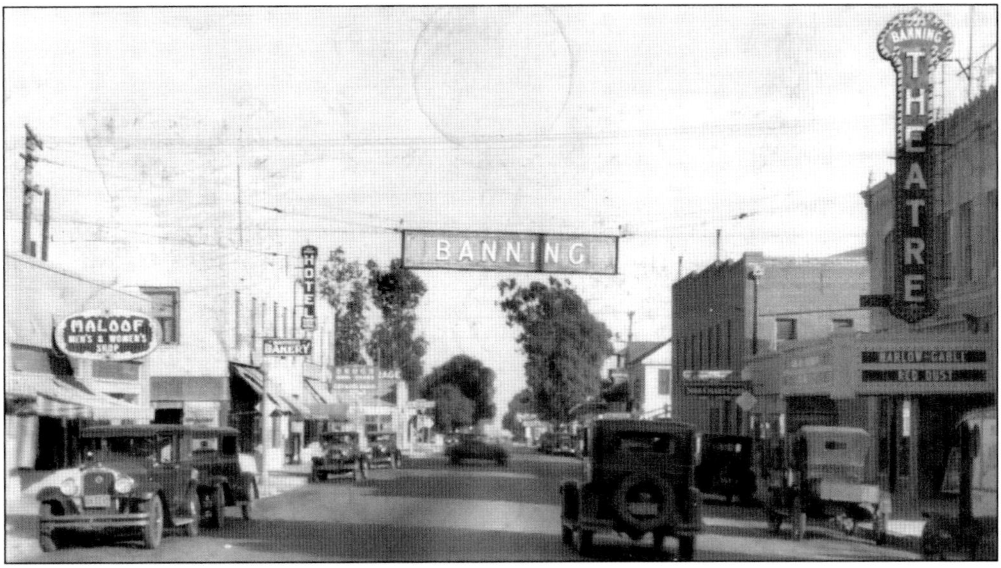

This early 1930s street scene in the heart of Banning shows a car in the center of Ramsey Street, traveling at a right angle to the other cars, south on San Gorgonio Avenue. The marquee of the Banning Theatre lists the 1932 movie *Red Dust*, the earliest of the Gable/Harlow movies. (Courtesy of Steve Lech.)

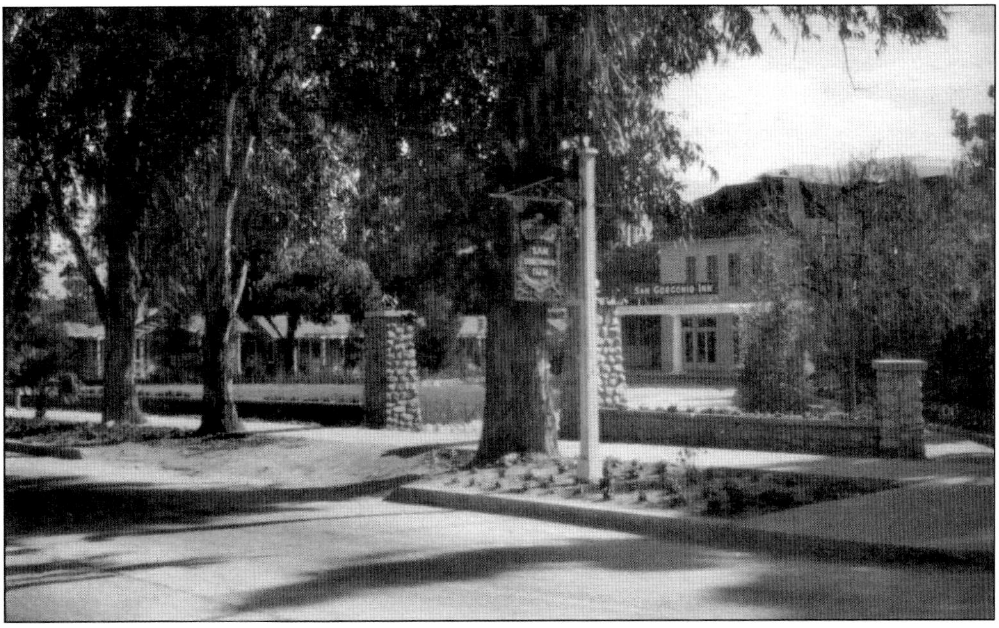

This is an early photograph of the San Gorgonio Inn. When first built in 1884, it was called the Bryant House. In 1888, Captain and Mrs. Fraser bought it and renamed it The Banning. In 1920, John Livacich and J. Kurtal purchased it and renamed it the San Gorgonio Inn. It was heavily damaged by fire on April 15, 1930, but soon rebuilt. The small stand sign, seen out front, has today been replaced by a large neon one. (Courtesy of Steve Lech.)

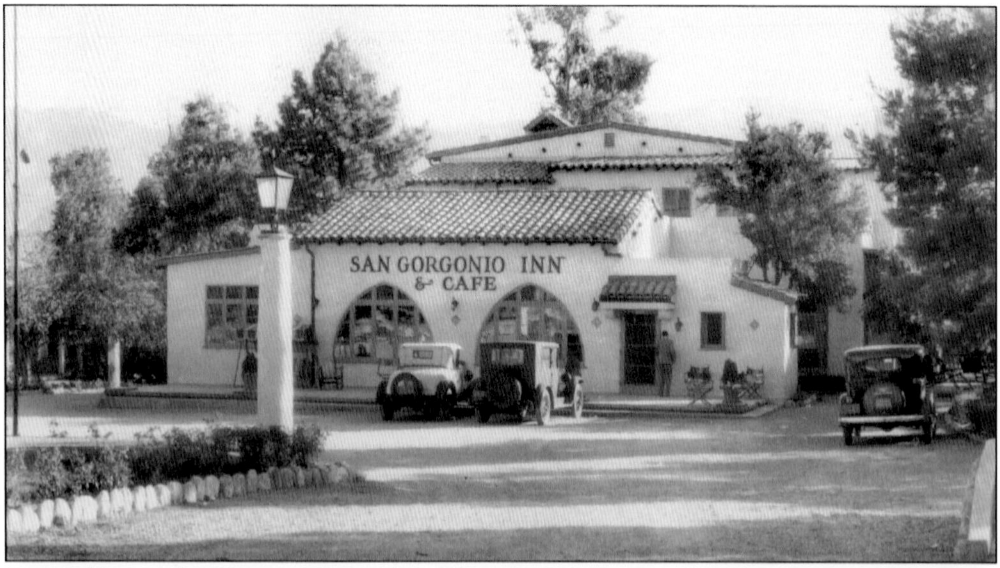

Pictured here is the Gorgonio Inn in the early 1930s, after it was rebuilt. Seems like a few people have stopped for lunch, as evidenced by the old cars. The structure is depicted before the additions that are seen today. To the left is one of the bungalows that once surrounded the restaurant. Presidents Cleveland and Grant both dined here. (Courtesy of Steve Lech.)

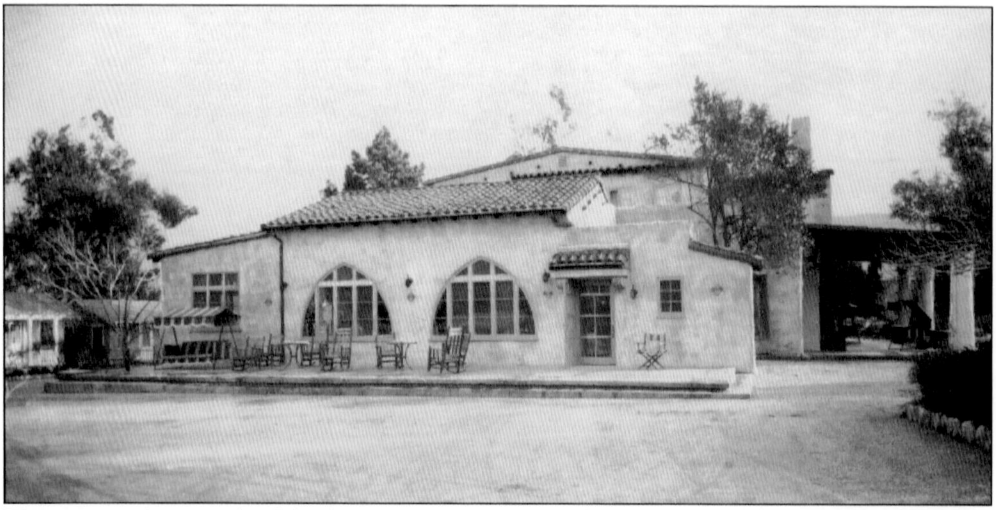

This prewar photograph of the San Gorgonio Inn was taken near the outbreak of World War II. Sometime after the war, it was remodeled and a large addition was constructed to the right side of the building, which includes a meeting hall. At left, note the bungalows that still remained at this time. It is owned and operated by Chris Dallas, with the help of his son Jack. (Courtesy of Jack Dallas.)

Banning resident and artist Norman McGary had a long relationship with the movie industry, working for Walt Disney for 17 years (1957–1973) and for Hanna-Barbera Productions. In Disney's children books, he was credited on illustrations of *Sleeping Beauty*, *101 Dalmatians*, and numerous other wholesome stories. He has also painted successfully as a freelance artist. McGary, who lived in Banning as a child but moved away, now resides here. He recently used his artistic abilities to illustrate Jeremiah Film's award-winning video, *God's Story: From Creation to Eternity*, sweeping the world in over 137 languages. (Courtesy of Norman McGary.)

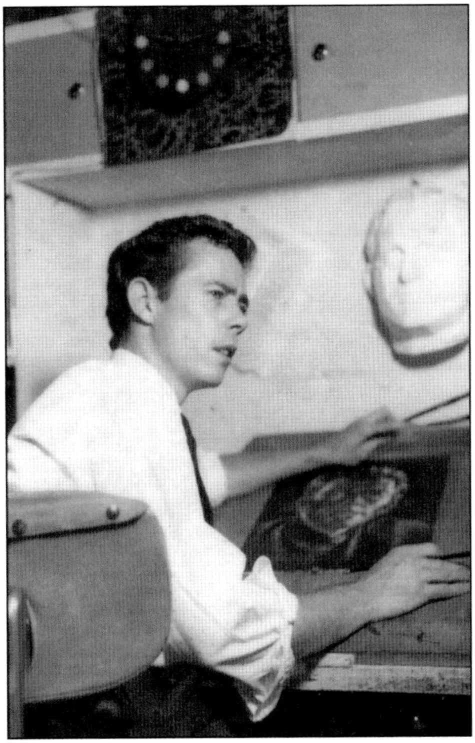

Banning resident Joni Rhoades poses here for a staff photograph of Bob Hope's 1972 Christmas Tour to U.S. troops in Vietnam. Joni is at right center, behind Bob Hope. In 1968, Joni wrote several scripts for the Bob Hope television show. She later became the show's director and directed through 1972, retiring at the early age 55. (Courtesy of Joni Rhoades.)

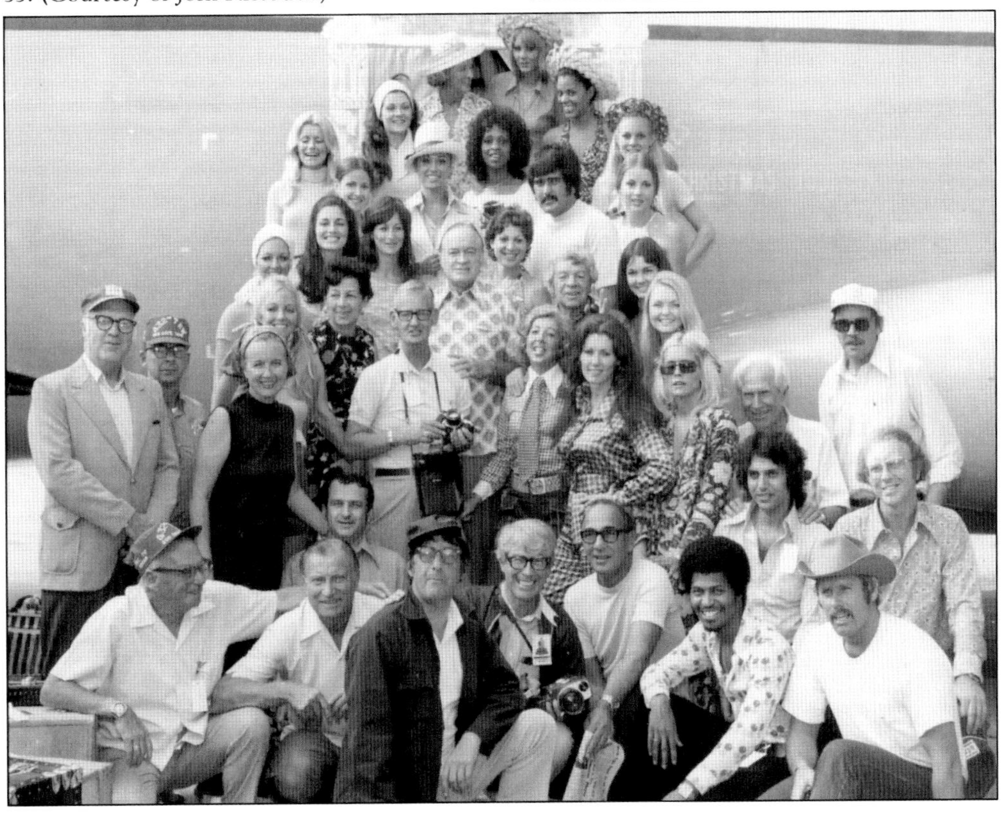

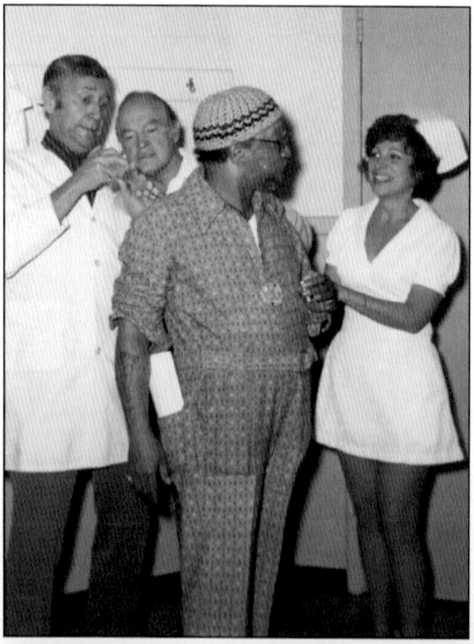

In 1973, Joni Rhoades stands next to Redd Foxx during a stint as a nurse on one of his television shows. Behind them are guest Bob Hope and a cast member. Rhoades directed many of Redd Foxx's shows during this era. In 1968, she worked as a variety-comedy writer for the Glen Campbell and Sunny and Cher shows, and later was a member of the writing staff with Steve Martin and Chevy Chase, before they became actors. Joni was born in Chicago, where her first job was in a music-recording studio. She came to California in 1965, went to work at KBIG-FM radio station on Sunset Boulevard in Hollywood, and often flew by seaplane to the station's Avalon radio tower to make new musical arrangements. (Courtesy of Joni Rhoades.)

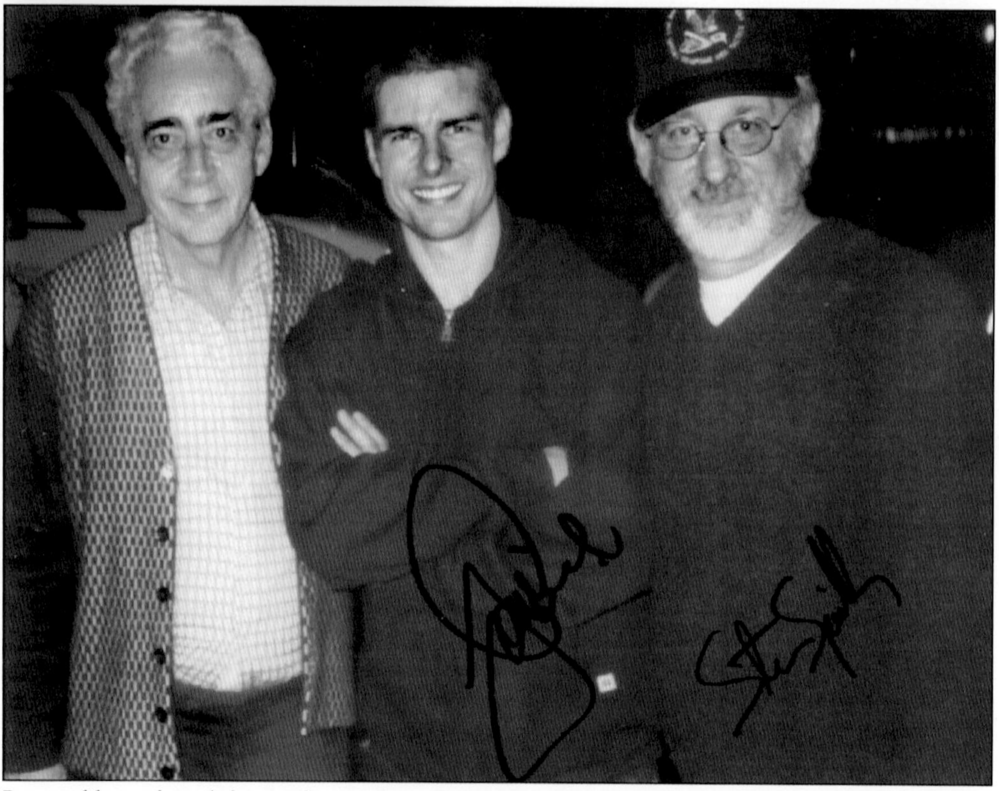

Pictured here, from left to right, are Jerry Perchesky, Tom Cruise, and Steven Spielberg. Jerry is a radio, television, and movie celebrity who came to Banning to live with his wife, Julie. Born on January 1, 1928, in New York City, he was reared in the central California coast town of Watsonville. Early in his career, he started a local radio music program featuring jazz and became the authority of old time radio, which was popular at this time. (Courtesy of Jerry Perchesky.)

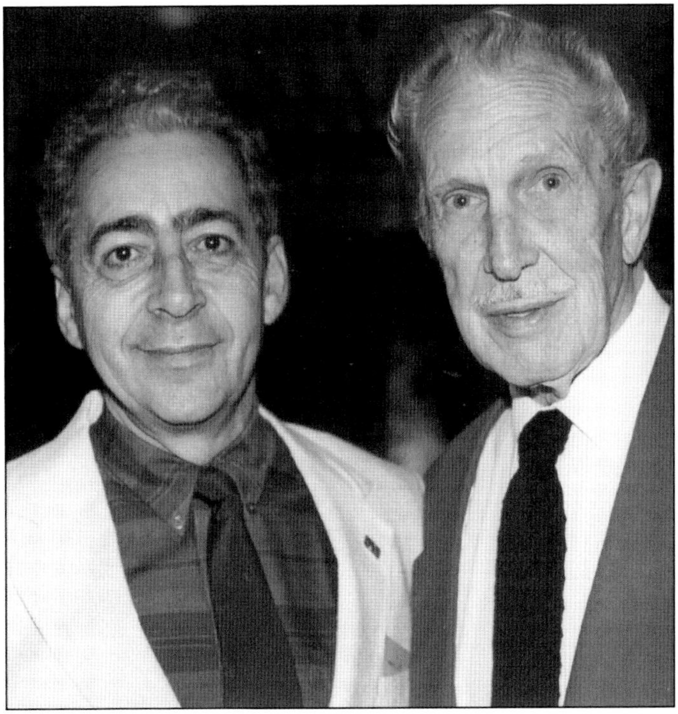

Jerry Perchesky is shown here beside Vincent Price. Jerry appeared in films such as *Bounce*, *Stigmata*, *Minority Report*, and others, and had parts in over 75 television shows. He became a member of Pacific Pioneer Broadcasters in Hollywood, ultimately acquiring a tape collection of radio shows numbered in the thousands. During his interviews with Hollywood celebrities, he became acquainted and fast friends with many of them, including such greats as Red Skelton, Bing Crosby, and George Burns. For a while, Jerry did public relations work for comedian Jerry Lewis. (Courtesy of Jerry Perchesky.)

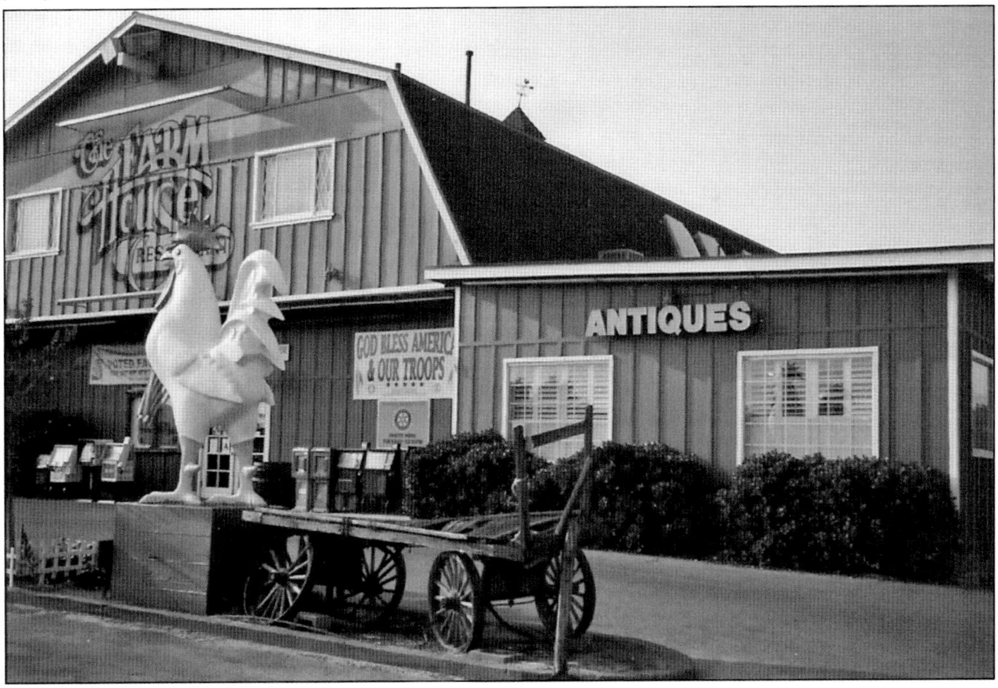

This building houses the Farm House Restaurant and a popular antique store in Banning. The restaurant is owned and operated by Jackie Palmer Kennedy, and the popular antique store is run by Bob and Susanne Adamson. Rolley the rooster stands as its mascot. It has been stolen several times as a prank but was always recovered. The Farm House is a charming place where both residents and tourists can come to eat and shop for antiques. (Courtesy of the author.)

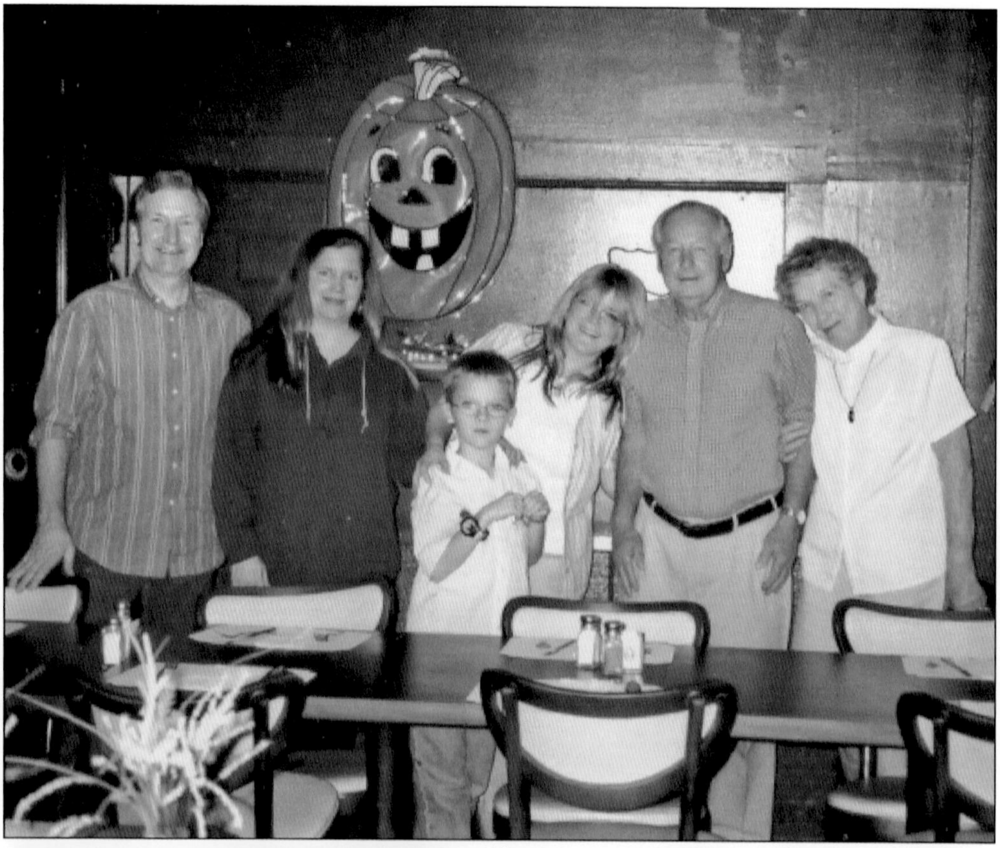

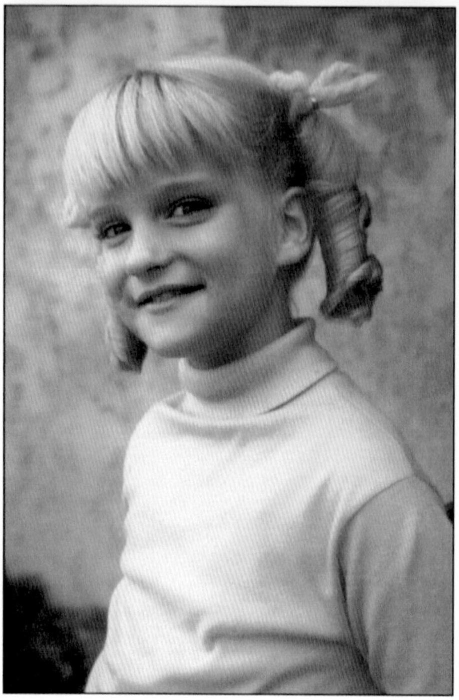

This recent group photograph was taken after a dinner at the historic San Gorgonio Inn. Pictured, from left to right, are John Uwens; Diane Olson; Michael Olson, Susan's son; Susan Olson; Ken Holtzclaw, the author, and his wife, Margaret. The Olson sisters have a vacation home in Banning and come here often. Both have spent years in show business. Susan was Cindy Brady on the popular, well-known *Brady Bunch* television show, and Diane is no stranger to television either. (Courtesy of the author.)

Pictured at left is Susan Olson as a young girl in the role of Cindy Brady in the popular television series, *The Brady Bunch*. The series was first seen in September 1969, on Friday nights on ABC. Susan still remains in constant contact with the Brady family. Since 1969, their popularity has remained, with television reruns, appearances, movies, and special events. Susan looks back on the era with fond remembrance. (Courtesy of Susan Olson.)

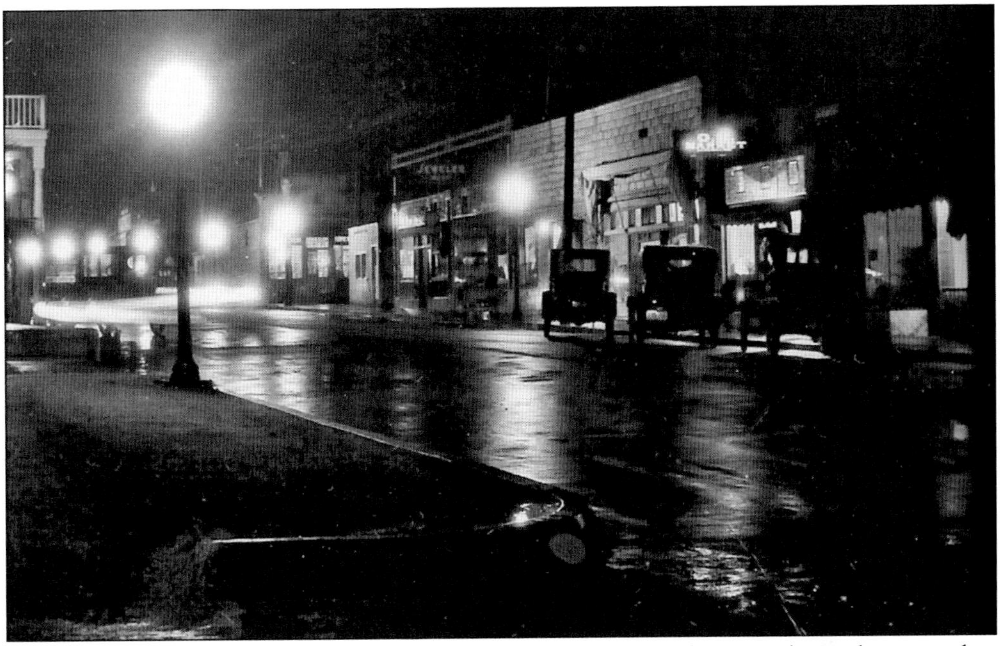

This is a night scene in the heart of Banning, taken soon after electricity began being used to light the streets. In the 1940s, during World War II, blackouts were introduced in many areas, for security reasons. Banning residents were happy, though, because the demarcation line was between the city limits of Beaumont and Banning. Banning could enjoy its nightlife, while Beaumont was blacked out. (Courtesy of Norman McGary.)

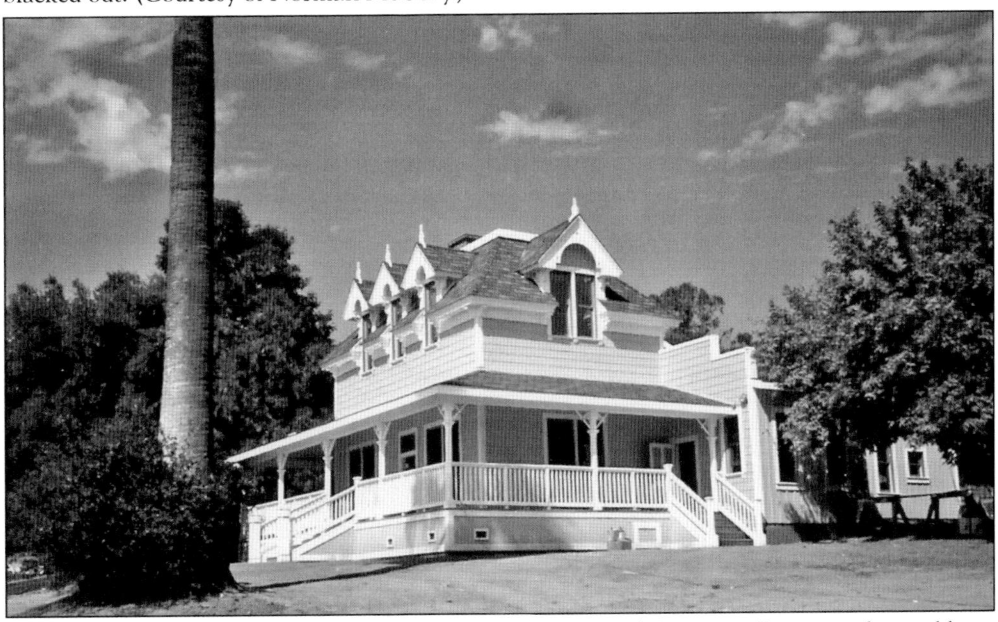

This photograph depicts the newly constructed Gilman Ranch House in Banning after a ribbon-cutting ceremony on September 29, 2005. Originally built between 1879 and 1883, it served as a focal point for the community from the early days of stagecoaches. On March 23, 1977, the original residence burned to the ground. It is a great addition to the Gilman Historic Ranch and Wagon Museum and a great landmark for the San Gorgonio Pass. (Courtesy of the author.)

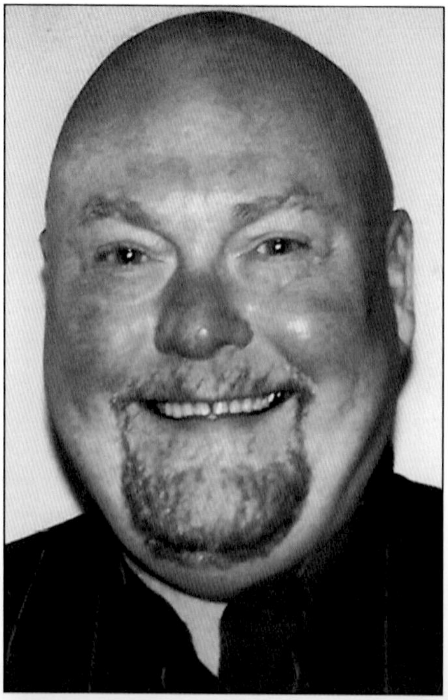

Charles G. Ferrell is editor and associate publisher of the *Record Gazette*, the newspaper that serves the San Gorgonio Pass Area communities of Beaumont, Banning, Cherry Valley, and Cabazon. Ferrell has been a journalist most of his professional life, working for various papers in Southern California. He is a third-generation Southern Californian who has lived here all his life. He was born in Calexico, near the Mexican border, where his father and grandfather were also born. His father served as a paratrooper in World War II at the battles of Normandy in France and Okinawa in the Pacific. Ferrell and his wife, Kerrie, recently celebrated their 22nd anniversary. They live in Beaumont. (Courtesy of Charles G. Ferrell.)

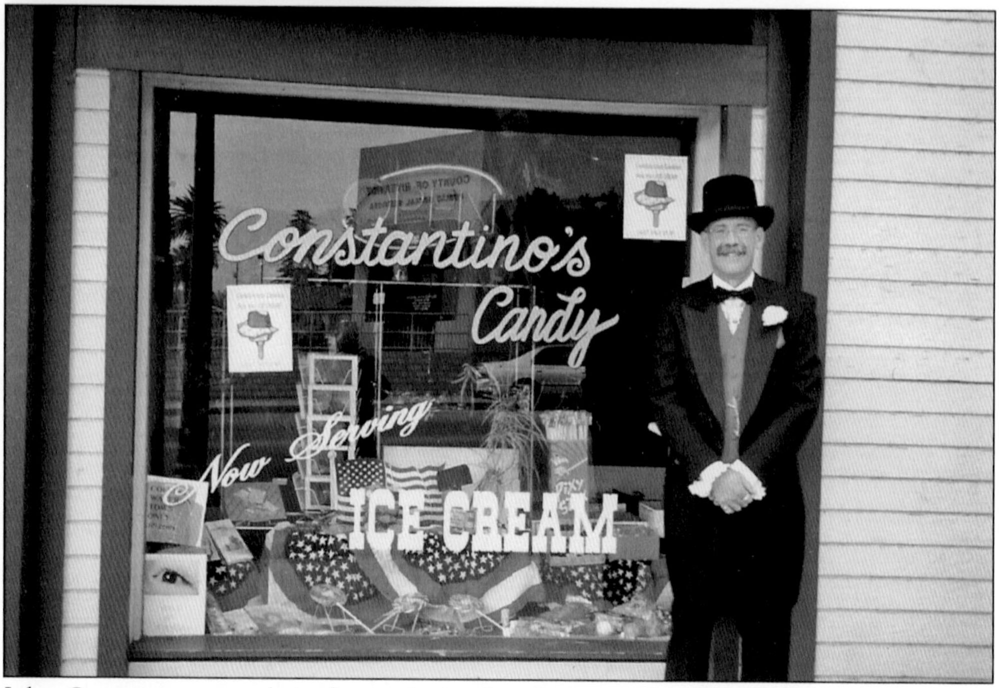

John Constantino stands in front of a landmark store—the oldest, continuously owned business in Banning. Since 1932, Constantino's candy store has been making and selling candies. John's grandfather came to Chicago from Italy in 1921, moved to Banning in 1932, and operated the store until 1945, when his son George and wife, Rachael, took the reins. George passed away recently, and John has become a third-generation candy maker. (Courtesy of John Constantino.)

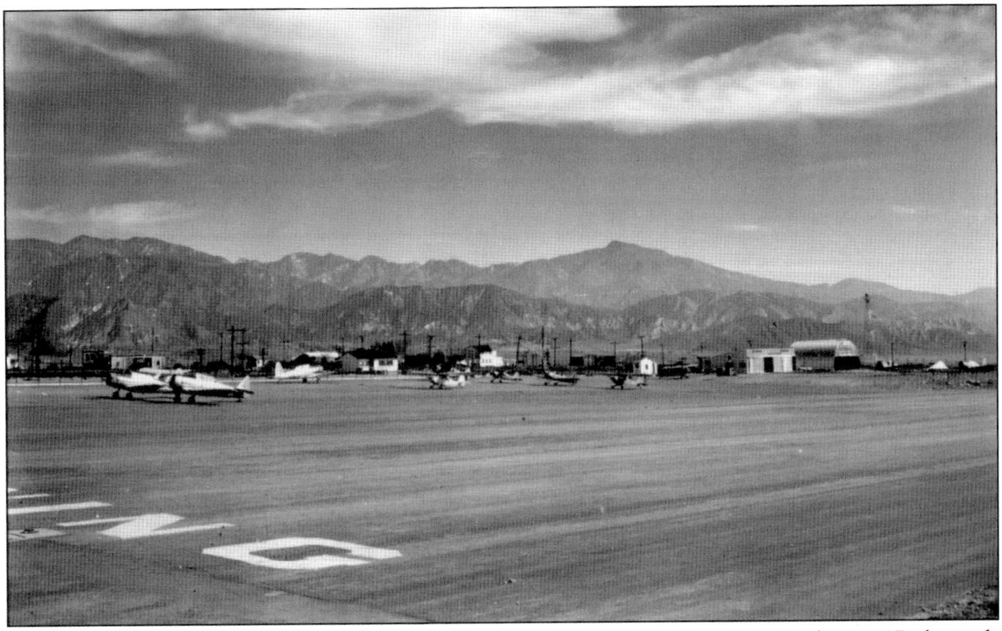

Banning's airport, shown here, had its inception at a Kiwanis Club meeting in late 1927, through the initiative of George L. Wing. A hangar was built and the airport operated for a few years. However, financial problems deemed it necessary to move the hangar to the Tri-City Airport in Colton. The old airport was rejuvenated when General Patton came to Banning in the mid-1940s, making it active during the war. (Courtesy of Steve Lech.)

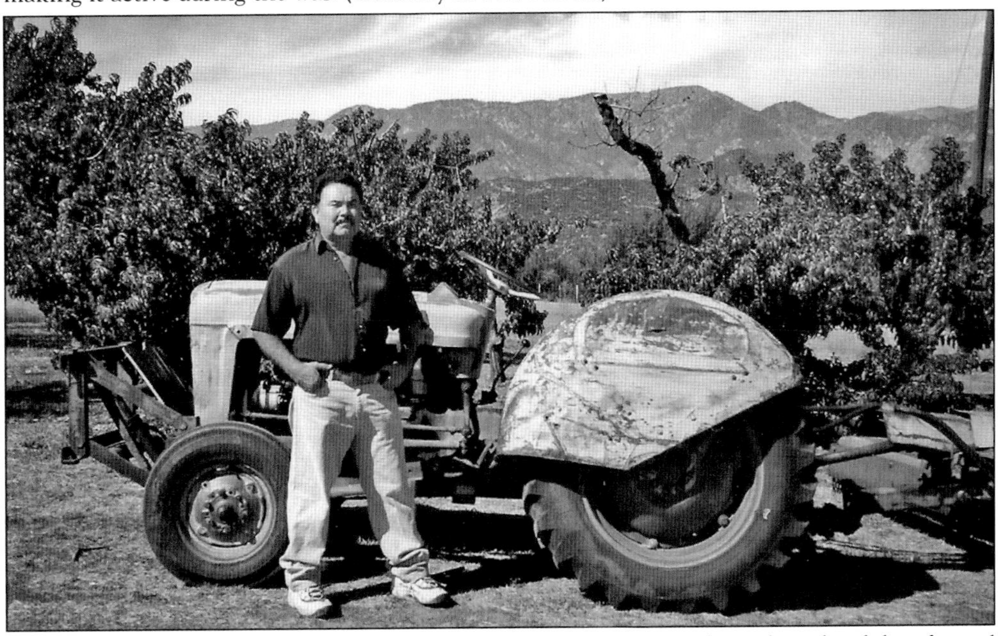

Fernando Rios, shown here against the backdrop of his tractor and peach orchard, has farmed peaches on the Banning Bench for about 30 years. In the 1950s, around 700 acres of peaches covered the bench. At one time, there were about six packing sheds and maybe 10 orchards operating on the plateau overlooking the San Gorgonio Pass. Today Rios is the only one left and declares he is staying as long as possible. (Courtesy of Fernando Rios.)

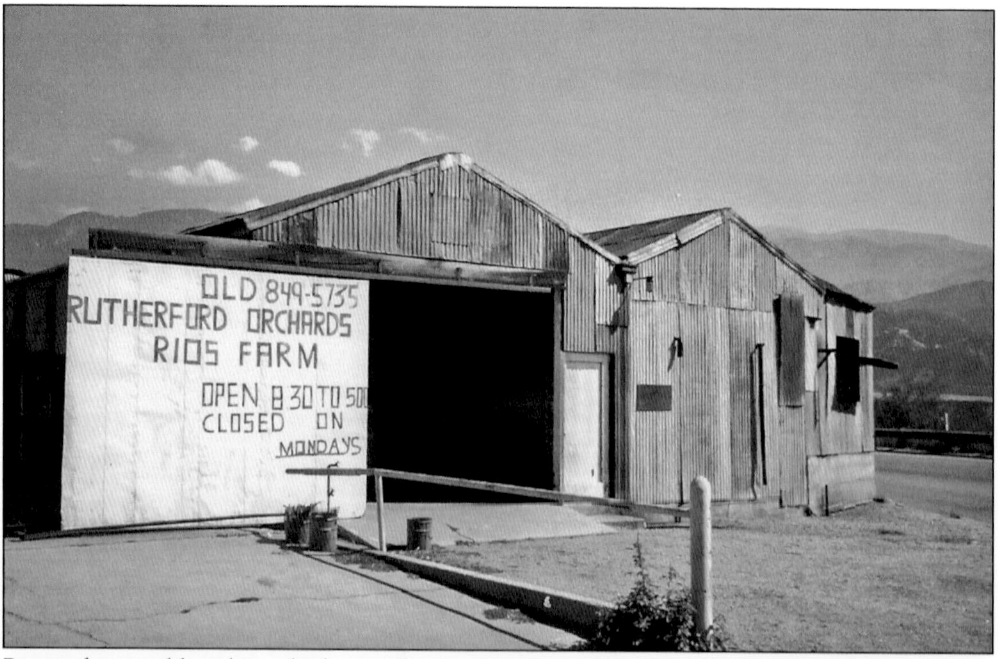

Pictured is an old packing shed—a tall, corrugated metal barn on the Banning Bench. A sign on its front still denotes the Rutherford Orchards and Rios Farm. The building dates back to the early 1930s, when Bob Rutherford's grandfather first planted a peach orchard. Bob was a third-generation peach grower until he retired in 1983. Fernando Rios now manages the farm for a group of investors who own it, but is able to raise crops for himself on some of the land. (Courtesy of Bob Rutherford.)

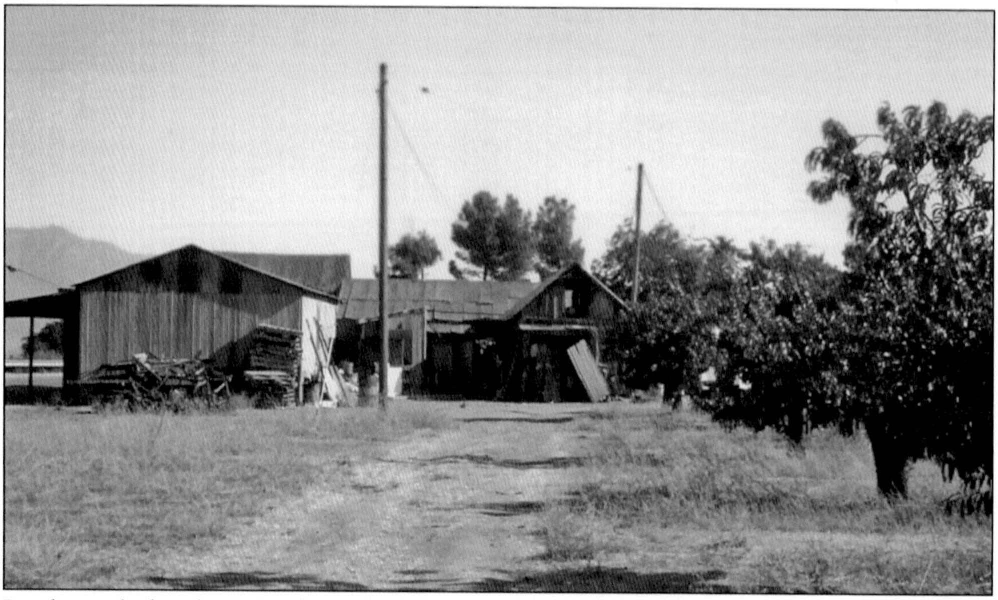

Peaches picked in the orchard were brought to the back of the Rutherford and Rios packing shed, along with other fruits and vegetables grown on the farm. Peaches are a favorite fruit sold here by Fernando Rios, but tomatoes are a specialty crop and many people come from Banning and afar to buy them. (Courtesy of the author.)

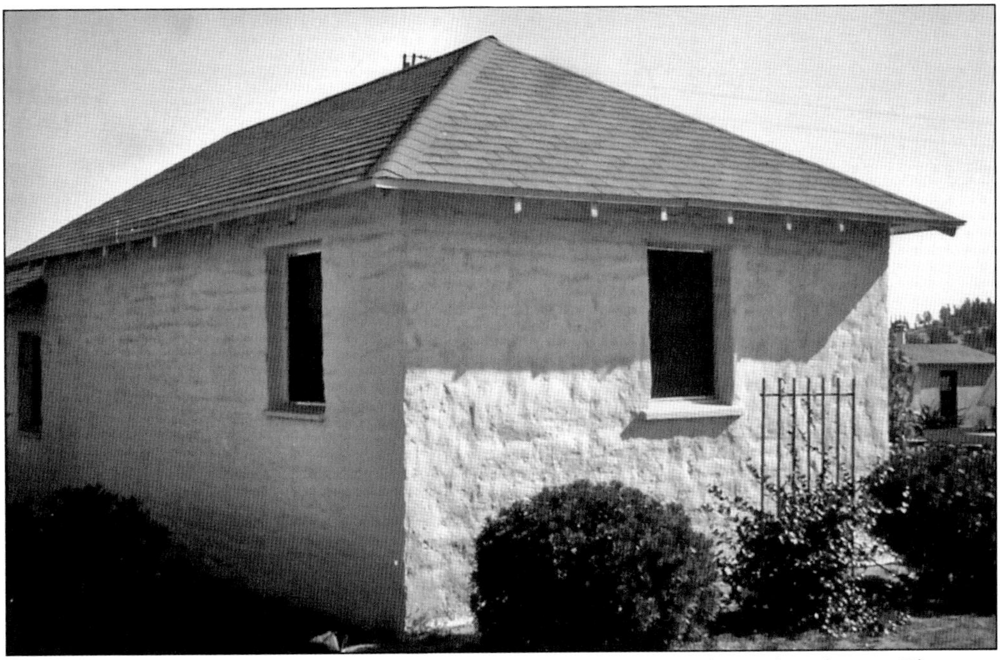

This adobe house on the bench was supposedly the first house built on this plateau. The view from the bench is superb, but especially so when Mount San Gorgonio and Mount San Jacinto are snowcapped several months of the year. Many people now live on the bench, forming the pleasant community seen today. (Courtesy of the author.)

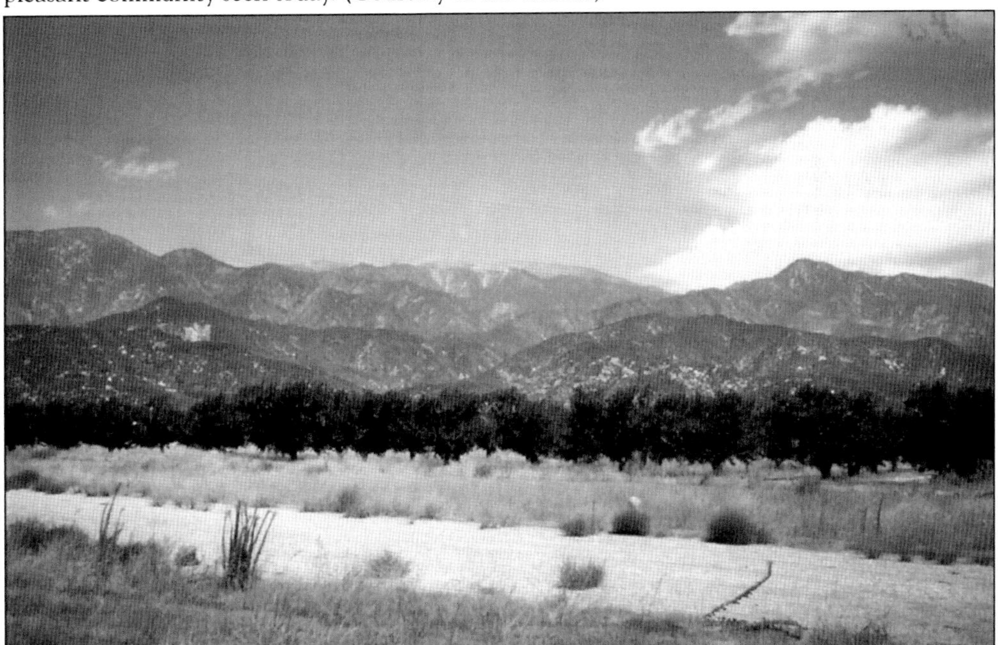

Peach trees, like those shown here on the old Rutherford and Rios farm, are thriving well. The large, unincorporated area of the bench has acres of relatively level land that warrant fruit growing. It is high above Banning and reaches out to the lower slopes of the San Gorgonio Mountain range, providing a climate that is conducive to fruit and vegetable farming. (Courtesy of the author.)

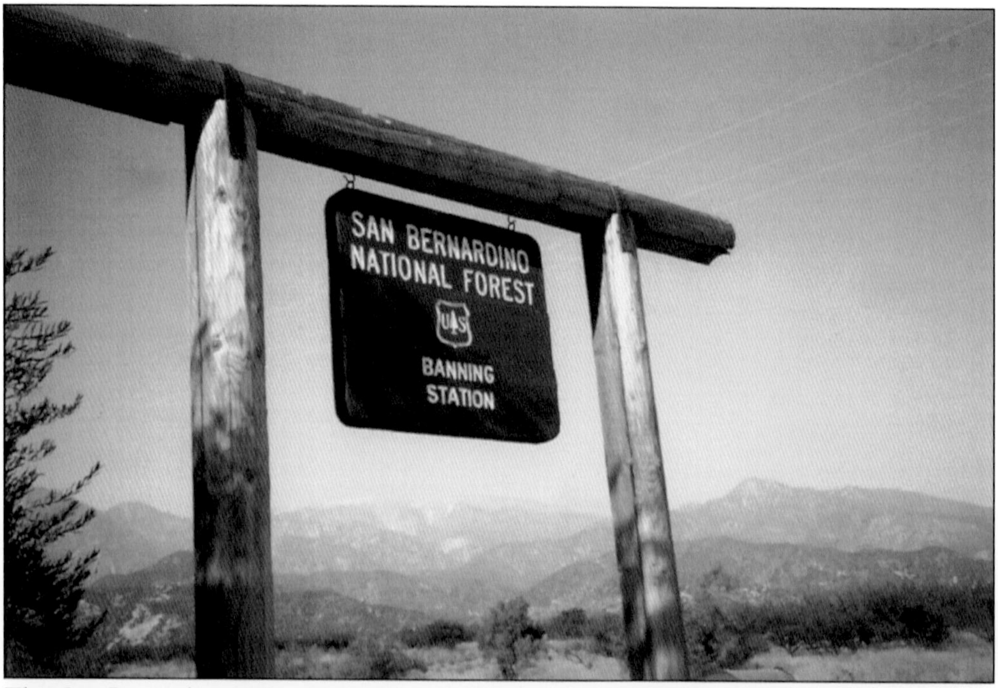

This San Bernardino National Forest sign advertises the nearby Banning U.S. Forest Station. The station protects a portion of the surrounding San Bernardino National Forest. It lies within the bounds of the unincorporated area of the Banning Bench. Recently, though, the Banning City Council has approved two large housing projects on bench acreage—Loma Linda and Black Bench Ranch acreages. (Courtesy of the author.)

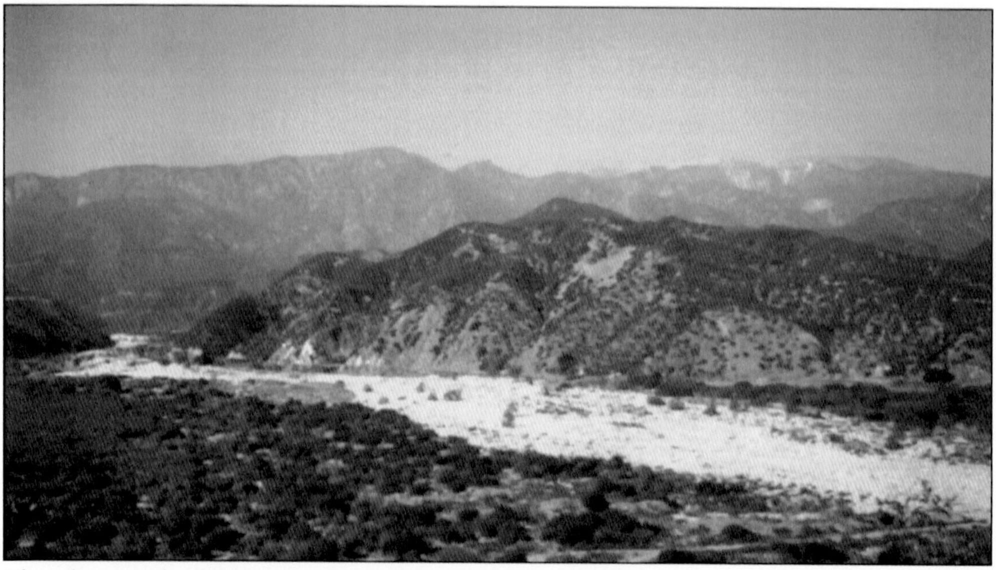

This photograph of Water Canyon, taken during the summer, shows no water rushing down its pathway, but during the snow and rainy season, water flows down and over its sprawling rock bed. Small lakes do remain in some areas throughout summer, though. The deep gorge is a divide that separates the major west portion of the bench from its eastern counterpart. (Courtesy of the author.)

Seven

Morongo Indian Reservation

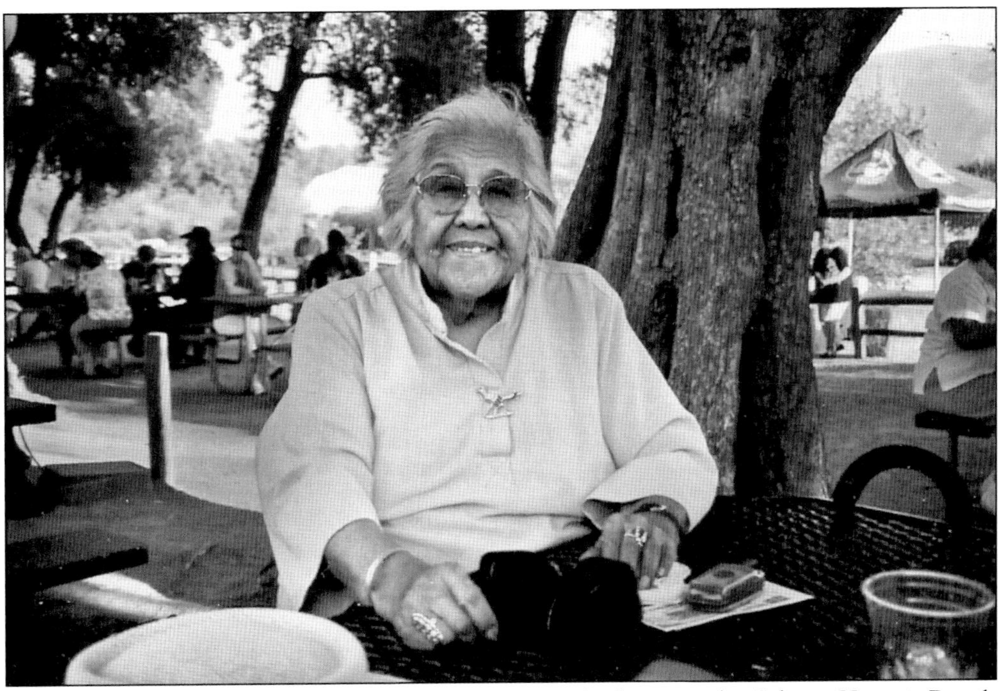

Katherine Siva Saubel is pictured here during a recent barbecue at the Gilman Historic Ranch and Wagon Museum. This site is familiar to her because she used to play as a child around the nearby creek. She was born on the Los Coyotes Reservation and is currently its tribal leader. Katherine was the first Native American to be inducted into the National Women's Hall of Fame. She was born on the Morongo Indian Reservation. (Courtesy of the author.)

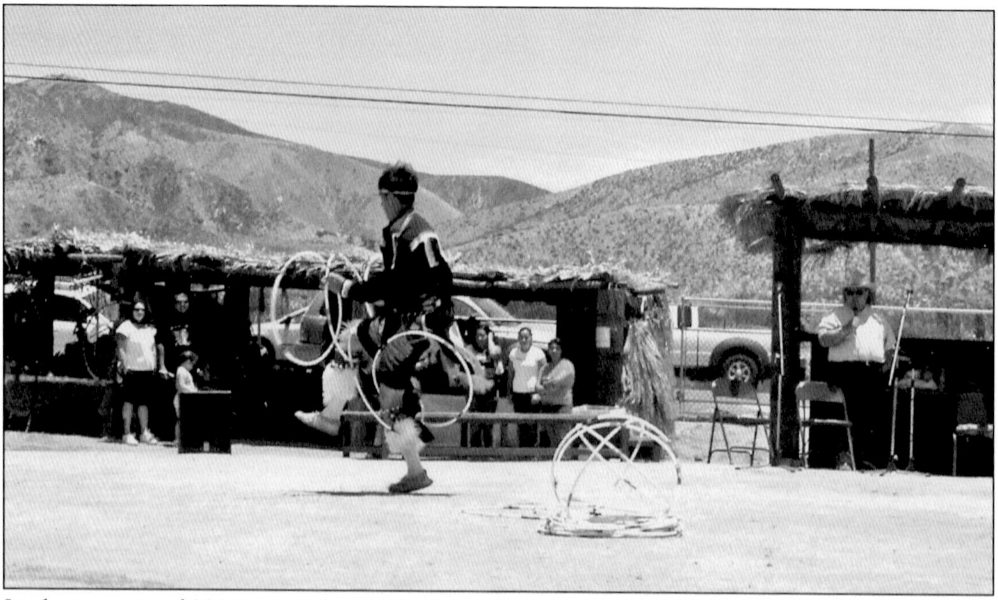

In the summer of 2004, a member of the Hoop Dancers performs a ring dance during the 40th annual fiesta on the grounds of the Malki Museum. Hoop dancers are always a delight to watch during events. Kevin Siva, master of ceremonies for the event, introduced other colorful and exciting entertainment throughout the day. (Courtesy of Debra Garcia.)

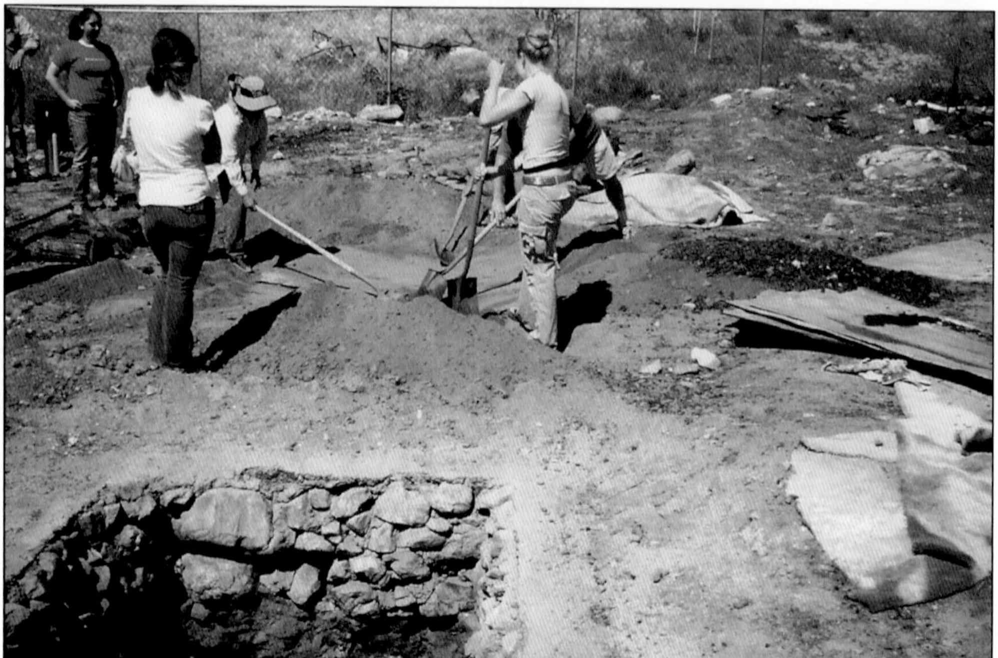

Preparation is being done for the April 23, 2005, agave roast at the Malki Museum compound. Over 40 people gathered on the nearby desert at Tewanet to hunt and dig up enough agave plants for the feast. In the foreground is an open pit used to cook the agave. Another pit in the background is being covered with soil that will let the partially cooked agave to simmer over coals. (Courtesy of Debra Garcia.)

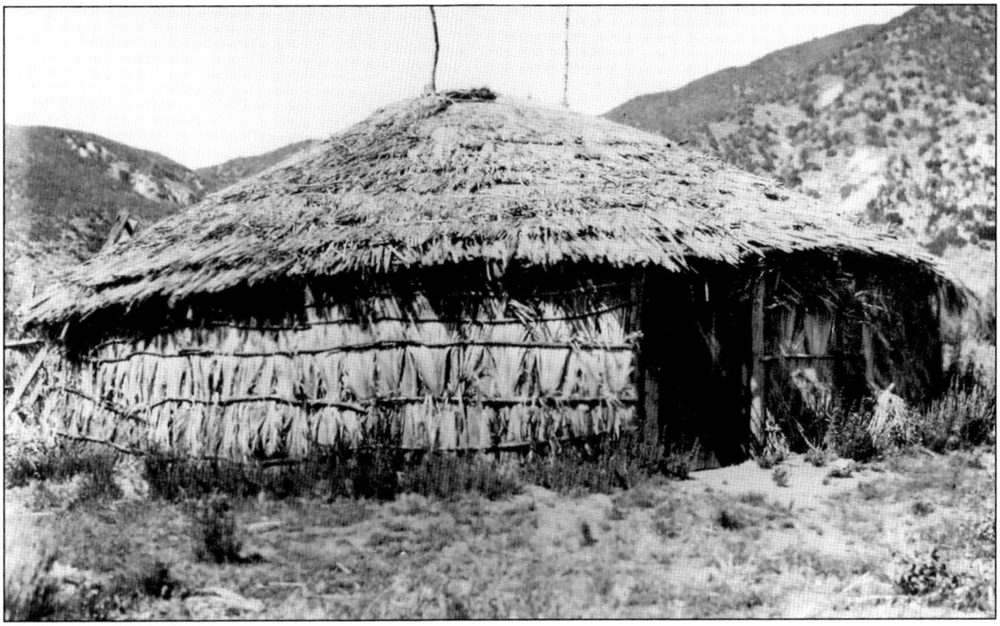

This Native American ceremonial house, used for special events, was once located on the Morongo Indian Reservation. In the Cahuilla culture, perhaps one of the most important special events was an annual, weeklong ceremony to commemorate those who had died that year. Before the arrival of the Spaniards, most structures were round, including ceremonial houses. (Courtesy of Katherine Siva Saubel.)

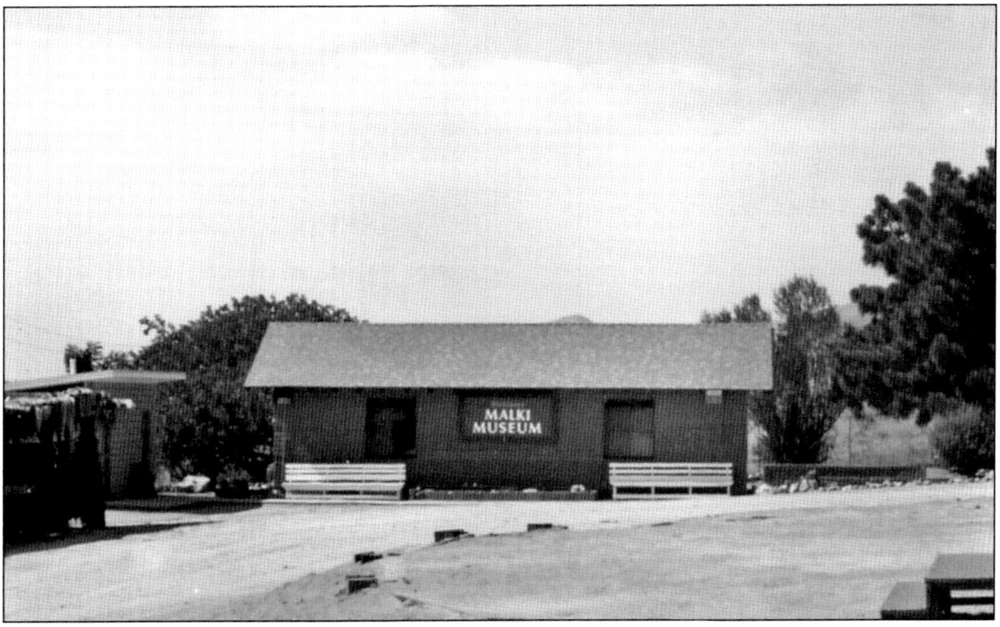

The Malki Museum, shown here, is a landmark on the Morongo Indian Reservation that has survived for over 40 years. It began because of the inspiration of two Cahuilla women, cofounders Jane Penn and Katherine Siva Saubel. The museum's mission is to promote scholarship, cultural awareness, and understanding of Southern California Native American tribes. The museum has a large membership and many visit it yearly. (Courtesy of the author.)

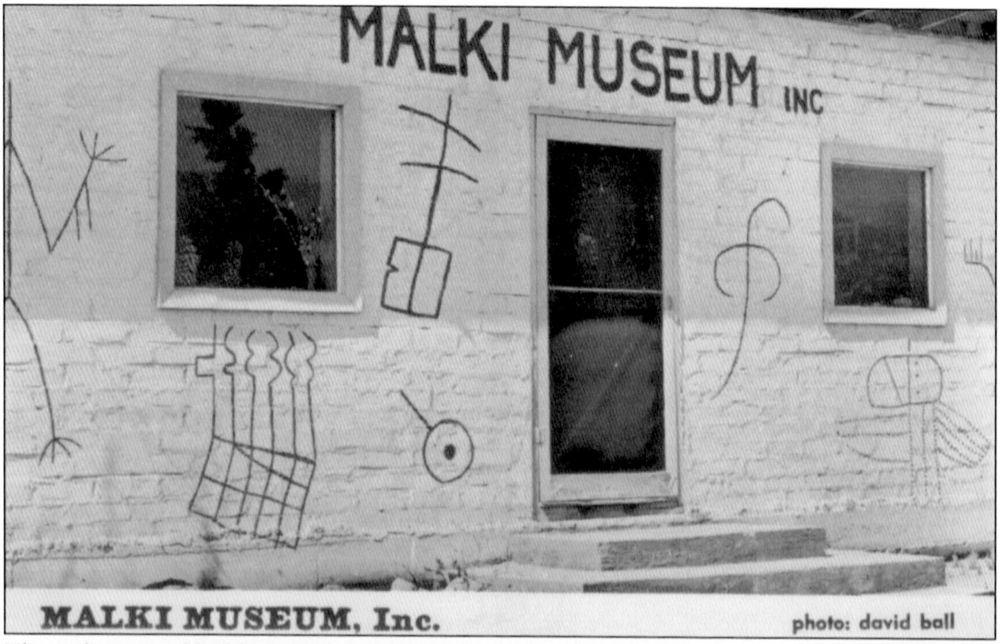

This is the original building that once housed the Malki Museum, before it moved to its new location just a short distance to the south. The remains of this building exemplify its meager beginning. This early effort has since produced a museum that evolved into a well-known institution, one which has incorporated its own quality press, the Malki Press. (Courtesy of Steve Lech.)

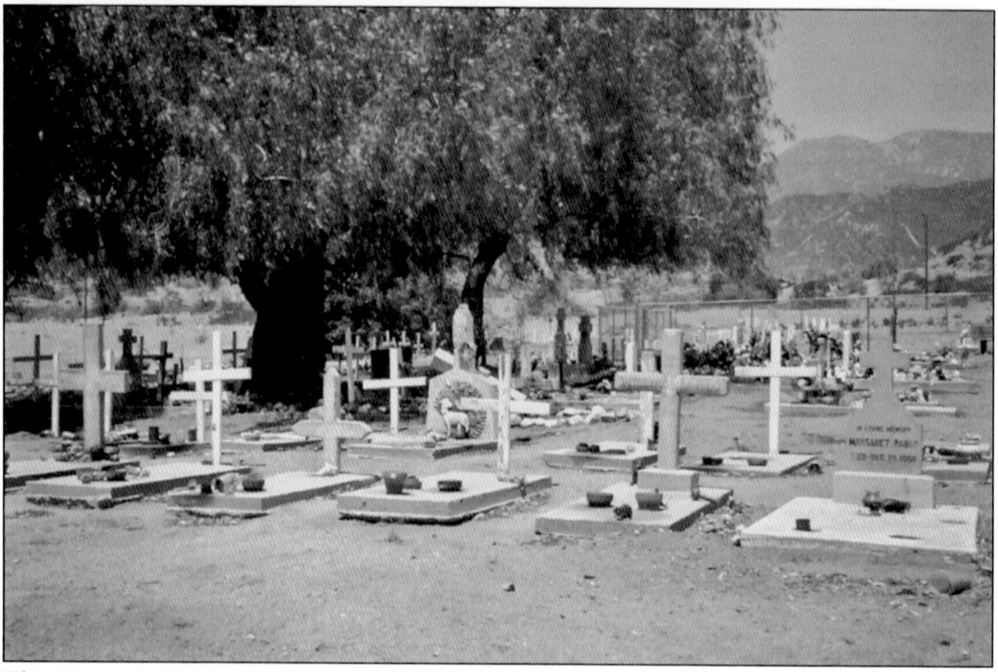

This cemetery is the oldest of the three that are located on the Morongo Indian Reservation. Located in a field directly across from the Moravian Church, it dates back to 1890, being one of the oldest churches in the San Gorgonio Pass. The church stems from a denomination organized in Germany in 1772. (Courtesy of the author.)

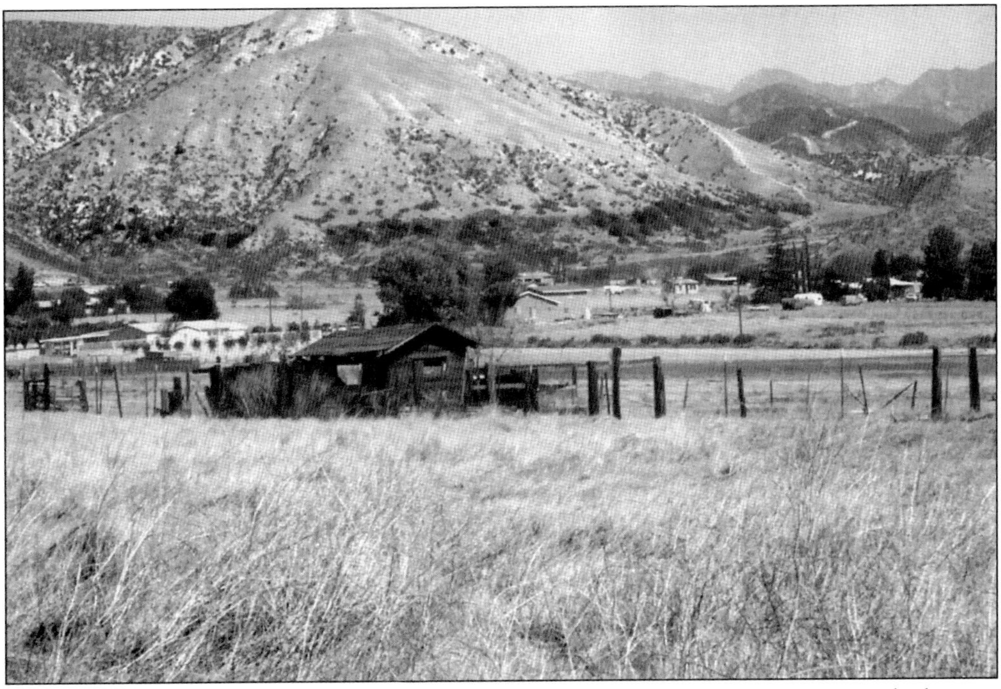

This is a scene of one of the more remote areas on the Morongo Indian Reservation, looking to the northeast. Tribe members once lived on small acreages like this one Note the small deserted barn in the center of the photograph. Here tribe members once farmed, cared for their animals and fruit trees, and raised their families. (Courtesy of the author.)

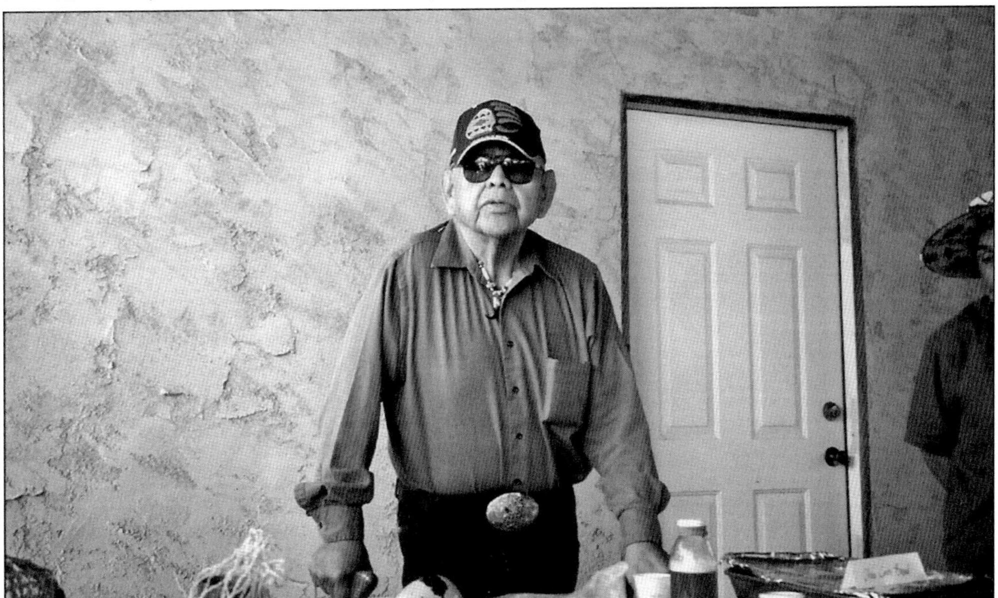

Alvino Siva is giving a presentation to participants at the agave roast lunch at the Malki Museum. His enlightening talk gave insight into the numerous foods the Native Americans feed upon in this area. The food served for lunch featured the agave plant, mesquite beans, and other staples of the desert. (Courtesy of the author and Alvino Siva.)

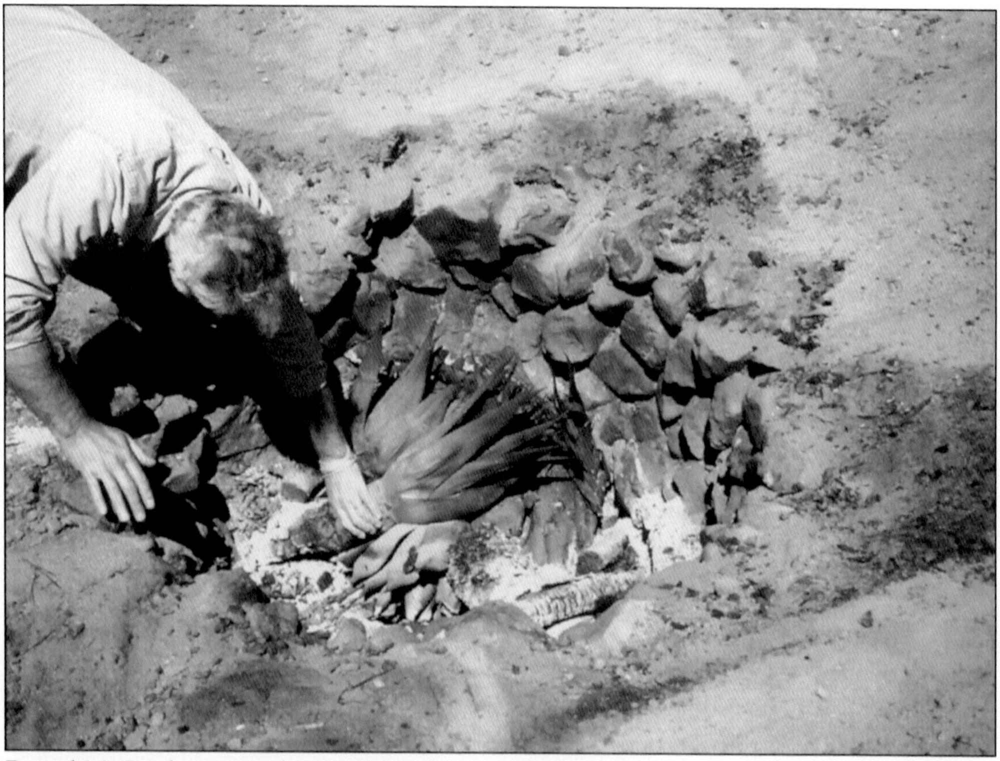

Daniel McCarthy is seen here rolling an agave plant over hot coals at the beginning of the roasting. It is placed directly on the coals just as it had been dug from the earth, uncovered in the beginning, to be covered later with soil for a slow roasting process. Preparation of agave to the edible stage consists of a long process. Not only does it have to be hunted and harvested, but also prepared in this manner. (Courtesy of the author.)

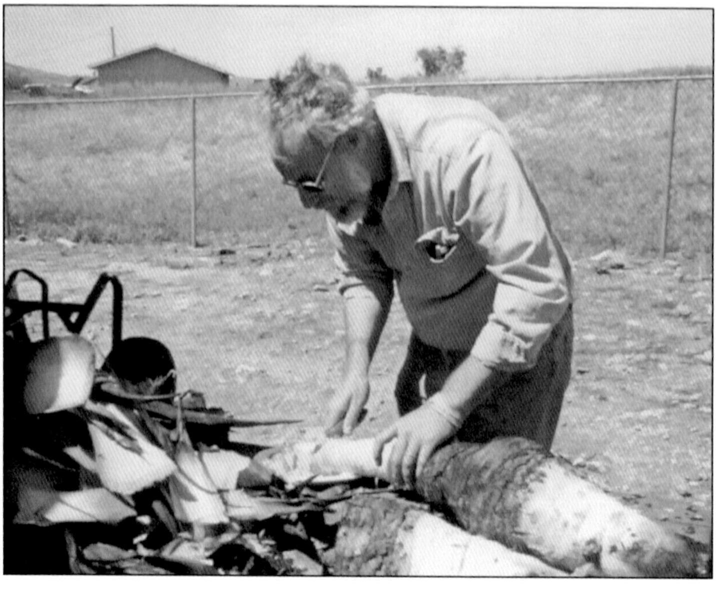

Daniel McCarthy is pictured here working hard to prepare agave for the 2005 Agave Roast at the Malki Museum. After roasting, the stalk of the agave plant is stripped of its leaves, cleaned, and sliced. This culmination was preceded a week earlier by the hard work of volunteers, who went to the surrounding desert area and harvested the agave plant. (Courtesy of the author.)

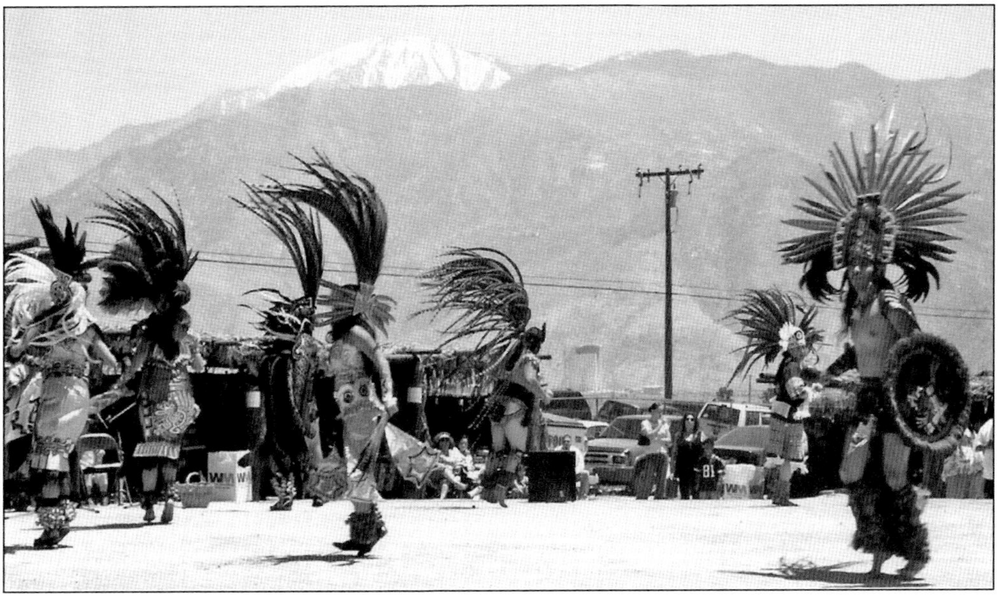

Attendees of the 40th Annual Fiesta of 2004 enjoyed watching the Aztec Dance Group, the Cupa Dancers, and the Hoop Dancers—all performing Native American dances. Here a vibrant dance is in session, with its members adorned in their feather headdress and dance regalia. (Courtesy of the author.)

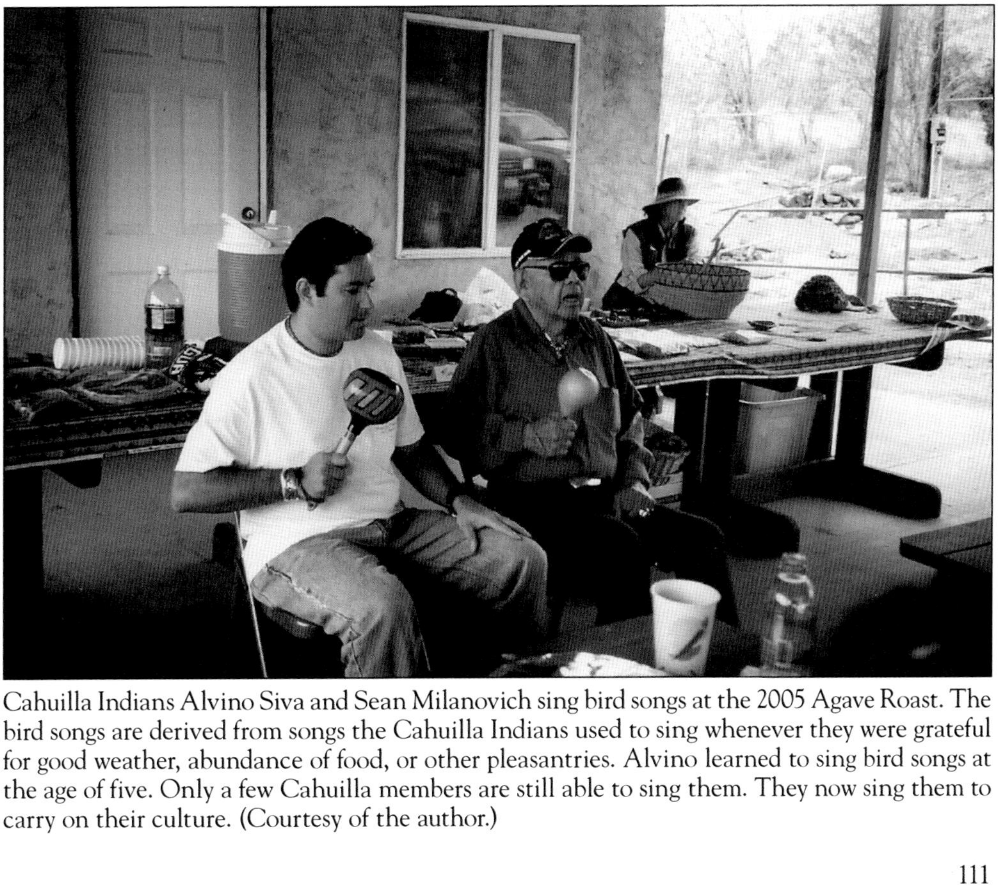

Cahuilla Indians Alvino Siva and Sean Milanovich sing bird songs at the 2005 Agave Roast. The bird songs are derived from songs the Cahuilla Indians used to sing whenever they were grateful for good weather, abundance of food, or other pleasantries. Alvino learned to sing bird songs at the age of five. Only a few Cahuilla members are still able to sing them. They now sing them to carry on their culture. (Courtesy of the author.)

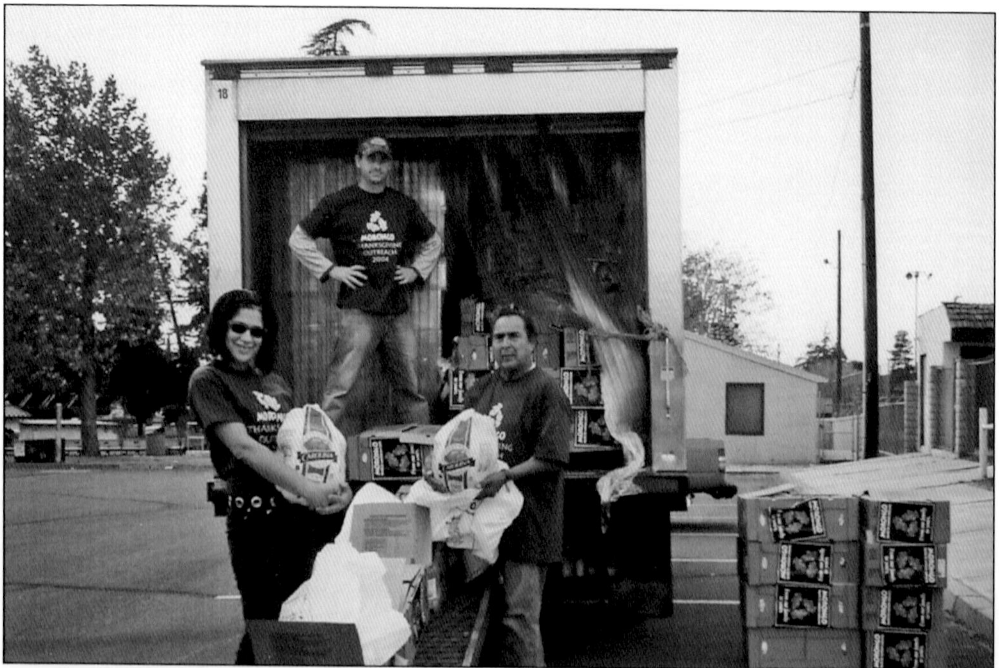

For Thanksgiving 2004, the Morongo Indian Reservation donated around 6,000 turkeys to needy residents in Banning and surrounding areas. Trucks, like the one shown here, were used as distribution centers. This one, stationed near the senior center in Banning, has volunteers ready to start handing out turkeys. (Courtesy of the author.)

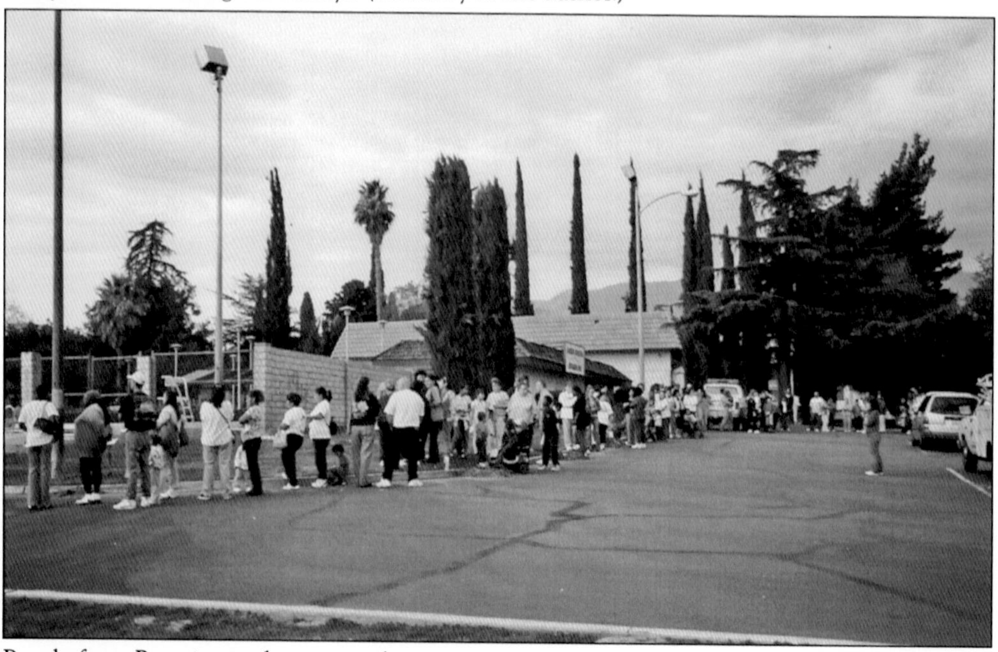

People from Banning and areas nearby came to receive a free turkey donated by the Morongo Indian Reservation. A truck full of turkeys had just pulled into the parking lot and the volunteers were preparing to hand out turkeys. It is apparent that the truck had caught the eye of those at the front of the line. (Courtesy of the author.)

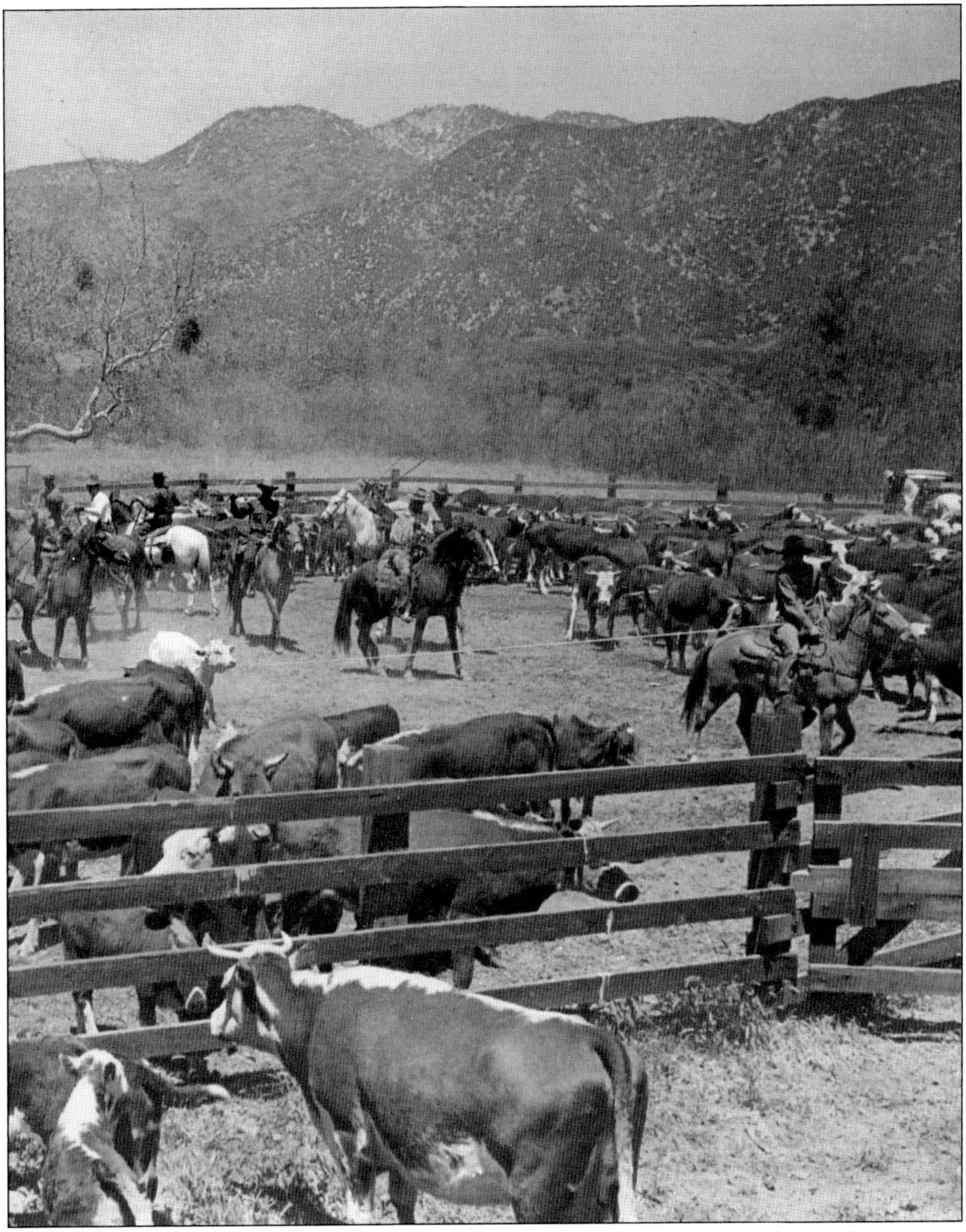

Pictured here is the lower corral on the Morongo Indian Reservation around 1950. Reservation range cattle were rounded up yearly for market in this manner. It was a joint effort, incorporating Native American cowboys from some of the nearby reservations of Los Coyotes, Palm Springs, and Saboba, as well as more distant tribes. It became an anticipated event each year, viewed by many people. (Courtesy of the author.)

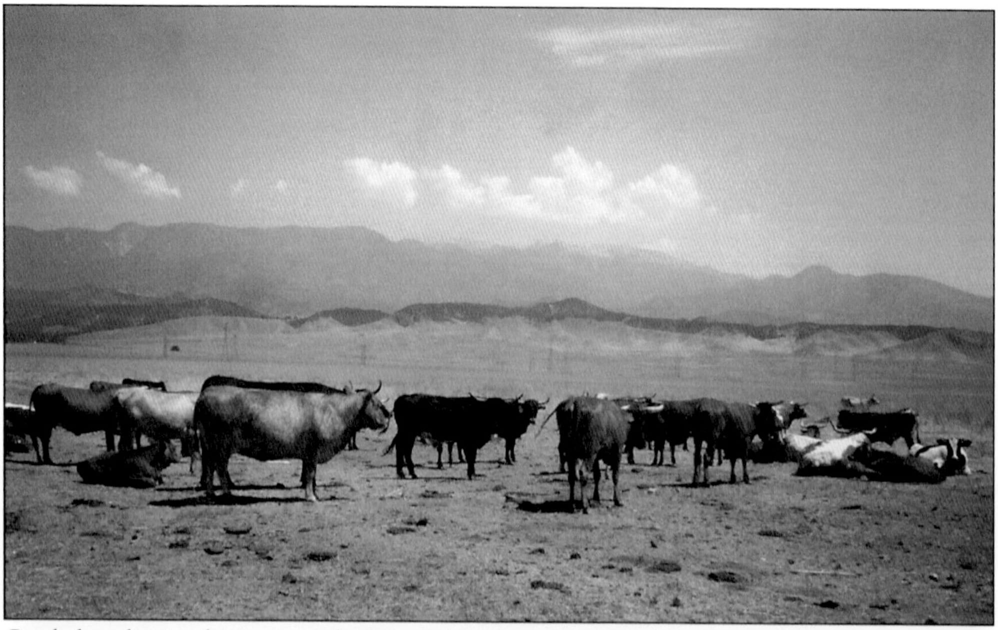

Cattle breeding and raising on the Morongo Indian Reservation has slowed down drastically in the last few decades. However, small groups of cattle can still be seen on the reservation, like the herd shown here. It is still a pleasure for one to spot them on the range and see their picturesque, casual stance. (Courtesy of the author.)

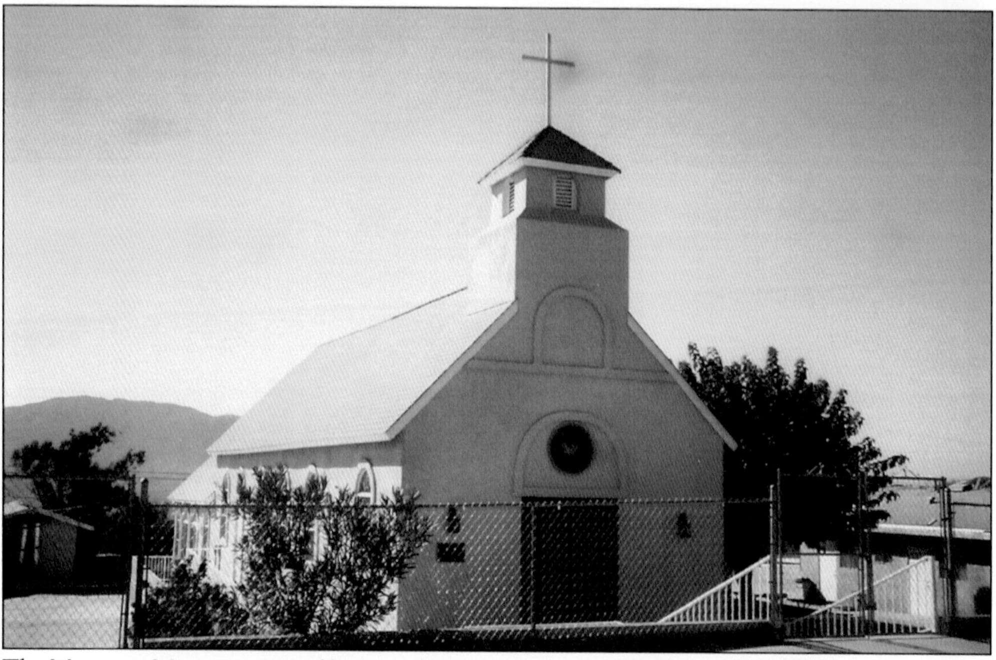

The Moravian Mission, pictured here on the reservation, was established by the Woman's National Indian Association at the Banning Potrero on June 7, 1889, under charge of the Rev. W. H. Weinland. A year later, the association turned the mission over to the Moravian church on the reservation grounds, and in 1914, the government issued a patent to the land. The church dates from the martyrdom of John Huss, 60 years before the Protestant Reformation. (Courtesy of the author.)

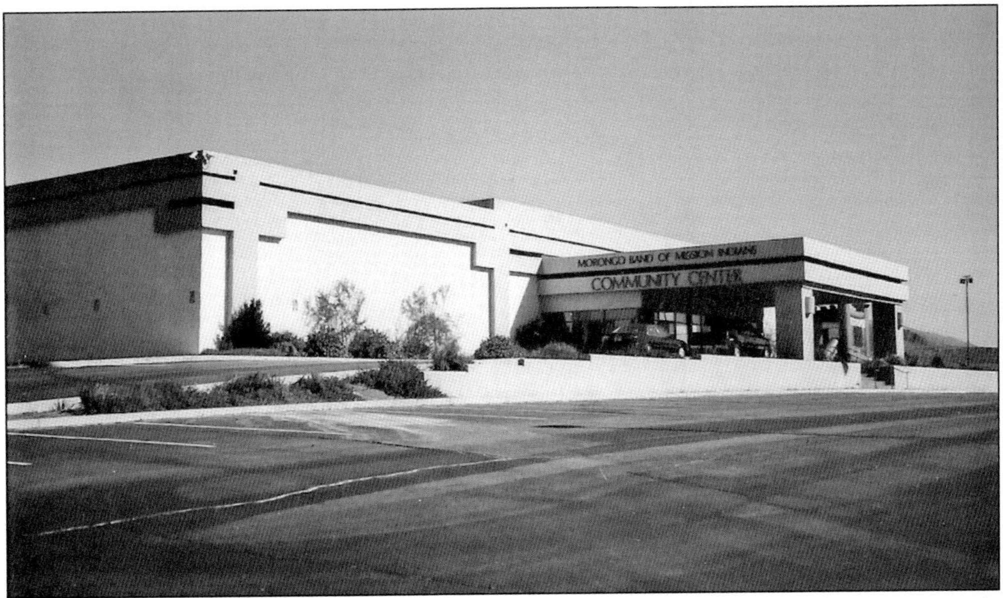

The first casino on the Morongo Indian Reservation was established in this building on Field's Road, now home to the Morongo Band of Moreno Indians Community Center. On the north side of I-10, the reservation's second casino (Casino Morongo) was recently replaced by a $250 million high-rise resort and casino (Morongo Casino), just a short distance to the west. (Courtesy of the author.)

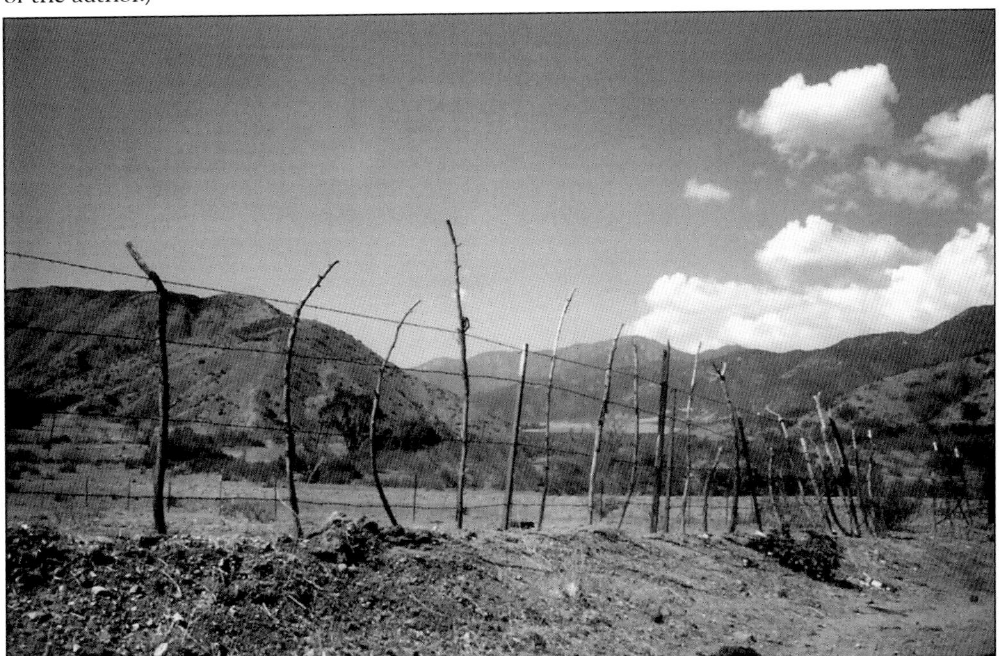

Some of the graze land on the Morongo Indian Reservation is centered behind this fence and runs far up into the Portero Canyon. The tree-limb fence perhaps exemplifies the ingenuity of the Native Americans, who, throughout the years, have used articles of nature to their great advantage. The fence separates two of the reservation's cemeteries. (Courtesy of the author.)

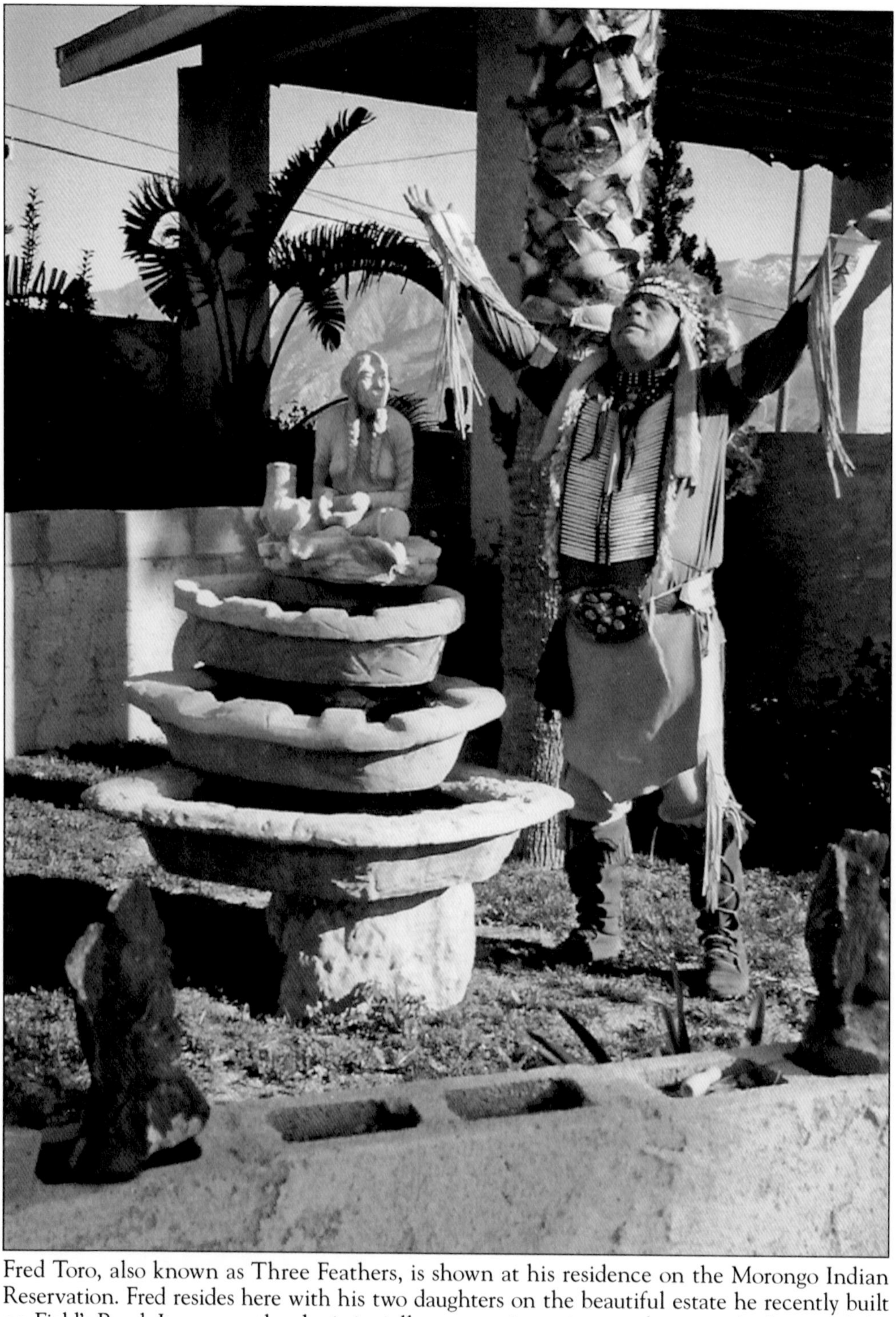

Fred Toro, also known as Three Feathers, is shown at his residence on the Morongo Indian Reservation. Fred resides here with his two daughters on the beautiful estate he recently built on Field's Road. It appears that he is jovially summoning rain or welcoming the beautiful sky above. Fred has worked in movies with Steven Seagal. He sometimes adorns this regalia for school performances and other activities. (Courtesy of Fred Toro.)

Eight

Cabazon

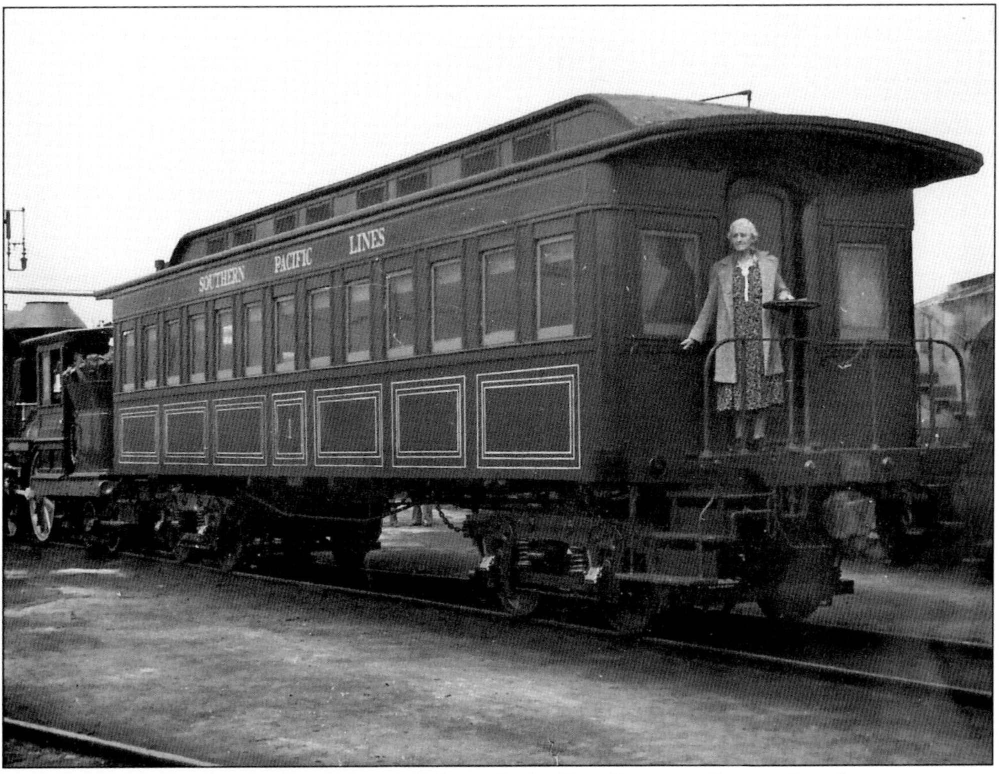

This Southern Pacific coach once passed through the San Gorgonio Pass and made routine stops at Beaumont, Banning, and Cabazon. Cabazon's telegrapher, Nellie Bailiff, standing on the coach platform, enjoyed working for the railroad and was held in high esteem by the company. She liked riding the train and sometimes would take her grandchildren short distances to Banning or Beaumont, just for the thrill of the ride. (Courtesy of Marianne Bailiff.)

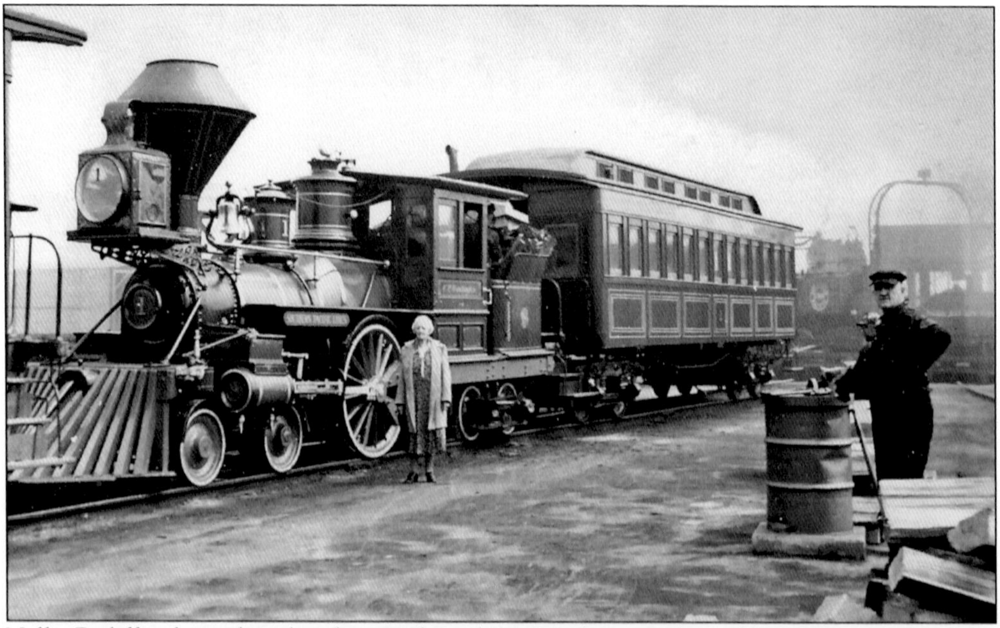

Nellie Bailiff is shown here beside one of Southern Pacific's prized wood burners. Note the wood extending from the bin behind the engineers compartment. Nellie had a great liking for the railroad's trains and enjoyed riding them whenever she could. Her pride is evident as she stood to be photographed before this one. (Courtesy of Marianne Bailiff.)

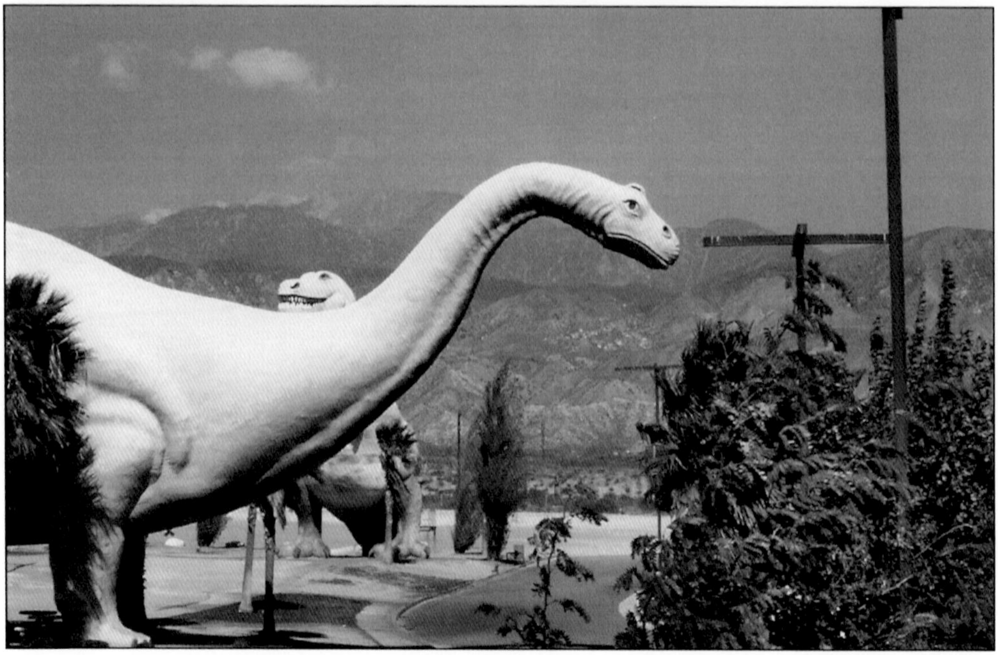

When travelers along I-10 come through the San Gorgonio Pass to Cabazon, their heads turn abruptly north to an unusual sight on the roadside. Here stands Dinny, the massive 150-foot, 150-ton brontosaurus that took Claude Bell 11 years to build. Its domination of the landscape is further enhanced by Rex, in the background. A gift shop is housed in Dinny's belly. (Courtesy of the author.)

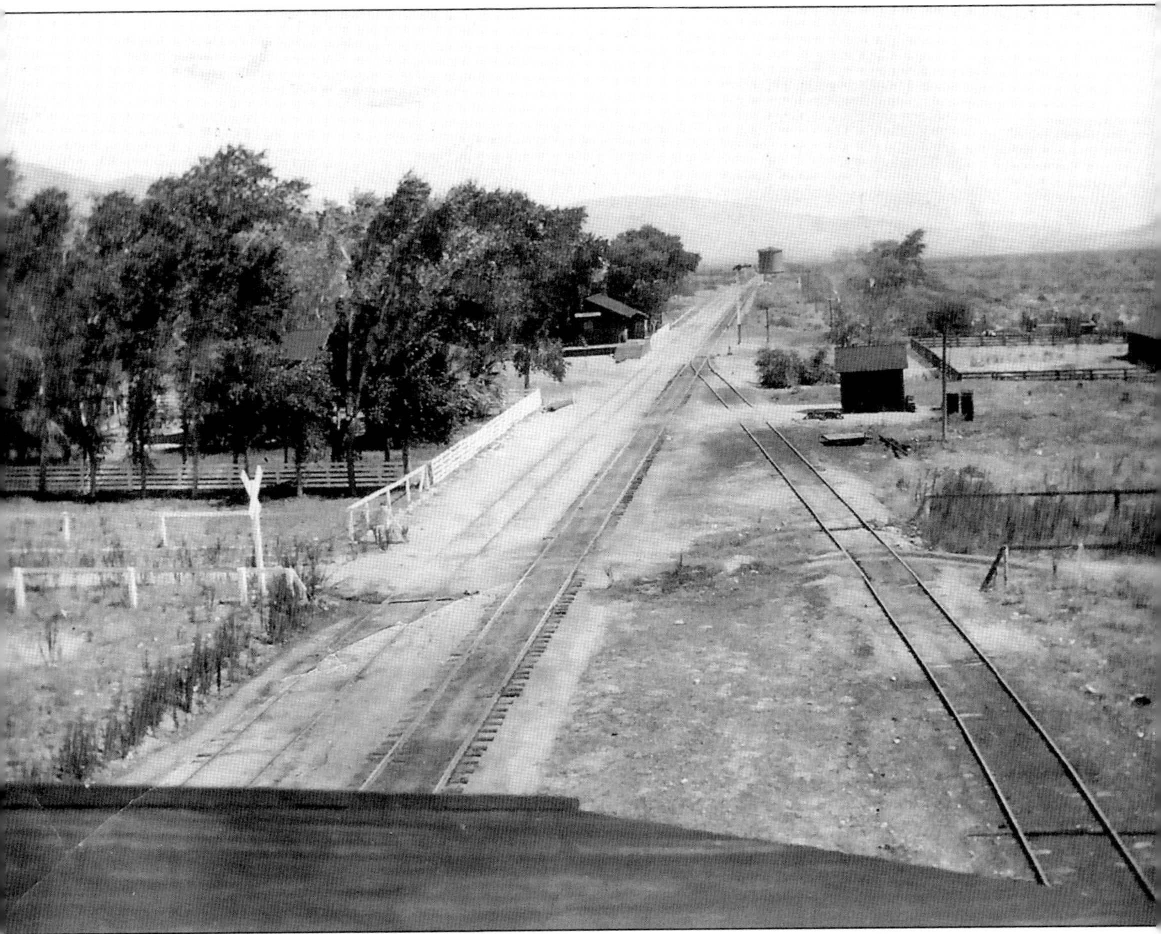

The Cabazon train station is shown in the center background of this photograph. The Cabazon sign on the train station indicates that the town of Cabazon was already formed, pulling away from its previous name of Hal's Siding. By this time, Hal City to the south was failing and fading into oblivion. Cabazon was beginning to take center stage. (Courtesy of Marianne Bailiff.)

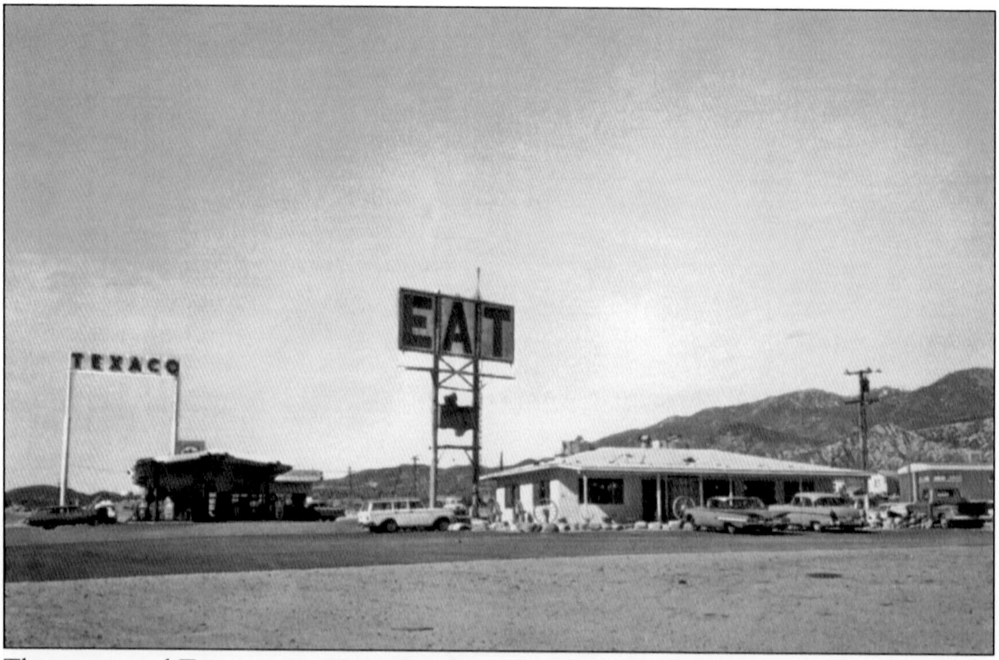

This eatery and Texaco gas station were along the Highway 99 in Cabazon before I-10 came through the San Gorgonio Pass. At this time, the town was small and undeveloped. However, it served as a great respite for the traveler coming through the lonely desert. Food and gasoline were welcomed items. (Courtesy of Steve Lech.)

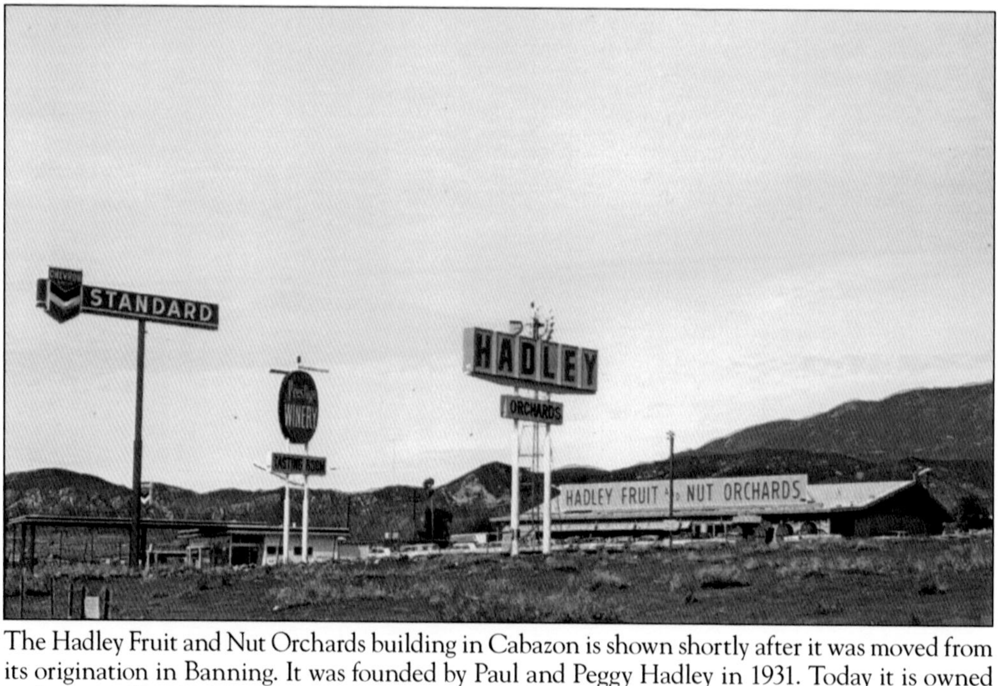

The Hadley Fruit and Nut Orchards building in Cabazon is shown shortly after it was moved from its origination in Banning. It was founded by Paul and Peggy Hadley in 1931. Today it is owned and operated by the Morongo Indian Reservation. Hadley's is a backpacker's dream market. Many hikers of the famous Pacific Crest Trail, crossing 6.5 miles to the east, come here to replenish their backpacks. (Courtesy of Steve Lech.)

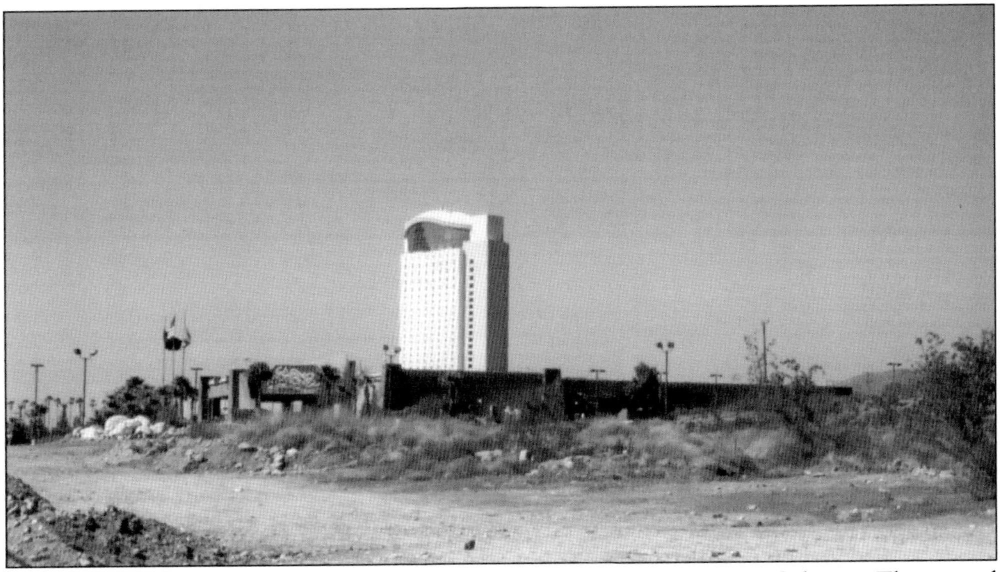

Shown in this photograph are the second and third Morongo casinos in Cabazon. The second one, the squatty Casino Morongo building in the foreground, is dwarfed by the third one, the new high-rise Morongo Casino. It sits on 44 acres and boasts a 685,000-square foot 27-story structure, with 272 rooms, 32 double bay suites, 9 restaurants, and a 316,000 gallon swimming pool. (Courtesy of the author.)

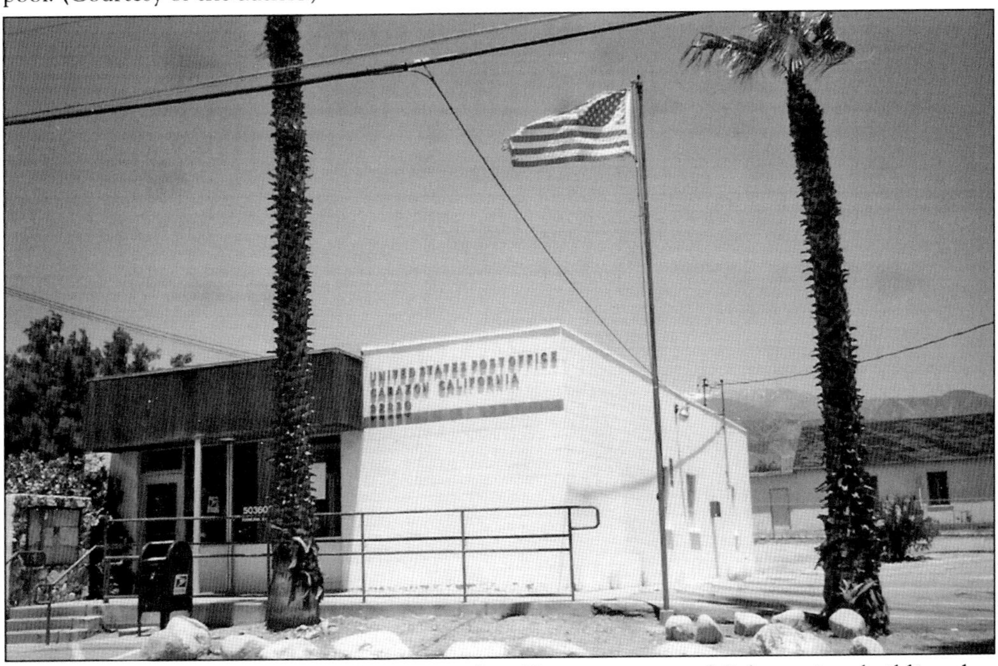

The Cabazon Post Office, shown here, is in the old town section of Cabazon in a building that was moved into at the southeast corner of Ramona and Broadway in 1957. It was the first time Cabazon had a postal building. The first post office was established on March 1, 1886, with W. A. Patterson becoming the first postmaster. This new building is located about five miles from the path of the Pacific Crest Trail's crossing to the east. Many hikers mail supplies here to pick up as they hike by. (Courtesy of the author.)

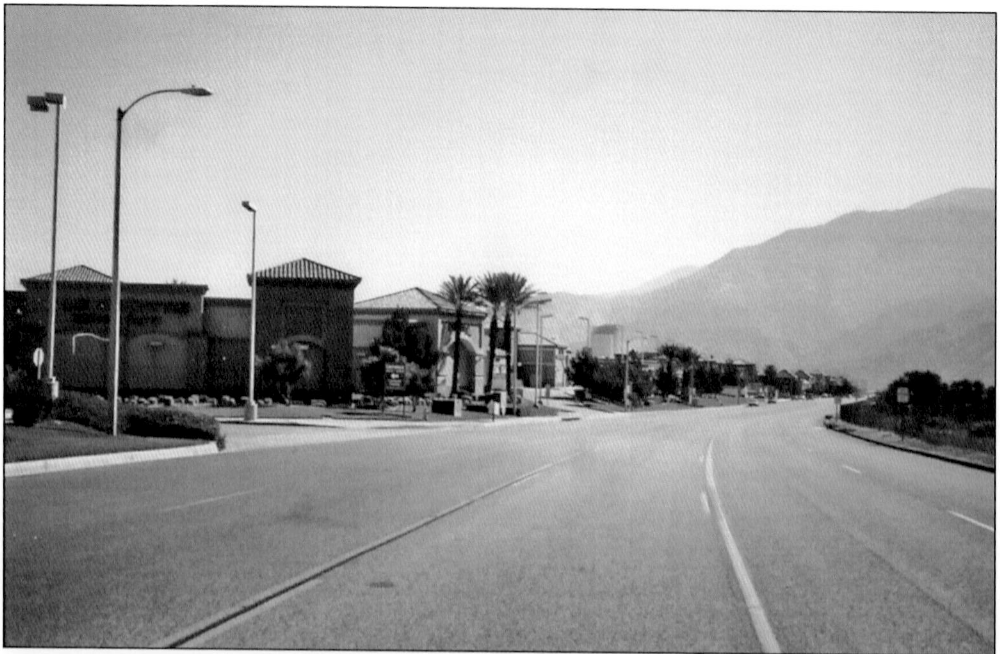

Running parallel to I-10 in Cabazon are the Desert Hill Premium Outlet Stores, with 300 shops, and Cabazon Outlets, to its east, containing even more stores. It is a shopper's paradise for area residents, travelers, and tourists. A large variety of items can be found here, representative of most popular brands. (Courtesy of the author.)

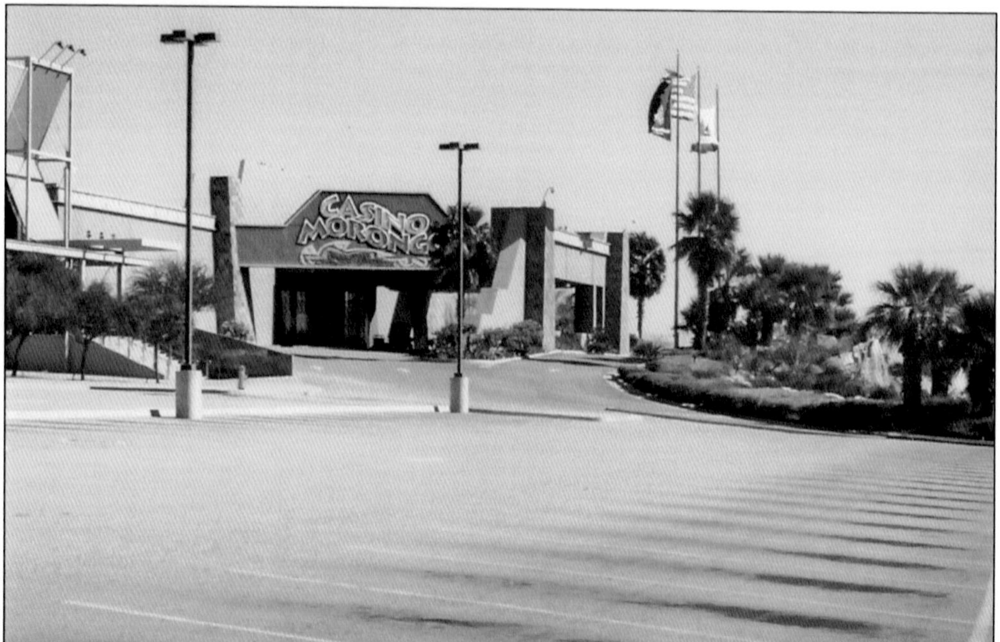

This is a close-up view of Casino Morongo, the second casino built in Cabazon. Since the new Morongo Casino opened, Casino Morongo has not been idle. It is now used as a large bingo hall that has become quite popular. Many reminisce about playing here before the new casino arrived. (Courtesy of the author.)

Nine

WHITEWATER

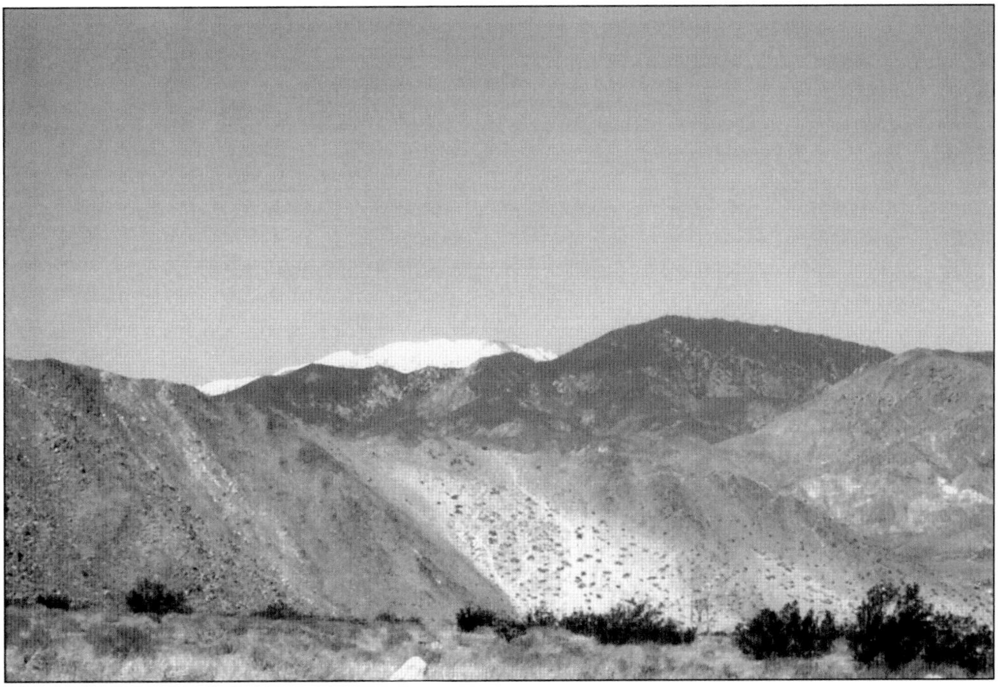

The sight pictured here often greets visitors on the road to Whitewater and its fish farm. The splendor of the snowcapped San Gorgonio Mountains in the distance to the northwest and the green trees that are nourished from water of the Whitewater River Canyon make a pleasant scene. The old stage stop at Whitewater, near I-10, has faded away, but its history remains. (Courtesy of the author.)

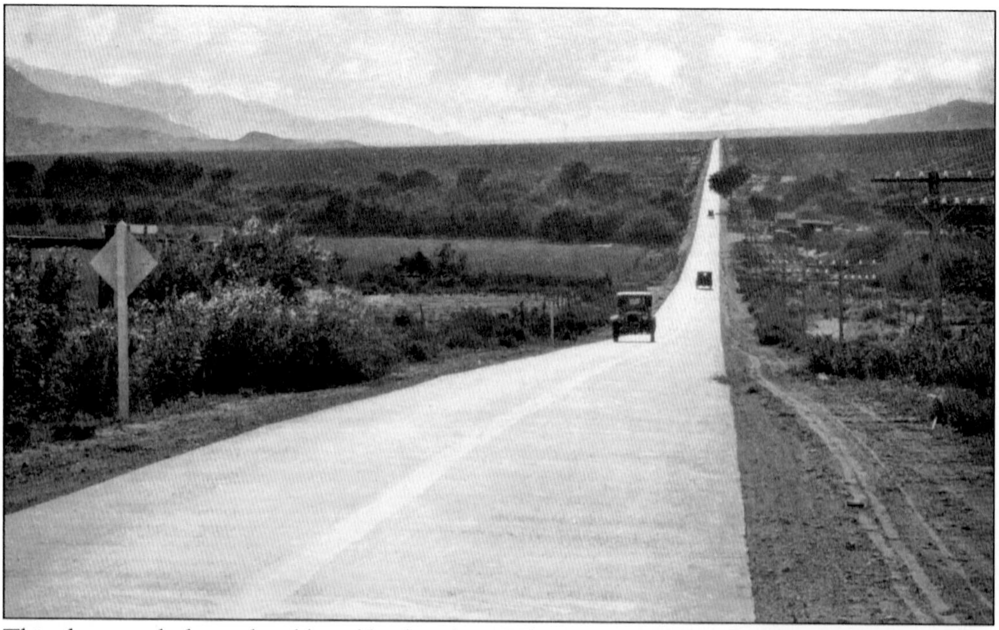

This photograph shows the old road leading from Whitewater to Indio. It is interesting to compare the three cars seen here at this time with what can be seen today on I-10, which now covers this same route. Note the sparsely spaced buildings along the way and the insulated pole line at right. (Courtesy of Steve Lech.)

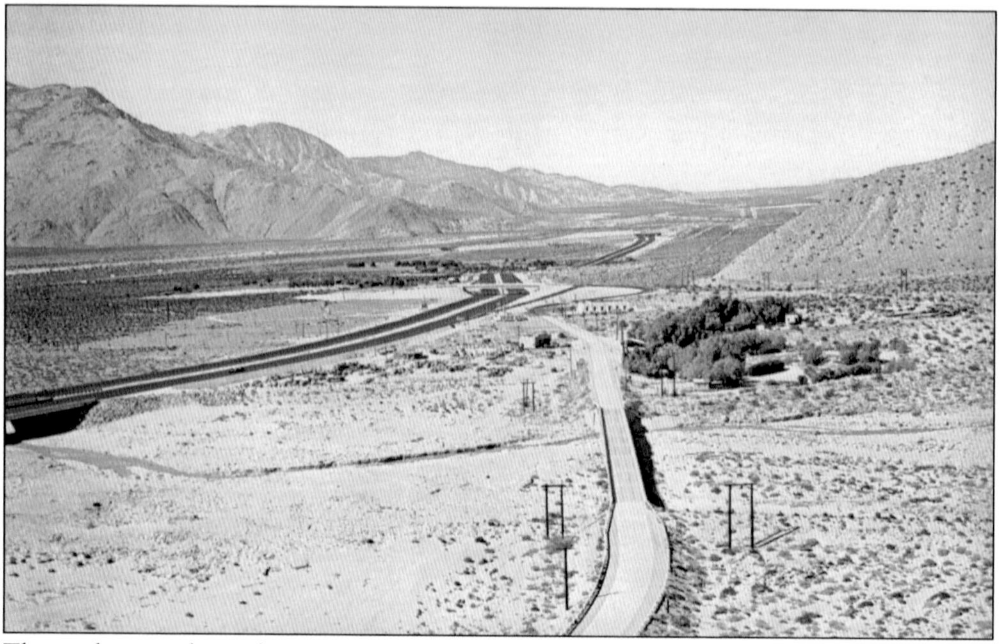

The road pictured at right passes Whitewater and leads onto the old Highway 99. Very little remains that can be associated with a stage stop. The trail of the Whitewater River is in the foreground of the picture, passing under Highway 99. It is relatively dry in the summer months. (Courtesy of Steve Lech.)

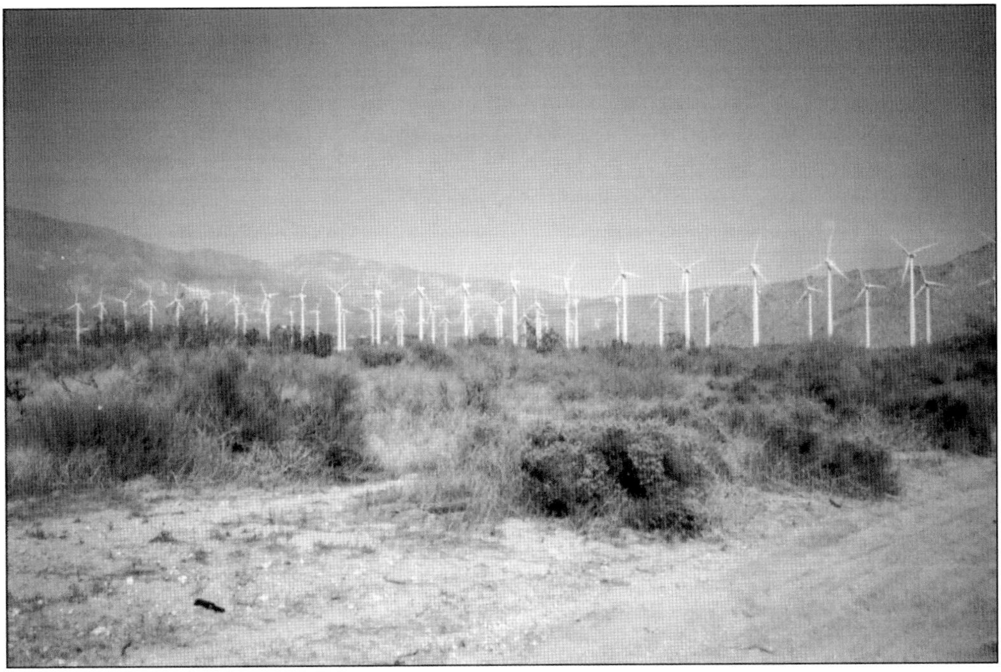

Wind turbines are a familiar sight near Whitewater and its surrounding area. One cannot approach Whitewater without bringing them into view. Hundreds of them generate electrical power daily. They are installed along the ridge to the west and in the lower clearing to the east. (Courtesy of the author.)

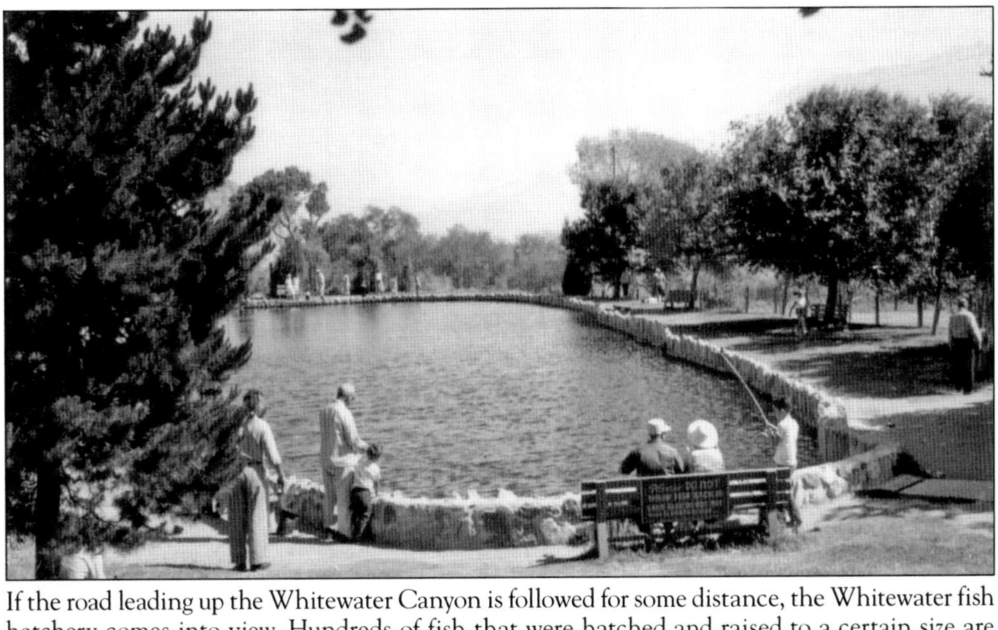

If the road leading up the Whitewater Canyon is followed for some distance, the Whitewater fish hatchery comes into view. Hundreds of fish that were hatched and raised to a certain size are loaded into this large pond. Fishermen are invited to catch fish and have them freshly cooked in a nearby restaurant. (Courtesy of Steve Lech.)

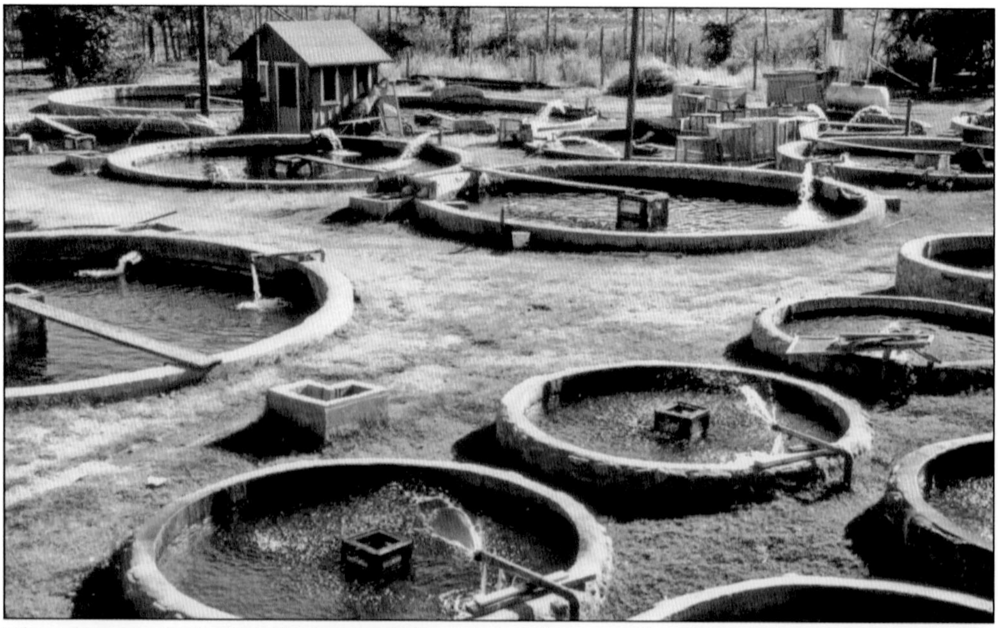

This photograph depicts the heart of the fish hatchery on the Whitewater Fish Ranch. The numerous cylindrical tanks on the farm contain thousands of small fish that are being cultured for the larger pond, to be placed there and made ready for market. Fish farming is a tedious operation because aeration of the water must always be maintained and feeding precisely monitored. (Courtesy of Steve Lech.)

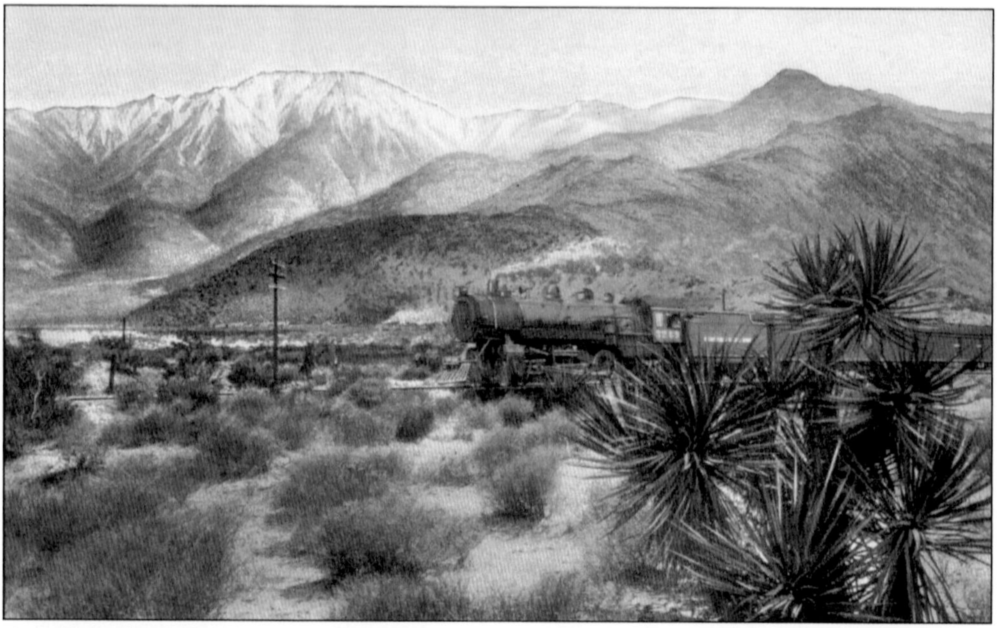

An old Southern Pacific train approaches west near Whitewater. It was not until 1876 that the first passenger train came through the San Gorgonio Pass. It fast replaced the stage lines that were running prior to its emergence. The first train passed through Beaumont (then known as Summit) and stopped at Cabazon. It continued to Indio, then known as Indian Wells. (Courtesy of Steve Lech.)